Quantitative Methods for Place-Based Innovation Policy

Quantitative Methods for Place-Based Innovation Policy

Measuring the Growth Potential of Regions

Edited by

Roberta Capello

Professor of Regional and Urban Economics, Politecnico di Milano, Italy

Alexander Kleibrink

European Research Centre for Anti-Corruption and State-Building, Hertie School of Governance, Berlin, Germany

Monika Matusiak

Senior Policy Officer, European Commission, Joint Research Centre, Seville, Spain

Cheltenham, UK • Northampton, MA, USA

Published by
Edward Elgar Publishing Limited
The Lypiatts
15 Lansdown Road
Cheltenham
Glos GL50 2JA
UK

Edward Elgar Publishing, Inc.
William Pratt House
9 Dewey Court
Northampton
Massachusetts 01060
USA

A catalogue record for this book
is available from the British Library

Library of Congress Control Number: 2020938636

This book is available electronically in the **Elgar**online
Economics subject collection
http://dx.doi.org/10.4337/9781789905519

ISBN 978 1 78990 550 2 (cased)
ISBN 978 1 78990 551 9 (eBook)

Typeset by Servis Filmsetting Ltd, Stockport, Cheshire
Printed and bound by CPI Group (UK) Ltd, Croydon, CR0 4YY

Contents

Contributors

Roberta Capello is Full Professor of Regional and Urban Economics at the Politecnico di Milano, Italy, past President of the Regional Science Association International (RSAI) (2009–2010) and President of the Italian Section of RSAI (AISRe) (2019–2022). She is also Editor-in-Chief of *Papers in Regional Science* (Wiley Blackwell) and author of many scientific papers and a textbook in regional economics, published in Italian (Il Mulino, Bologna), English (Routledge, London) and Chinese (Economy and Management Publishing House, Beijing).

Andrea Conte is Team Leader of the Regional Economic Modelling (REMO) team at the Joint Research Centre (DG JRC) of the European Commission. He holds a PhD and MSc in economics from CORIPE, University of Turin, Italy. He was Senior Research Fellow at the Max Planck Institute of Economics, Jena, Germany, before joining the European Commission (DG ECFIN) in 2008.

Nicola Cortinovis is Assistant Professor in Regional and Industrial Economics at Erasmus School of Economics, Erasmus University Rotterdam, the Netherlands.

Teodora Dogaru has a PhD in regional economics and is currently an independent researcher. She specialises in urban analysis for regional growth policies, societal discourses, trade networks and innovation.

Susana Franco is a Researcher at the Orkestra-Basque Institute of Competitiveness, Spain, where she conducts quantitative and qualitative research that has been published in international academic journals, books and reports. Her areas of interest include clusters, competitiveness, regional development, employment and well-being.

Enric Fuster is a Senior Consultant at SIRIS Academic, Spain, specialising in science and innovation policy. He has been involved in higher education, regional development and smart specialisation strategies and projects across Europe and, with colleagues at SIRIS Academic, he is developing new uses of open data, data analysis, natural language processing and data visualisation to support science and innovation policy design, monitoring and communication.

Carlo Gianelle is Scientific Officer at the European Commission's Joint Research Centre, Seville, Spain. He holds a PhD in economics from the University of Siena, Italy and studied at the University of California Berkeley, USA, specialising in applied economics. He has been involved in the implementation of the Smart Specialisation policy of the European Commission from its inception in 2011, contributing in particular to the development of analytical methodologies and impact assessment.

Hugo Hollanders is an Economist and Senior Researcher at Maastricht University, the Netherlands. He has over twenty-five years of experience in innovation studies and innovation statistics and is the lead author of the European Innovation Scoreboard. Since 2010 he has also been working with Eurostat redesigning the Community Innovation Survey. More recently, he has been working with the Joint Research Centre developing a methodology for diagnosing the potential of European regions to strengthen their economic and innovation performance.

Alexander Kleibrink is currently working in international development on good governance and local economic development. He was formerly an advisor of regional and national governments on place-based innovation policies while working at the European Commission. He is the author of more than 30 policy briefs, articles and book chapters on governing innovation, and a member of the Advisory Board of the journal *Policy Design and Practice*.

Henning Kroll is Head of the Business Unit Innovation Trends and Knowledge Dynamics at the Fraunhofer Institute for Systems and Innovation Research, Germany, as well as Adjunct Professor of Economic Geography at the Leibniz Universität Hannover, Germany, and Visiting Professor at the University of the Chinese Academy of Sciences. His areas of work include regional innovation systems and regional development policies.

Camilla Lenzi has been Associate Professor of Regional and Urban Economics at Politecnico di Milano, Italy, since 2015. She has a PhD in economics from the University of Pavia, Italy, and a Master of Science in industry and innovation analysis from SPRU – University of Sussex, UK. She is the author of many papers published in various international refereed journals in the fields of regional and innovation studies, urban economics, highly skilled worker mobility, and entrepreneurship.

Giovanni Mandras is an economist at the Joint Research Centre of the European Commission, a member of the Regional Economic Modelling (REMO) team on regional data analysis, and a specialist in economic impact analysis with a specific focus on regional economics and macro-economic modelling.

Francesco A. Massucci is the Director of R&D at SIRIS Academic, Spain. He holds a MSc in physics (2007) and a PhD in applied mathematics (2012) in the field of complex systems. He is the co-author of several scientific publications in major peer-reviewed international journals and he has been a speaker in many international top scientific conferences. At SIRIS, he helps strategic decision-making for research and development initiatives by devising tools built on data science and natural language processing techniques.

Monika Matusiak is Senior Policy Officer at the European Commission's Joint Research Centre, Seville, Spain, where she leads work streams on the development of smart specialisation methodology for the European Union's Enlargement and Neighbourhood Countries and Smart Specialisation for Sustainable Development Goals. She is the focal point for the United Nation's Inter-Agency Task Team for Science, Technology and Innovation Roadmaps for Sustainable Development Goals. She holds a PhD from Poznań University of Economics and Business, Poland, where she held the post of Assistant Professor before joining the European Commission.

Asier Murciego is a data scientist and engineer at the Orkestra-Basque Institute of Competitiveness, Spain. He was the co-founder of Captiva Soluciones y Seguridad, a cybersecurity firm. He is a collaborator in many scientific papers regarding territorial benchmarking and index composition, and the developer of data management and visualisation web platforms such as Orkestra's Regional Competitiveness Observatory.

Jeroen van Haaren is Senior Researcher in Urban Economics at the Erasmus Centre for Urban Port and Transport Economics at Erasmus University Rotterdam, the Netherlands. He is currently working on a dissertation on the value of urban amenities and their capitalisation in house prices.

Frank van Oort is Full Professor in Urban and Regional Economics at the Erasmus School of Economics, Erasmus University Rotterdam (EUR), the Netherlands. He is a Research Fellow at the Tinbergen Institute, and Academic Director of the Institute of Housing and Urban Development Studies at EUR. He is editor of the *Cambridge Journal of Regions, Economy and Society* and the *Journal of Economic and Social Geography* (*TESG*).

1. Mapping industrial and territorial dimensions for the design of place-based innovation policies: the rationale of the book

Roberta Capello, Alexander Kleibrink and Monika Matusiak

1.1 MAPPING INNOVATION AS A RECENT NEED FOR THE DESIGN OF POLICY: AIM OF THE BOOK

Smart specialisation is now a well-known strategy of the European Union (EU), due to its implementation in the 2014–2020 period to boost the competitiveness of Europe and its regions. Prior to this, innovation activities were related primarily to research and development (R&D) expenditure. Smart specialisation aimed to change this, by embracing a much larger concept of innovation, insisting on the idea that entrepreneurial discovery was not based only in high-tech industries and in R&D activities. The one-size-fits-all policy of the Lisbon and Europe 2020 agenda was totally replaced, and the idea that innovation strategies had to be place-based (Barca, 2009), as a result of bottom-up processes based on the self-discovery of entrepreneurial capability, drove the present programming period 2014–2020 (Giannitsis, 2009; Foray, 2009; Foray et al., 2009).

The new policy strategy was therefore calling for an attempt to supersede the old innovation policy style, based on centralised planning methods for the identification of industrial development priorities. The new strategy was aiming to ensure the appropriateness of the logic and design of the policy, as well as the relevance of the local context, rather than this being imposed by an external (supra-regional) body, as with a place-based policy *à la* Barca (Barca, 2009).

In addition to this redirection of innovation policy style, smart specialisation was asking for the identification of priorities, a policy prioritization capable of boosting growth, since it is based on regional context conditions. As one of the founding fathers of smart specialisation, Dominique Foray claimed that contemporary innovation strategies ought to be 'largely about the policy process to select and prioritize fields or areas where a cluster of activities should be developed, and to let entrepreneurs discover the right domain of future specialization' (Foray et al., 2011, p. 7).

The new approach towards innovation policies was well received by scientists and experts, since it was interpreted as being based on innovative, modern and shareable principles. They viewed it as a cultural leap in the design and implementation of innovation (and competitiveness) policies, moving away from an R&D-based policy that over past years has demonstrated all its fragility and inefficiency (Capello and Kroll, 2016).

However, as with all paradigmatic changes, the implementation of this policy model was much more complicated than expected (Capello and Kroll, 2016; Camagni and Capello, 2020). Most notably, the achievement of its goals – mainly the identification of the 'smart domain' in which to look for and encourage an entrepreneurial discovery – emerged as the primary difficulty in the implementation of the new strategy, as the first evaluations of the strategy highlighted (Iacobuci and Guzzini, 2016).

In particular, place-based innovation policy design requires an in-depth understanding of territories and their complexity. Traditional statistics, with low public availability of data at disaggregated (sub-sectoral and regionalised) level, often do not provide enough information. Therefore, new methods and approaches are called for by scientists and experts that can inform decision-makers and stakeholders in choosing priorities and directions for their innovation strategies. The 'mapping' of innovation, of its modes, features, potentialities, is a fundamental tool for providing policy-makers with the right information on which to build a smart innovation strategy.

This book provides new reflections on the conceptual approaches for the identification of innovation priorities, the data required, the methods with which to turn data into useful information, and the mapping of the information available. On the conceptual side, new reflections have been launched on the concept of innovation itself. On the empirical and methodological side, new technologies have made it easier and cheaper to gather and process massive and novel kinds of data. On the policy side, legislation and soft regulation is increasingly defining how evidence should be used to design development policies.

This book builds on the experience of more than 100 innovation strategies for smart specialisation which regional and national governments have designed in the EU since 2012. In what one of the leading industrial relations scholars, Charles Sabel, has labelled 'the biggest experiment in innovation and industrial policy' in the world, mapping various dimensions of the innovation system was a critical and legally required element.

The book presents four basic dimensions of mapping for innovation policies and how they can be meaningfully combined and complemented. It shows how the economic, scientific, innovation and societal potential of cities, regions and countries can be measured, and how these insights can inform policy-making. Mapping is understood as a quantitative analytical exercise using available data presented at the territorial (sub-national) level.

Mapping methodologies and techniques are the tools that policy-makers and innovation analysts use to design appropriate policies for different contexts and development levels of countries and their regions. Numerous methods and data sources can be useful in meeting the growing interest in the evidence-base of the numerous facets of innovation policies. Which methods governments and analysts ultimately use to justify choices and investments depends on the level of socio-economic development, the policy objectives and their analytical capabilities. This book provides a comprehensive menu of options that are applicable to both emerging economies and Organisation for Economic Co-operation and Development (OECD) countries, albeit with different degrees of suitability. While each territory has its own unique characteristics, recent developments in analytical techniques enable us to collect new data and link them in novel ways. The book shows how to reap these potentials to deal with economic and societal challenges, in both dynamic metropolitan and remote rural areas. Mapping the socio-economic fabric of territories contributes to better innovation strategies by bringing together the pieces that make up effective innovation systems and providing a strong evidence base for informed decisions.

This book pays strong attention to the preparation of 'knowledge bases' for policy discussions and their uptake by practitioners. To do this, the book considers 'what if' type approaches that reflect on a number of potential options, discussing 'holes and gaps' and thus pushing for experimenting with different methods for different purposes. Uniquely, this book considers innovation:

- As requiring a policy design and evidence base to be developed in a way which leads to successful competitive strategies.
- As place-based. It is contingent on spatially clustered socio-economic activities and actors, and therefore all methods presented pay attention to this spatial dimension.
- As based on the sectoral dimension. Increasingly attention is paid to developments inside and across economic sectors. Yet to date no

systematic book has discussed this at a sufficient level of detail. Only a sectorial and cross-sectorial picture allows us to see how different industries develop and link over time.

● As requiring specific information to develop innovation policies. Policy-makers should understand what is being done, as well as how and why certain phenomena are mapped. Mapping in this case is concerned with the uptake and how public administrations can employ these methods themselves.

The timing of this book is fortunate, since the design of the next generation of more than 100 innovation strategies in Europe is beginning, making it a timely and useful reference for practitioners and academics alike. Given the increasing interest in the EU's smart specialisation approach across the world, from Mexico to Australia, the book has the potential to inform discussions and policies at a larger scale.

The value added of this book lies in the presentation of new conceptual thinking, new data and methods for their interpretation. Especially, the book shows how both conceptual and methodological developments have changed the way it is possible to map interesting information for policy-makers and stakeholders for sustaining place-based innovation policies.

1.2   MODERN CONCEPTUAL APPROACHES TO INNOVATION

In the mid-1990s, the conceptual approach to the interpretation of the innovation process became more complex. Technological change required increasing systemic knowledge and integration of different technological competences in order to produce one single product. The 'linear model' of innovation – referring to a logical sequence between creativity and knowledge, invention, innovation and economic performance – was highly criticised for its unrealistic idea that rational and orderly innovation processes could exist (Edgerton, 2004), and was replaced by a systemic approach.

The process of knowledge acquisition was supposed to be influenced by the complexity and systemic nature of innovation; it therefore was expected to call for an interactive process of new knowledge acquisition. Learning necessarily required cooperation and interaction between firms and the local scientific system, between different functions within the firm (between production and research and development, between marketing and research and development), between producers and customers, and between firms and the social and institutional structure, in either formal or informal ways, the former imposing interactive forms of organizational learning, the latter based on direct experience or that of others, which came about through activities focused on finding solutions to specific technological, productive or market problems.

The consequence of such cooperation and interaction was that the innovative process was strongly localised: it resulted from the variety of traditions, norms, habits, social conventions and cultural practices that constituted what has been called 'institutional thickness'.[1] Innovation therefore could not be understood properly unless it was examined within the socio-cultural and institutional context in which it took place; in particular, innovation required 'institutional proximity', meaning the set of norms, codes and rules of behaviour which help economic actors (people, individual firms, public and private institutions) to adopt forms of organisation that facilitate interactive learning. 'Institutions are here defined as the sets of habits, routines, norms and laws that regulate the relations between people and thus shape human interaction and learning' (Lundvall and Johnson, 1994, p. 33).

On the basis of the systemic nature of innovation, and of the context conditions that guarantee interactive and collective learning processes, a series of theories emerged emphasising the importance of 'proximity' among innovative actors as a condition for cooperation to take place. In the 2000s, a conceptual framework was put forward where the concept of 'cognitive proximity' was emphasised as a crucial element for explaining innovation capacity. In order to create new technological solutions and new innovation, firms have to share complementary knowledge. At the same time, firms have to share a common knowledge base that guarantees a common language and mutual understanding among firms. In the literature, this condition was labelled 'related variety', and it was defined as a variety of interrelated technological solutions with a common knowledge basis.[2]

This theory was recognised as a useful approach to identify a smart innovation strategy for a region. This approach, in fact, underlines that the innovation process is strongly shaped by a specific knowledge base

---

[1]   See Amin and Thrift (1994). The term 'institution' should of course be understood in the sense given to it by North's and Williamson's institutional economics, namely as a set of societal norms and 'rules of the game' (North, 1990, p. 3).

[2]   The first author to deal with the concept of 'related variety' was Nooteboom (2000), but it is thanks to the Dutch school of evolutionary economic geography that the concept has developed and received empirical evidence. For advanced studies on this concept, see Boschma (2005), Frenken et al. (2007), Boschma and Iammarino (2009) and Boschma et al. (2012).

and the combinations of economic sectors in regions. A diversification of the regional innovation path is possible, but within the existing innovation trajectories and knowledge base. Existing specialisations and knowledge bases in regions provide options for diversification, but what has to be avoided by the region is the development of new economic structures from scratch (Boschma, 2014). The related variety concept has become rather useful in the identification of possible entrepreneurial discoveries within the region (Van Oort et al., Chapter 3 in this book); when empirically applied, it may become a useful tool to identify the innovative domains in which 'a region is likely to excel given its existing capabilities and productive assets' (Foray et al., 2011, p. 7).

Even if clear merits can be attributed to the related variety concept, this theory has an important intrinsic limitation, in that it reduces cognitive aspects to the industry dimension. In fact, learning processes occur within the industry, and the condition for them to occur is the simultaneous presence of a knowledge complementarity and a common knowledge basis. But this means that they occur in the same way wherever the industry is located, and therefore that the learning process is separated from the economic and territorial context (Capello, 2019).

Recently, the idea that the industrial dimension was not sufficient to explain the regional innovation capacity has been strongly advocated (Capello, 2019). When applied at regional level, in fact, the industrial logic showed two kinds of limits. The first one referred to the fact that this logic risked pushing towards the interpretation of formal knowledge as the main source of innovation; instead, a variety of informal elements, such as face-to-face meetings, informal cooperation, creativity and collective learning processes are behind a learning process. The second limit referred to the idea that only knowledge stemming from local sectors was a source for local innovation; instead, a large literature highlighted the role of knowledge coming from outside the region as a fundamental source for innovation.

In order to overcome such limits and restore the territorial elements to the centre of the explanation of innovation processes, a new concept was recently proposed: that is, regional patterns of innovation, defined as the spatial breakdown of the single, logical phases of the innovation path – from invention based on new knowledge, to innovation, ending with development – built on the presence/absence of territorial preconditions for knowledge creation, knowledge attraction and innovation.[3]

---

[3] On the concept of regional patterns of innovation, see Camagni and Capello (2013) and Capello and Lenzi (2013).

The different components of the cognitivist, linear model of innovation were broken down, separated, allocated differently in time and space, and recomposed at the end following a relational logic of interregional cooperation and exchange.

The concept of regional patterns of innovation was translated into empirics, and the identification of such patterns in the real world is extremely useful in the identification of smart innovation strategies (Capello and Lenzi, Chapter 5 in this book). In fact, as will be largely explained in Chapter 5, by grouping regions on the basis of similarities in innovation processes, a taxonomy of innovative regions can operationally serve the purpose of defining innovation pathways by preventing unlikely local strategies and undue use of public resources (Capello and Camagni, 2013; Camagni et al., 2014).

1.3   THE EVOLUTION OF DATA ON INNOVATION

Using data and information to design development strategies is by no means new to place-based policy-making. How to systematically gather data and analyse them has been a concern for urban and regional planning for more than a century. In the mid-19th century, Scottish town planner Sir Patrick Geddes had already pointed out the need for panel data and accompanying maps in the context of industrial development. He was acutely aware that, 'What was needed to start was an adequate collection of maps: maps describing town conditions before the industrial revolution, maps a generation later when industrial expansion was in full swing, and maps for current conditions' (Boyer, 1986, p. 72). Nowadays there is arguably a lack of neither data nor maps. The sheer amount of potentially relevant data and the increasing variety of processing techniques have likely surpassed even Geddes's expectations. The new challenge lies in deciding upon the right questions to ask about what kind of data are needed.

For industrial and later innovation policies, the guiding questions or *Erkenntnisinteresse* of policy-makers has changed over time. Since the 1980s it has been increasingly clear that differences between countries matter, in terms of economic structure, R&D capabilities, institutional set-up and innovation performance. These ideas were embodied by the concepts of national innovation systems and industrial policy (Lundvall, 1992; Freeman and Soete, 1997; Piore and Sabel, 1984). This bias towards nation-states held until the 1990s when interest in intra-country diversity started to grow. In the academic and policy discourse, national innovation systems were no longer seen as monolithic and homogenous entities.

Rather, the view that states consisted of different regional innovation systems put the territorial dimension into the limelight (Cooke, 2014; Morgan, 1997; Ohmae, 1993). Three main reasons explain this renewed interest in questions of place:

- Available data and experience indicated that regions and cities are different with respect to industrial specialisation patterns and innovation performance (Porter, 2003).
- Research on knowledge spillovers, relatedness between sectors and their role in innovation processes highlighted the importance of local interactions (Asheim, 2012; Boschma, 2017).
- On the policy side, powers to design or implement industrial and innovation policies have been increasingly devolved to regions and cities in many countries (Tödtling and Trippl, 2005).

However, many place-based economic and innovation policies have not performed as expected (Rodríguez-Pose, 2018; Barca, 2009). This is, at least in part, a consequence of their lack of attention to local conditions and history. It turned out that a vision for the future is not enough to create local economic growth, even if it is accompanied by large public investments. Robust information about the state of the local economy is necessary to identify realistic and promising avenues of development, as well as the barriers that need to be overcome and the local actors that need to be engaged. Only by having this kind of information is it possible to target local economic development policies effectively and have a proactive industrial policy for places (Foray, 2015; Hausmann and Rodrik, 2003).

The predominant emphasis on the national level, at least at the beginning, partly determined what kind of data and evidence would be used for industrial and innovation policies at the regional level. Regional analysis has been widely dependent on established industrial statistics, but a variety of new data sources are gaining recognition, and more and more analytical methods are being developed to use them. Compelling new efforts for mapping combine established industrial data (employment, firm number and characteristics, sectoral gross value added, and so on) and science, technology and innovation (STI) indicators (patents, research funding, publications, and so on) with novel open data on firms and start-ups and interaction data from digital platforms (Kleibrink and Mateos, 2017). Advances in social network analysis now make it possible to visualise large networks of companies, research institutes and universities. Figure 1.1 depicts the evolution of dominant data use over time.

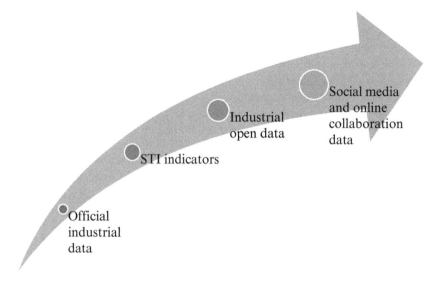

Source: Based on Kleibrink and Mateos (2017).

Figure 1.1 Evolution of data sources for place-based innovation policies

Yet how exactly was this kind of data used for innovation policy-making? European regions have been designing territorial innovation strategies over the last 25 years. In the mid-1990s, the European Commission (EC) integrated innovation support into the European Regional Development Fund (ERDF). This laid the foundation for what we understand today as 'regional innovation strategies'. Innovative actions were further developed in the period 2000–2006. In parallel, pre-accession countries in Eastern Europe benefited from similar support to develop place-based innovation strategies. In total, more than 120 regions participated in these strategy exercises (Charles et al., 2000). Since these early beginnings, learning and feedback exercises have become an inherent part of regional innovation policies (European Commission, 2007). While these initiatives brought greater levels of cooperation, transparency and expertise to regional administrations, there was little emphasis on the quality of strategy design and the robustness of data used to inform policy choices. Evaluations have indeed shown that this was one of the main weaknesses of the first generations of place-based innovation strategies. It turned out that the identification of relevant societal needs and capabilities at the beginning of strategy-making is critical. The successful cases from those years had a relatively precise idea of the region's endowments, which in turn made it easier to develop appropriate solutions to overcome identified bottlenecks (Socintec and Inno, 2005).

In the 1990s and 2000s, obtaining detailed data at the local and regional level was rather difficult, except for traditional industrial statistics. Nowadays, data arguably abound, at least in OECD countries. The problem is much less one of data availability, but rather of deciding what data are relevant and, as a final step, having the skills to analyse them properly. Many if not most local and regional administrations do not have sufficient competencies and resources to examine overly complex or unstructured data. Analytical capacities are often unevenly distributed across regional and local authorities, thus aggravating sound policy analysis (Borrás, 2011; Borrás and Jordana, 2016). Except for some vanguard regions such as Catalonia and Wales, most regional administrations have not developed modern open data tools to monitor local STI developments.[4] This is one of the key goals of this edited volume: to inspire and explore the possibilities of new data sources and analysis for regions in Europe and beyond.

1.4   NEW DATA FOR A NEW POLICY PERSPECTIVE: QUANTITATIVE MAPPING

The unfulfilled expectations of place-based economic and innovation policies triggered a reflection process in the European Union. Despite large public investments, success was partial and ambiguous at best. Regional inequalities inside EU member states and globally have been on the rise (Iammarino et al., 2019; OECD, 2016). Investments were not strategic in the sense of identifying realistic and promising avenues of development. It became clear that a truly territorial policy must pay attention to local conditions and history, regional bottlenecks, and the needs and capacities of local actors who need to be engaged. To achieve this, acquiring robust information about the state of the local economy became an essential first step.

In EU policy cycles, consensus emerged that targeted local economic development policies and a proactive industrial policy needed a stronger evidence base than before (Barca, 2009). This is why the ERDF regula-

---

[4]   Catalonia's RIS3-MCAT Platform is an interactive tool visualising the development of sectorial and technological specialisations and the networks among STI organisations (http://catalunya2020.gencat.cat/en/plataforma-ris3-mcat). Arloesiadur is an open data platform developed jointly by innovation charity Nesta and the Welsh Government to map industry, research and technology networks (https://arloesiadur.org).

Table 1.1   Fulfilment criteria for smart specialisation in current and proposed EU legislation

2013 A national or regional smart specialisation strategy is in place that:	2018 Smart specialisation strategy shall be supported by:
Is based on a SWOT or similar analysis to concentrate resources on a limited set of research and innovation priorities	Up-to-date analysis of bottlenecks for innovation diffusion, including digitalisation
Outlines measures to stimulate private RTD investment	Existence of a competent regional/ national institution or body, responsible for the management of the smart specialisation strategy
Contains a monitoring mechanism	Monitoring and evaluation tools to measure performance towards the objectives of the strategy
	Effective functioning of entrepreneurial discovery process
	Actions necessary to improve national or regional research and innovation systems
	Actions to manage industrial transition
	Measures for international collaboration

Source: Based on REGULATION (EU) No 1303/2013 (on the left) and the proposal for the new regulation COM(2018) 375 final (on the right).

tion and the common framework provisions defined compulsory steps to build a strong evidence base and the continuous involvement of relevant stakeholders in 2013. This conditionality, known as 'smart specialisation', had far-reaching consequences: in cases of non-compliance, the European Commission could suspend funds for research, technological development and innovation. It triggered a policy learning process across the whole continent (Foray, 2015). Some leading scholars and practitioners described it as an 'ambitious experiment' (Sabel and Kuznetsov, 2017, p. 52). The concept is also part of the current proposal for the EU multi-annual budget 2021–2027, where it is one of several 'enabling conditions'. Table 1.1 compares the fulfilment criteria for the current and proposed conditions. The new proposal prescribes in more detail which aspects are of particular relevance for a successful economic transformation. Instead of the original strengths, weaknesses, opportunities, threats (SWOT) analysis, an up-to-date analysis of bottlenecks for innovation diffusion is now demanded, with a special emphasis on digitalisation. Furthermore, the required monitoring mechanism is described in greater detail, including 'evaluation tools to measure performance towards the objectives of the strategy'. Data requirements are now even more ambitious, since the proposal explicitly calls for measures to manage industrial transition and foster international collaboration. In the proposed regulation the European Commission continuously monitors compliance and can suspend funds in case of non-fulfilment at any time. The need for high-quality data and quantitative methods to make sense of those data has increased.

This European concept of place-based innovation policy has met interest globally in Eastern Europe, Africa, the United States (US), Latin America and Australia (Dosso et al., 2018; Wilson, 2016; Radosevic and Ciampi Stancova, 2018; Kleibrink and Matusiak, 2018; Aranguren et al., 2014; Wessner and Howell, 2018; Office of the Economic Development Board, 2018; Kleibrink et al., 2017). The World Bank, the United Nations and OECD are either supporting countries with their effort to develop smart specialisation or contributing to its conceptual development (World Bank, 2016; OECD, 2014; UN IATT, 2019). International demand for localised data and analyses is on the rise.

The use of data and quantitative analysis is not only about comparing numbers. It is meant to convey a narrative that is able to engage a broader set of actors in the strategy's transformational agenda both within and outside the respective territory (Kleibrink and Gianelle, 2016; Mendez, 2013; Kleibrink and Magro, 2018). Two examples from Austria and Germany illustrate these two functions. The regional government of Lower Austria collects and organises relevant data on regional economic and innovation policy in a comprehensive yet concise balanced scorecard that allows for detailed and timely analytical monitoring.[5] For assessing its position in comparison to other German and European regions, the government of Baden-Württemberg resorts to its own tailor-made innovation index which supports a robust narrative on innovation leadership in Europe, together with a sound analysis of innovation performance dynamics.[6]

Another more prominent example is from the US. In terms of advocacy, the Silicon Valley region in California has long been at the forefront of innovation communities worldwide. The multi-stakeholder organisation

---

[5]   See Interreg project KNOW-HUB for more information, http://www.know-hub.eu/blog/application-of-the-balanced-scorecard-methodology-in-lower-austrias-economic-and-innovation-policy.html.

[6]   For the Innovation Index 2018, see https://www.statistik-bw.de/Presse/Press emitteilungen/2018291.

Silicon Valley Joint Venture has been publishing an index of the broader socio-economic developments in the region since 1995. This index aggregates 26 indicators of trends in Silicon Valley's economy and quality of life, reported on an annual basis (Saxenian and Dabby, 2004). Over time, this index has been increasingly tailored to stakeholder needs, and has contributed to a feeling of joint ownership in a region that is otherwise very much characterised by competition and individual achievements. In fact, it supported a narrative that framed policy and business debates by pinpointing gaps where action was required.

The outcome of the new conceptual approaches and of the new quantitative methods to treat data and information is a quantitative mapping of the degree of innovation capacities, of innovation priorities and of local conditions guaranteeing the success of local innovative policies. For a meaningful discussion with stakeholders, quantitative mapping is valuable as it provides the evidence and facts for an informed dialogue. This way of proceeding is an important one, since it informs stakeholders and policymakers of the necessary conditions. However, this all has to be reinforced by qualitative interpretations, not treated in this book.

1.5 STRUCTURE OF THE BOOK

The book is structured around two complementary parts. Part I contains methods and data that allow an understanding to be gained of the industrial fabric of territories on which innovation should be anchored. In fact, knowing all the relevant puzzle pieces of a territory's economic fabric is an essential first step for any strategic policy support. It is also a precondition for having informed dialogues and discussions with stakeholders, be they firms, associations, research institutes or universities.

Three chapters develop such a theme. Chapter 2, by Henning Kroll, presents a method with which to map economic specialisation. The chapter puts forward the idea that, according to EC guidelines and much early literature, the main rationale of smart specialisation activities is to provide innovation strategies for economic transformation. During the first period of its promotion, however, many strategies instead focused on research, and their monitoring on traditional STI indicators. Such analyses, however, do not necessarily provide a good indication for economic transformation, as in most regions outside leading clusters, scientific and economic activities remain structurally disconnected. Hence, future smart specialisation strategy monitoring needs to focus more on the state of local economies and their potential interfaces with science. This chapter suggests a process to achieve such monitoring.

Chapter 3, by Frank van Oort, Nicola Cortinovis, Teodora Dogaru and Jeroen van Haaren, introduces the concepts of related variety and relatedness in the European Union, and discusses how this links to the entrepreneurial search process and innovative structural change in regional contexts. Throughout the chapter, the authors argue that although relatedness is a key element for supporting place-based innovation processes and policies, their interdependence and functioning requires more attention in both scientific and policy circles. The authors illustrate this by presenting new empirical research which puts skill-relatedness on the local (sub-regional) map of the Netherlands. The patterns of mapped relatedness are linked to policy implications at the local and regional level, and show that diversification strategies may be more complex to actively pursue when they have to comply with existing entrepreneurial, educational, industrial organisation, infrastructural and social network conditions.

Chapter 4, by Giovanni Mandras and Andrea Conte, deals with the phenomenon of global value chains (GVCs), representing networks of production and trade across countries, and therefore the complex industrial fabric of a global and interconnected world economy. In recent years, in fact, GVCs have become the new paradigm for the production of goods and services since production is increasingly internationally integrated. GVCs are directly identifiable by domestic exports, and indirectly by those regions that provide intermediate inputs to final exporting regions. Considering that trade in intermediate inputs accounts for two-thirds of international trade, a complete analysis of the magnitude of both direct and indirect contributions is needed to assess the position of regions and the degree of their participation in different types of GVCs, such as European value chains (EVCs), where the deepening of the European single market has fostered the process of economic integration.

Part II of the book deals with the mapping of regional innovation and the territorial conditions that favour innovation activities. Chapter 5, by Roberta Capello and Camilla Lenzi, provides a taxonomy of innovative regions that can be a useful policy tool to support fully decentralised regional innovation policy approaches, such as the smart specialisation strategy, so as to mitigate the multiple risks arising from the implementation of innovation policies. The chapter presents the most recent taxonomy of innovative regions, produced through a scientific effort based on the overcoming of several limitations that characterised the existing taxonomies. The chapter also demonstrates how the regional innovation pattern taxonomy, as it is called, is useful for suggesting innovation strategies specific to each group of innovative regions, which are aimed at the reinforcement and upgrading of the existing regional innovation mode.

Chapter 6, by Hugo Hollanders and Monika Matusiak, presents a method to identify smart specialisation priority domains through an economic analysis that is able to highlight economic specialisations using detailed industry-level data on employment, value added, wages and exports. A second step involves the identification of the innovation potential of these preliminary priority domains by implementing an innovation potential mapping exercise. Mapping the innovation potential of regions should move from a generic and horizontal view of innovativeness, embodied in questions such as: 'What is the share of innovative companies in the national/regional economy?', to a more granular picture.

Chapter 7, by Susana Franco, Carlo Gianelle, Alexander Kleibrink and Asier Murciego, starts from the idea that innovation policy is inherently a highly experimental endeavour. In an increasingly complex, intertwined, fast-changing and uncertain world, policy-makers pursuing public policy innovations in support of economic development need to engage in a systematic process of policy learning. Benchmarking with peers is a powerful learning channel in regional innovation policy, provided that the identification of suitable peer regions is based on similarity in the structural dimensions influencing innovation policy. While several regional benchmarking methodologies and toolsets are currently available, regions are most often chosen for comparison based either solely on innovation and economic performance measures, paying insufficient attention to the context in which performance is or can be achieved, or on a mix of variables of different nature not suitable for supporting effective learning. To overcome those limitations, the chapter proposes a methodology to identify peer regions in the European Union focused on similarity in innovation-relevant structural characteristics. A novel database is presented covering all European Union regions, and a full matrix of regional pairwise distances resulting from the aggregation of several dimensions is constructed. The chapter ends by discussing selected cases and the related policy implications for the design and implementation of regional innovation policy.

Finally, Chapter 8, by Enric Fuster, Francesco A. Massucci and Monika Matusiak, focuses on new methods that can be used at the interface of science and policy for the identification of the localised domains of specialisation in science and technology. The authors explore semantic methodologies which, by analysing the textual content of science and innovation-related documents (such as policy and project descriptions, scientific publications, patents, clinical trials) go beyond classifications, allowing emergent topics and domains to be identified, as well as mapping and benchmarking the local capabilities in specific domains of interest.

REFERENCES

Amin, A. and N. Thrift (1994), *Globalization, Institutions and Regional Development in Europe*, Oxford: Oxford University Press.

Aranguren, M.J., S. Franco and J.R. Wilson (2014), 'Conectando Estrategias de Especialización Inteligente y Clústeres: ¿Un Reto Clave Para América Latina?', in Red Interamericana de Competitividad (ed.), *Señales de Competitividad de Las Américas 2014*, Washington, DC: Organization of American States, pp. 38–42.

Asheim, B. (2012), 'The Changing Role of Learning Regions in the Globalizing Knowledge Economy: A Theoretical Re-Examination', *Regional Studies*, **46** (8), 993–1004. https://doi.org/10.1080/00343404.2011.607805.

Barca, F. (2009), 'An Agenda for a Reformed Cohesion Policy: A Place-Based Approach to Meeting European Union Challenges and Expectations', Independent Report, prepared at the request of Danuta Hübner, EU Commissioner for Regional Policy.

Borrás, S. (2011), 'Policy Learning and Organizational Capacities in Innovation Policies', *Science and Public Policy*, **38** (9), 725–734. https://doi.org/10.3152/030 234211X13070021633323.

Borrás, S. and J. Jordana (2016), 'When Regional Innovation Policies Meet Policy Rationales and Evidence: A Plea for Policy Analysis', CIRCLE Papers in Innovation Studies, no. 2016/12. http://wp.circle.lu.se/upload/CIRCLE/work ingpapers/201612_Borras_Jordana.pdf.

Boschma, R. (2005), 'Proximity and Innovation: A Critical Assessment', *Regional Studies*, **39** (1), 61–74.

Boschma, R. (2014), 'Constructing Regional Advantage and Smart Specialisation: Comparison of Two European Policy Concepts', *Scienze Regionali*, **13** (1), 51–68.

Boschma, R. (2017), 'Relatedness as Driver of Regional Diversification: A Research Agenda', *Regional Studies*, **51** (3), 351–364. https://doi.org/10.1080/00 343404.2016.1254767.

Boschma, R. and S. Iammarino (2009), 'Related Variety, Trade Linkages, and Regional Growth in Italy', *Economic Geography*, **85** (3), 289–311.

Boschma, R., A. Minondo and M. Navarro (2012), 'Related Variety and Regional Growth in Spain', *Papers in Regional Science*, **91** (2), 241–256.

Boyer, C. (1986), *Dreaming the Rational City: The Myth of American City Planning*, Cambridge, MA, USA and London, UK: MIT Press. https://www. amazon.de/Dreaming-Rational-City-American-Planning/dp/0262521113.

Camagni, R. and R. Capello (2013), 'Regional Innovation Patterns and the EU Regional Policy Reform: Towards Smart Innovation Policies', *Growth and Change*, **44** (2), 355–389.

Camagni, R. and R. Capello (2020), 'Contributions by Italian scholars to regional science', *Papers in Regional Science*, **99** (2), 359–388, DOI: 10.1111/pirs.12510.

Camagni, R., R. Capello and C. Lenzi (2014), 'A Territorial Taxonomy of Innovative Regions and the European Regional Policy Reform: Smart Innovation Policies', *Scienze Regionali – Italian Journal of Regional Science*, **13** (1), 69–106.

Capello, R. (2019), 'Theories of Innovation in Space: Path-breaking Achievements in Regional Science', in R. Capello and P. Nijkamp (eds), *Handbook of Regional Growth and Development Theories*, 2nd edn, Cheltenham, UK and Northampton, MA, USA: Edward Elgar Publishing, pp. 240–456.

Capello, R. and H. Kroll (2016), 'From Theory to Practice in Smart Specialization Strategy: Emerging Limits and Possible Future Trajectories', *European Planning Studies*, **24** (8), 1393–1406.

Capello, R. and C. Lenzi (2013), 'Territorial Patterns of Innovation in Europe: A Taxonomy of Innovative Regions', *Annals of Regional Science*, **51** (1), 119–154.

Charles, D.R., C. Nauwelaers, B. Mouton and D. Bradley (2000), 'Assessment of the Regional Innovation and Technology Transfer Strategies and Infrastructures (RITTS) Scheme', Final Evaluation Report, Newcastle upon Tyne: CURDS (University of Newcastle) and MERIT (University of Maastricht) with PAIR and OIR.

Cooke, P. (2014), 'Systems of Innovation and the Learning Region', in M.M. Fischer and P. Nijkamp (eds), *Handbook of Regional Science*, Berlin and Heidelberg: Springer, pp. 457–474. http://link.springer.com/10.1007/978-3-642-23430-9_28.

Dosso, M., A. Kleibrink and M. Matusiak (2018), 'Smart Specialisation in Sub-Saharan Africa: Opportunities and Challenges', in F. Pazisnewende Kabore, W.G. Park and S. Kati-Coulibaly (eds), *Proceedings of EAI International Conference on Technology, R&D, Education and Economy for Africa*, Côte d'Ivoire, Abidjan, pp. 67–74.

Edgerton, D. (2004), 'The Linear Model did not Exist: Reflections on the History and Historiography of Science and Research in Industry in the Twentieth Century', in K. Grandin, N. Worms and S. Widmalm (eds), *The Science Industry Nexus*, Sagamore Beach, MA: Science History Publications, pp. 31–57.

European Commission (2007), 'Innovative Strategies and Actions: Results from 15 Years of Regional Experimentation', Brussels: Directorate-General Regional Policy.

Foray, D. (2009), 'Understanding Smart Specialisation', in D. Pontikakis, D. Kyriakou and R. van Bavel (eds), *The Question of R&D Specialisation*, Brussels: JRC, European Commission, Directorate General for Research, pp. 19–28.

Foray, D. (2015), *Smart Specialisation: Opportunities and Challenges for Regional Innovation Policy*, Abingdon, UK and New York, USA: Routledge.

Foray, D., P. David and B. Hall (2009), 'Smart Specialisation – the Concept', Knowledge Economists Policy Brief, no. 9.

Foray, D., P. David and B. Hall (2011), 'Smart Specialisation: From Academic Idea toPolitical Instrument', MTEI working paper, Lausanne.

Freeman, C. and L. Soete (1997), *The Economics of Industrial Innovation*, 3rd edn, Cambridge, MA: MIT Press.

Frenken, K., F.G. van Oort and T. Verburg (2007), 'Related Variety, Unrelated Variety and Regional Economic Growth', *Regional Studies*, **41** (5), 685–697.

Giannitsis, T. (2009), 'Technology and Specialization: Strategies, Options, Risks', Knowledge Economists Policy Brief, no. 8.

Hausmann, R. and D. Rodrik (2003), 'Economic Development as Self-Discovery', *Journal of Development Economics*, **72** (2), 603–633.

Iacobucci, D. and E. Guzzini (2016), 'Relatedness and Connectivity in Technological Domains: The "Missing Links" in S3 Design and Implementation', *European Planning Studies*, **24** (8), 1511–1526.

Iammarino, S., A. Rodriguez-Pose and M. Storper (2019), 'Regional Inequality in Europe: Evidence, Theory and Policy Implications', *Journal of Economic Geography*, **19** (2), 273–298. https://doi.org/10.1093/jeg/lby021.

Kleibrink, A. and C. Gianelle (2016), 'Monitoring Innovation Strategies:

Co-Creating Sustainable Policy Cycles Together with Stakeholders', in D. Kyriakou, M.P. Martinez, I. Periáñez-Forte and A. Rainoldi (eds), *Governing Smart Specialisation*, Abingdon, UK and New York, USA: Routledge.

Kleibrink, A. and E. Magro (2018), 'The Making of Responsive Innovation Policies: Varieties of Evidence and Their Contestation in the Basque Country', *Palgrave Communications*, **4** (74). https://www.nature.com/articles/s41599-018-0136-2.

Kleibrink, A. and J. Mateos (2017), 'Searching for Local Economic Development and Innovation: A Review of Mapping Methodologies to Support Policymaking', in B. Huang, K. Cao and E.A. Silva (eds), *Reference Module in Earth Systems and Environmental Sciences*, Amsterdam, the Netherlands; Oxford, UK; Waltham, MA, USA: Elsevier, pp. 59–68. https://doi.org/10.1016/B978-0-12-409548-9.09674-3.

Kleibrink, A. and M. Matusiak (eds) (2018), *Supporting an Innovation Agenda for the Western Balkans: Tools and Methodologies*, Luxembourg: Publications Office of the European Union.

Kleibrink, A., P. Larédo and S. Philipp (2017), *Promoting Innovation in Transition Countries: A Trajectory for Smart Specialisation*, JRC Science for Policy Report, Luxembourg: Publications Office of the European Union.

Lundvall, B.-Å. (1992), *National Systems of Innovation: Toward a Theory of Innovation and Interactive Learning*, London: Pinter. http://dx.doi.org/10.7135/UPO9781843318903.

Lundvall, B.-Å. and B. Johnson (1994), 'The Learning Economy', *Journal of Industry Studies*, **1** (2), 23–42.

Mendez, C. (2013), 'The Post-2013 Reform of EU Cohesion Policy and the Place-Based Narrative', *Journal of European Public Policy*, **20** (5), 639–659. https://doi.org/10.1080/13501763.2012.736733.

Morgan, K. (1997), 'The Learning Region: Institutions, Innovation and Regional Renewal', *Regional Studies*, **31** (5), 491–503. https://doi.org/10.1080/00343409750132289.

Nooteboom, B. (2000), *Learning and Innovation in Organizations and Economies*, Oxford: Oxford University Press.

North, D.C. (1990), *Institutions, Institutional Change and Economic Performance*, Cambridge: Cambridge University Press.

OECD (2014), *Innovation-Driven Growth in Regions: The Role of Smart Specialisation*, Paris: OECD Publishing. https://www.oecd.org/sti/inno/smart specialisation.htm.

OECD (2016), *Regions at a Glance 2016*, Paris: OECD Publishing.

Office of the Economic Development Board (2018), 'Smart Specialisation: Insights for a Future Industry Policy', Adelaide: Economic Development Board South Australia and Department of State Development.

Ohmae, K. (1993), 'The Rise of the Region State', *Foreign Affairs*, **72** (2), 78–87.

Piore, M. and C. Sabel (1984), *The Second Industrial Divide: Possibilities For Prosperity*, New York: Basic Books.

Porter, M.E. (2003), 'The Economic Performance of Regions', *Regional Studies*, **37** (6–7), 549–578. https://doi.org/10.1080/0034340032000108688.

Radosevic, S. and K. Ciampi Stancova (2018), 'Internationalising Smart Specialisation: Assessment and Issues in the Case of EU New Member States', *Journal of the Knowledge Economy*, **9** (1), 263–293. https://doi.org/10.1007/s13132-015-0339-3.

Rodríguez-Pose, A. (2018), 'Commentary: The Revenge of the Places That Don't Matter (and What to Do About It)', *Cambridge Journal of Regions, Economy and Society*. https://doi.org/10.1093/cjres/rsx024.

Sabel, C.F. and Y. Kuznetsov (2017), 'Managing Self-Discovery: Diagnostic Monitoring of a Portfolio of Projects and Programs', in S. Radosevic, A. Curaj, R. Gheorghiu, L. Andreescu and I. Wade (eds), *Advances in the Theory and Practice of Smart Specialization*, London and Oxford, UK; Cambridge, MA and San Diego, CA, USA: Academic Press, pp. 51–72.

Saxenian, A. and N.C. Dabby (2004), 'Creating and Sustaining Regional Collaboration in Silicon Valley? The Case of Joint Venture: Silicon Valley', Working Paper 2004-05, Institute of Urban and Regional Development, University of California at Berkeley.

Socintec and Inno (2005), 'Ex-Post Evaluation of the RIS, RTTs and RISI ERDF Innovative Actions for the Period 1994–99', Final Synthesis Report to the European Commission.

Tödtling, F. and M. Trippl (2005), 'One Size Fits All? Towards a Differentiated Regional Innovation Policy Approach', *Research Policy*, **34** (8), 1203–1219. https://doi.org/10.1016/j.respol.2005.01.018.

UN IATT (2019), 'A Guidebook for the Preparation of STI for SDGs Roadmaps: An Input to the Fourth STI Forum, New York', New York: United Nations Inter-Agency Task Team on Science, Technology and Innovation for the SDGs (IATT). https://sustainabledevelopment.un.org/content/documents/22724Guidebook_STI_for_SDG_Roadmaps_Draft_for_STI_Forum.pdf.

Wessner, C.W. and T.R. Howell (2018), 'Smart Specialization in US Regional Policy: Successes, Setbacks and Best Practices', Background paper for an OECD/EC Workshop, 15 October, workshop series 'Broadening Innovation Policy: New Insights for Regions and Cities', Paris.

Wilson, B. (2016), 'Smart Specialization and Innovation: A View from Beyond Europe', in A. Nikina, J. Piqué and L. Sanz (eds), *Areas of Innovation in a Global World: Concept and Practice*, Malaga: International Association of Science Parks and Areas of Innovation, pp. 1–7.

World Bank (2016), *Toward an Innovative Poland: The Entrepreneurial Discovery Process and Business Needs Analysis*, Washington, DC: World Bank.

PART I

Understanding the Economic Fabric
of Territories

2. Establishing the basis for RIS3 regional innovation policies: mapping economic specialisation*

Henning Kroll

2.1 INTRODUCTION

According to official guidelines of the European Commission (EC) and much of the early academic literature, smart specialisation strategies constitute 'place-based economic transformation agendas' (Foray et al., 2012; Foray, 2014). Rather than focusing on the development of technologies per se, they are intended to identify specific current and possible future domains of technology uptake and application that can help to close Europe's productivity gap vis-à-vis the United States across a variety of industries (Rodrik, 2004; Foray et al., 2009). By increasing performance across various regional industries, they should help policy-makers to enhance growth dynamics in the 'real economy' (Landabaso, 2012, 2014) and safeguard local jobs.

In practice, however, the Research and Innovation Strategies for Smart Specialisation (RIS3) strategy process was communicated as one to design 'innovation strategies' which, in many member states, resonated more strongly with research policy than with economic development (Kroll, 2015, 2016). Accordingly, many – although admittedly not all – strategies abandoned their original intent, and became strategies of at best research and innovation or, in some cases, more or less straightforward research. Accordingly, many of the concrete RIS3 monitoring activities that we have witnessed during the 2014–2020 support period have centred around traditional innovation indicators such as publications and patents,

* The author thanks Alexander Kleibrink, then working for the European Commission's Joint Research Centre in Seville, for providing practical support throughout the analytical process in Serbia. He acknowledges continuous support of his colleagues Đerđ Horvat and Esther Schnabl in the development and execution of the statistical analysis. Finally, he would like to thank Hugo Hollanders and Đuro Kutlača for methodological inspiration.

accompanied by traditional, thematically unspecific European Structural and Investment Fund (ESIF) reporting on outcomes, results and socio-economic impacts. Conversely, the conceptually required analysis of interfaces between industries and technologies has only been pursued in rare cases, because this is methodologically more challenging, and also because such questions of broader societal impact are more difficult to engage with politically (Foray et al., 2011; Iacobucci, 2014; Kroll, 2018, 2019a).

Furthermore, both the EC's smart specialisation guidelines and a growing strand of literature emphasise the need to focus technology deployment on solving local, socio-economic challenges, and where necessary employing source technologies from outside the region to do so. In short, smart specialisation is – or at least should be – about deploying technologies, even those sourced from outside the region, for local purposes (Foray et al., 2012; Kroll, 2019b). Quite evidently, therefore, it cannot be useful to conduct an isolated analysis of regional science, technology and innovation (STI) indicators that does not consider the local socio-economic basis (Kleibrink et al., 2016). At the very least, this requires a complement: an analysis of regional economic indicators and a subsequent analysis of areas that may be in need of and display at least some capacity for technological upgrading. So far, however, such a needs-oriented perspective on regional economic development has rarely been taken (Gianelle and Kleibrink, 2015; Kroll, 2016). While interregional collaboration is commonly promoted in smart specialisation discourses, this is most often promoted as a collaboration between the strong, rather than one in which innovators from more advanced regions qualify industries in less advanced environments (Vanguard Initiative, 2016).

Against this background, this chapter outlines a conceptual framework that complies with the current academic discourses in regional science and economic geography. Subsequently, it illustrates how a suitable approach can be implemented based on the data available at most national statistical offices.

2.2   CONCEPTUAL FRAMEWORK

Since Michael Porter's seminal contributions in 1990 and 1998 (Porter, 1990, 1998), but actually dating back much earlier to Alfred Marshall (1920), regional science literature has established that the agglomeration of economic activities can be and has been beneficial for industrial productivity, efficiency and growth (Beaudry and Schiffauerova, 2009). Against this background, a broad range of cluster literature and subsequent contributions on smart specialisation have advanced what are, in principle, variants of the old Marshall–Arrow–Romer (MAR) proposition (Glaeser et al., 1992; Saxenian, 1994): that specialised industrial agglomeration expedites economic growth as it facilitates the 'exchange of knowledge, ideas, and information on products and processes through imitation, business interactions, and the inter-firm circulation of skilled workers' (Beaudry and Schiffauerova, 2009, p.318). In the wake of Porter's writings, methodologies to identify such localised clusters have been put forward and have become common practice in both academia and policy-making.

At the same time, the counter-argument of Jacobs's (1969) proposition that unrelated agglomerations might be just as beneficial has been refined and corroborated in the related variety discussion. Following Frenken et al.'s (2007) as well as Hidalgo et al.'s (2007) much-noted contributions, a consensus has emerged that the best hopes for productive and meaningful industrial path development are in fact situations in which industrial capacities are thematically neither too fragmented nor too similar to stifle cross-fertilisation between different domains of knowledge (Boschma et al., 2017; Grillitsch et al., 2018; Isaksen and Trippl, 2016). Consequently, 'smart specialisation' can hardly be conceived of as an overspecialisation in specific industrial sectors. Overall, therefore, any useful RIS3 monitoring will have to allow this basic distinction.

More importantly, however, it has to provide at least some indication of whether the sectors in which a region is specialised are future-oriented in the sense that the region can productively leverage them to position itself in ongoing socio-technical and industrial change (Boschma et al., 2017). Depending on where the region stands initially, it can engage in different ways with different implications. Prior literature suggests that technology-driven path creation, which many intuitively aspire to, has generated sufficient socio-economic momentum to actually trigger a transformative impulse in only a few cases. Boschma et al. (2017) call this attempt at generating activity in novel fields 'saltation' and suggest that it is risky, as its build-up requires a very specific set of starting conditions and a broad range of capable actors, neither of which are present in the majority of regions. Moreover, isolated change in budding sectors can hardly be suitable to generate growth and jobs in a way that transforms the broader economy.

On the contrary, initiatives and interventions aimed at path renewal in existing industries which are in jeopardy of falling behind have quite often contributed fundamentally to a region's renaissance. According to Boschma et al. (2017), there are two variants: 'exaptation', in which new entrants renew and reinvigorate local development paths; and 'transplantation', in which local incumbents that had lost touch with recent developments of the dominant regime are reconnected. Thus, useful monitoring will have to collect a number of relevant indicators beyond concentration parameters. To explore the field beyond obvious high-tech hotspots, it must be able to differentiate sectoral concentrations that are locked into unsustainable paths beyond saving, from traditional industries that may in fact yield themselves readily to different types of path renewal. To this end, a number of key economic indicators can provide first guidance, while in a final step, further insights will have to be drawn from the relation of science and technology.

Since the early 1990s, a stream of contributions has developed the notion of regional innovation systems, in which the generation of technologies in localised interaction plays a central role alongside scientific efforts, economic activity and specific institutions (Cooke, 1992; Cooke et al., 1998). In line with the general tenets of innovation system research (Freeman, 1987; Lundvall, 1992; Edquist, 1997), technology in this context is considered one central element of a complex, iterative and, in many ways, recursive process of conceiving and introducing new solutions (Kline and Rosenberg, 1986). While this postulates strong relations between scientific research, technological development and economic value creation, these can never *ex ante* be conceived of as linear or localised. In a globalised economy, it is the exception rather than the rule if innovation processes are contained within regions (Coe and Yeung, 2015; Yeung, 2009; Asheim and Isaksen, 2002; Markusen, 1996).

As interactions between economic actors are influenced and driven by various forms of non-spatial proximity (Boschma, 2005), technological capacities relate in a multiscalar system across regions and, more often than not, develop a substantial share of their impact far from their place of origin (Asheim, 2012; Boschma, 2017). Accordingly, localised interactions between innovators and users are contingent on many factors, and not a ubiquitous opportunity (Bathelt et al., 2004; Foray, 2014). In the majority of regions addressed by smart specialisation strategies, therefore, local scientific capacities may matter less than internal dynamics within the business sector (Asheim and Coenen, 2006; Blažek, 2016; Isaksen and Trippl, 2017). Although it focuses on studying local manifestations of innovation processes, the regional innovation literature broadly acknowledges that interregional exchanges and networks of control constitute central driving forces of regional development (Coe and Yeung, 2015; Asheim, 2012; Asheim and Gertler, 2005; Bathelt et al., 2004).

In equal measure, however, the regional innovation systems literature has pointed out the need for a certain degree of localised thematic fit between technological and economic capacities as an essential, desirable characteristic and a precondition for endogenously driven regional development (Asheim et al., 2016; Asheim and Gertler, 2005; Cooke, 1998; Cooke et al., 1998). In regions without this fundamental ability to relate technological capacities to local industrial dynamics, any consideration of innovation indicators may well be of an academic nature and not very relevant to regional economic transformation in practice. Precisely because these local matches between technological and economic activity can never be taken as a given, they should be considered a key element in all relevant monitoring approaches, to establish whether and where local innovation may be useful for industrial development.

Against this background, analyses that inform socio-economically relevant processes of entrepreneurial discovery should contain three main elements:

- Requirement 1: they must outline the current specialisations and absolute relevance of sectors in the local fabric of economic activities. This conveys a basic message on where modernisation and path renewal could deliver the most momentum.
- Requirement 2: they need to qualify the identified key areas of activity with regard their current growth performance, productivity and wages paid in order to evaluate them with a view to their 'future-orientation' and attractiveness as fields of development.
- Requirement 3: they must analyse which local technological activities could contribute to local development and path renewal in those domains of activities that were identified as relevant during the first two steps of analysis either directly or from a related variety perspective.

2.3   DATA AND METHOD

2.3.1   Approach and Data Sources

A monitoring approach in the RIS3 context requires reliable and valid data that are available from official statistics sources. That said, the approach presented in the following does assume a good level of collaboration between the researchers conducting the monitoring and those administratively responsible for data collection at national or regional levels. Quite commonly, the detailed information needed for the subsequent analysis will not be directly available in the required format or disaggregation, so that specific efforts are required on the part of the analysts and those processing and storing the data.

Based on the experiences from different countries, the relevant data sources for the three main steps of the analysis include:

- labour force survey (employment, wages);
- structural business statistics (firm numbers, employment, value added);
- innovation survey data;
- patent statistics;
- publication statistics.

In general, it is useful to begin the analysis with labour force survey data, to not unduly exclude the agricultural or relevant sections of the service sector. However, structural business statistics may provide more detailed information on the nature of industrial specialisations concerning the important relations between firm numbers, employment and value added. Innovation survey data are only useful if they can be disaggregated to Statistical Classification of Economic Activities in the European Community

(NACE) level at least to some extent to facilitate later matchings; and patent and publication statistics should ideally be translated from their International Patent Classes and Web of Science (IPC/WoS) classifications to NACE categories based on existing methodologies.

2.3.2 Steps of Analysis and Variables

Based on the requirements outlined above, this chapter proposes a successive three-step approach to identifying the economic potentials for smart specialisation as outlined in Figure 2.1.

Step 1: identifying specialisations
With a view to the first requirement, the first step of the analysis needs to identify areas of sectoral concentration in the local economy. One fundamental decision to make in this context is in choosing the framework of reference. From a domestic policy perspective, it can be reasonable to define specialisations within a national framework. Generally, however, it is more useful to define them internationally with a view to the actual playing field of industrial competition. While this complicates the search

Figure 2.1   General approach of economic monitoring

for adequate data in practice, it is certainly worthwhile from a conceptual standpoint.

While much has been said about the limited suitability of NACE classifications in this context, NACE remains the baseline differentiation of all public statistics. Hence, any implications of its structural datedness must be addressed at the level of interpretation rather than being built into the analysis *ex ante*. To a degree, this approach already seeks to address this issue by working at a high level of disaggregation (NACE3). This is able to distinguish specific types of activities that can then be aggregated in different ways. To capture relevant aspects of sectoral concentration, the first step of the analysis considers the following.

First, specialisation proper: that is, whether a sector is more important for the regional economy than the national average in relative terms. A typical measure to determine this specialisation is the location quotient (LQ),[1] which compares the share of a sector in the local economy with the share of this sector in the national economy.

Second, absolute size: the mere fact that a sector is more important regionally than nationally in relative terms may be irrelevant for regional economic policy if it is too small in absolute terms. Hence, absolute size is another important threshold criterion to be defined in relation to the overall size of the national economy.

Subsequently, it is important to correct for statistical artefacts resulting from the high level of disaggregation that is conceptually advisable. At NACE3 level, it is easily possible to 'gain' specialisations in single years, due to idiosyncratic investment; or to lose them due to closures or reclassification of single plants. Hence, sectoral data should be analysed based on time-series and only those sectors confirmed as potentially relevant specialisations that appear at least three times in a single year during a defined period of observation. When using structural business statistics, it may be advisable to select only those specialisations that occur simultaneously with a view to firm numbers, employment or value added.

The end of this first step identifies a list of possible smart specialisation priorities at NUTS 3 level. Before proceeding, standard economic and government functions (administration, wholesale, retail, transportation, and so on) should be removed from this list, and certain types of activities considered from a normative perspective (gambling, weapons and ammunition, and so on).

---

[1] $LQ = [e_{NACE\,X} / e_{total}] / [E_{NACE\,X} / E_{total}]$ with e = (sectoral) employment in region and E = (sectoral) employment in nation.

Step 2: qualifying specialisations

To assess the relevance and potential promise of the identified list of potential priority domains, a number of further, qualifying sources of information can be considered, following two different fundamental rationales.

First, potential domains should be considered with a view to their current dynamism, including recent growth and productivity:

- Recent growth in employment: sectors showing a recent positive development are more likely to be on a development path that is either still dynamic or provides sufficient opportunity for path renewal.
- Labour productivity: ideally, this should be expressed in relation to industry averages, to avoid classification by capital intensity, and instead provide evidence of how technologically up-to-date regional actors are. If this is not possible, however, even raw productivity values can – in an inter-sectoral comparison – indicate a specific sector's current state of development.
- Exports: under many – although not all – framework conditions, exports provide additional evidence of the competitiveness of domestic industries. Unless they are driven purely by labour costs or natural advantages, goods and services are usually exported if their quality or performance is better than that of foreign alternatives.

Second, potential domains should be considered with a view to the contribution that an improvement of the economic dynamics in this specific field would make to the socio-economic transformation of the region or nation in question.

- Total employment: although potential domains were selected based on minimum thresholds, more detailed information about the absolute number of jobs involved can indicate what economic development effects future political intervention could have in this specific area. Typically, this is the criterion under which path renewal activities would score better than path creation ones.
- Sector-specific wages: while a sector can be important for a regional economy, it will only be worthy of support if it offers the local population sufficient wages to at least keep them from migrating. Where wage levels are already low, this becomes even more important. In this respect, path renewal activities can become problematic and at least some share of path creation activities becomes more appealing.

● Value added: beyond employment and wages, it is important that an industry which could be supported by smart specialisation strategies is amenable to technological input – and is not just assembly-oriented. The value added generated locally provides a good first indication of a sector's value chain position. Again, industrial averages of turnover–value added relations would sharpen the reference, but these are usually more difficult to identify than for productivity.

At the end of this second step, it is possible to evaluate different sectors with a view to different characteristics. This allows an estimation of not only their general suitability, but also their potential position as complementary elements within future smart specialisation strategies. In line with the conceptual section, a non-exclusive list of such possible functions includes: (1) pockets of dynamism in emerging industries, that is, global path creation; (2) sectors that perform well but with below-average value creation, whose position in global value chains could be improved by locally driven path renewal; and (3) sectors that play a substantial role for employment, where path renewal could safeguard competitiveness, even if external technology infusion is involved.

Step 3: juxtapose techno-scientific and economic capacities
In a third step, the analysis addresses the essential question of whether and which local capacities in research and innovation can be productively combined with regional economic capacities. As outlined above, the conceptual literature suggests that a fundamental match of such capacities is required to enable the development of concrete solutions for specific application environments. Moreover, the presence of field-specific technological capacities can facilitate – or even be required to enable – the adaptation of general-purpose technologies.

The central components of this third step are the analysis of bibliometric data (which are not easy to translate into NACE categories) and patent data (which can usually be translated into NACE categories with limited effort). The former is best understood as an analysis of complementary activities. It clarifies which of the (broad range of) academic capacities that a particular industrial sector can profit from are present in the region. Accordingly, publication data need not necessarily be translated into NACE categories directly. Instead, the available correspondence tables should be used as a guide. These relate to capacities that reside primarily within industry itself, so that a generic translation of IPC-based information into NACE should be attempted where possible. Although this does not enable the analysts to attribute patents to their actual sources within a specific environment, it does give a clearer indication of which locally present technological activities are potentially relevant for which sector. If survey data on innovation activities are available disaggregated by economic sector, even this last caveat can be reduced since de facto information on specific local industries' innovation capacities is then available. Despite all their generic methodological shortcomings, innovation surveys are thus the only approach that can help to detect nascent pockets of activity in dynamic sectors that cannot yet be identified in a Step 1-type economic analysis.

Methodologically, the precise approach taken can be adapted to the available data to a certain degree. Usually, data quality will be good for publication and patent data because these can be sourced from centralised repositories. In this case, the respective analyses of scientific and technological capacities should replicate Step 1 of the analysis (or at least a reduced version of it) with different sets of data. Applying this analysis enables regional policy-makers to distinguish industries in which science–industry linkages and path renewal or path creation 'from within' are possible, from those for which external or broader networking solutions are needed to ensure technological upgrading.

2.3.3   Analysis of Serbia as a Case Study

In late 2016, the Fraunhofer Institute for Systems and Innovation Research (Fraunhofer ISI) was tasked with providing methodological assistance to the ongoing process of Serbia preparing for smart specialisation activities under the Technical Assistance and Information Exchange (TAIEX) instrument of the European Commission programme. During the course of 2017, the institute collaborated intensively with the European Commission's Joint Research Centre (JRC), the Ministry of Education, Science and Technological Development of the Republic of Serbia, and the Mihajlo Pupin Institute, to pilot the analyses described above. Variants of this process were later taken up by other states in the region (see, e.g., Hollanders, 2017 for Moldova), although it has not been replicated in full so far.

For the Serbian project, the Statistical Office of the Republic of Serbia and the Mihajlo Pupin Institute provided the experts with good-quality data from various sources on almost all the analytical dimensions, including detailed innovation survey data. Commonly, detailed data were provided by economic, technological and scientific fields of activity. Economic and technological information were provided in NACE three-digit categories (to which patent data were also translated), whereas scientific data remained in their original Web of Science/Frascati classification.

Following the JRC's mandate, the national level was defined as the framework of reference against which all Serbian regions were measured. On this basis, detailed analyses were carried out for four of Serbia's five regions. Since 2011, the official statistical system of Serbia has subdivided the country into five main regions:

- RS11: Belgrade.
- RS12: Vojvodina.
- RS21: Šumadija and Western Serbia.
- RS22: Southern and Eastern Serbia.
- RS23: Kosovo and Metohija.

These regions are relatively similar in size in terms of population (between 1.6 million and 2.0 million inhabitants) but their economic significance varies between an annual gross domestic product (GDP) of €12.5 billion in Belgrade and €4.5 million in Southern and Eastern Serbia and in Kosovo. The level of per capita income differs respectively as well. In relative terms, however, the economic capacity of the five Serbian regions does not vary more substantially than, for example, regions in Germany, Poland or France. Belgrade is the strongest region, with a GDP per capita of about €7500. Southern and Eastern Serbia displays the lowest GDP per capita of €2900. While Serbia has various industrial strengths, value added mainly stems from service industries. Although agriculture is unimportant with regard to value added, it accounts for high shares of employment. In Šumadija and Western Serbia, 30.9 per cent of jobs are in agriculture, and at least 18.0 per cent even in Vojvodina. Generally, no data are available for the de facto independent region of Kosovo and Metohija.

2.3.4   Step 1 of the Analysis

In the first step of the study on Serbia, industrial sectors were preliminarily considered as concentrations if their location quotient in the labour force survey employment was above 1.25 or 1.5 and, at the same time, they employed more than 5000 people. Additional analyses were conducted for relevant structural business statistics data with different absolute threshold values (250 for number of firms and RSD 10 million for value added).

A first overview of the sectors identified using this purely specialisation and critical mass-based analysis is given in Box 2.1. It is immediately apparent that this type of information can provide only a very cursory and preliminary basis for future economic development policies. In line with the methodology outlined above, the following sectors were excluded from the findings as basic economic functions: 46 (wholesale), 47 (retail), 80–84

BOX 2.1   LIST OF PRELIMINARY SPECIALISATIONS IN
                      SERBIAN REGIONS

RS11: Belgrade

LQ > 1.5

- C18.1 – Printing and service activities related to printing.
- C26.2 – Manufacture of computers and peripheral equipment.
- H49.3 – Other passenger land transport.
- J58.1 – Publishing of books, periodicals and other publishing activities.
- J62.0 – Computer programming, consultancy and related activities.
- K64.1 – Monetary intermediation.

LQ > 1.25 < 1.5

- I56.1 – Restaurants and mobile food service activities.
- M71.1 – Architectural and engineering activities and technical consultancy.
- Q86.1 – Hospital activities.
- Q86.2 – Medical and dental practice activities.

RS12: Vojvodina

LQ > 1.5

- A1.1 – Growing of non-perennial crops.
- C10.1 – Processing of meat and production of meat products.
- C19.2 – Manufacture of refined petroleum products.
- C20.1 – Manufacture of basic chemicals, fertiliser, plastics and synth. rubber.
- C22.2 – Manufacture of plastics products.
- C29.3 – Manufacture of parts and accessories for motor vehicles.

LQ > 1.25 < 1.5

- C10.7 – Manufacture of bakery and farinaceous products.
- C10.8 – Manufacture of other food products.

RS21: Šumadija and Western Serbia

LQ > 1.5

- A1.2 – Growing of perennial crops.
- A1.4 – Animal production.
- A1.5 – Mixed farming.
- C10.3 – Processing and preserving of fruit and vegetables.
- C14.1 – Manufacture of wearing apparel, except fur apparel.

- C16.1 – Sawmilling and planing of wood.
- C22.2 – Manufacture of plastics products.
- C25.4 – Manufacture of weapons and ammunition.
- C29.1 – Manufacture of motor vehicles.
- C29.3 – Manufacture of parts and accessories for motor vehicles.
- C31.0 – Manufacture of furniture.

LQ > 1.25 < 1.5

- C10.7 – Manufacture of bakery and farinaceous products.
- C25.9 – Manufacture of other fabricated metal products.
- F43.2 – Electrical, plumbing and other construction installation activities.

RS22: Southern and Eastern Serbia

LQ > 1.5

- C22.1 – Manufacture of rubber products.
- C24.1 – Manufacture of basic iron and steel and of ferro-alloys.
- D35.1 – Electric power generation, transmission and distribution.
- T98.1 – [Agricultural] activities of private households for own use.

LQ > 1.25 < 1.5

- A1.1 – Growing of non-perennial crops.
- C14.1 – Manufacture of wearing apparel, except fur apparel.

Source: Adapted from Kroll et al. (2017).

(security, administration, public services), 85 (education), 92 (gambling), 94 (associations), 96 (personal services) and 97 (activities of households).

2.3.5   Step 2 of the Analysis

Based on the data available from Serbian statistical sources, the Serbian analytical team at the Mihajlo Pupin Institute and the Statistical Office of the Republic of Serbia compiled a number of complementary indicators that further qualified the economic sectors identified in the first step. In the context of the project, the analysts had been explicitly asked to refrain from additional judgements (these were the object of subsequent discussions), so that the indicators featured in the final report were information-based only.

However, we can see quite clearly in Table 2.1 that only some of the identified sectors are relevant with a view to the international positioning

Table 2.1 Step 2: qualifying information on potential priority domains

	Employment[a]	Exports[b]	Wages[c]	Value added[d]	Labour productivity[e]	Employment growth (%)[f]
Belgrade						
C18.1 – Printing	4936	183	41352	3.91	1359	24.6
C26.2 – Computers	240	41038	136745	4.15	2191	19.6
H49.3 – Transport	16463	0	47674	13.66	1303	21.8
J58.1 – Publishing	4980	30282	64241	7.66	1441	31.4
J62.0 – Programming	10413	0	244641	28.45	2942	28.2
M64.1 – Monetary	15931	0	104359	x	x	26.9
I56.1 – Restaurants	16879	0	30319	4.37	583	19.0
M71.1 – Arch/Tech C	6115	1190	69809	12.90	1672	23.5
O84.1 – Administration	18745	0	53078	x	x	19.3
Q86.1 – Hospitals	20490	0	45152	x	x	15.6
Q86.2 – Med./Dental	14940	0	40583	x	x	19.5
Vojvodina						
A1.1 – N-P Crops	61889	486872	40624	x	x	24.7
C10.1 – Meat Proc.	9088	55458	33347	9.00	1415	25.3
C19.2 – Refining	2684	191548	133598	42.16	14092	29.7
C20.1 – Basic Chm.	2803	330834	65259	2.94	822	23.9
C22.2 – Plastics	6396	234372	52938	8.42	1738	20.2
C29.3 – Vehicle Part	9351	274958	39358	6.92	938	21.9
C10.7 – Bakery	10488	28438	27213	3.58	1061	19.5
C10.8 – Food Prod.	6347	213260	57331	7.54	2996	19.4
Šumadija and Western Serbia						
A1.2 – P. Crops	29306	49131	25512	x	x	24.9
A1.4 – Animal Prod.	47146	26876	25747	x	x	25.7

	a	d	c	e	f	b
A1.5 – Mixed Farm	136707	0	25890	x	x	24.0
C10.3 – Fruit Proc.	5584	221273	36595	7.51	1824	22.3
C14.1 – Apparel	11022	91073	24367	4.32	668	26.3
C16.1 – Sawmilling	4538	22779	30977	1.98	915	19.6
C22.2 – Plastics	6626	177013	38466	8.39	1844	19.2
C25.4 – Weapons	8015	88905	55707	9.94	1455	33.1
C29.1 – Vehicles	3821	1018810	50058	16.81	4057	28.5
C29.3 – Vehicle Part	4881	248821	36474	10.48	1083	12.3
C31.0 – Furniture	7084	113788	30689	4.72	1029	16.9
Southern and Eastern Serbia						
C22.1 – Rubber	4711	313158	60348	14.88	4708	27.0
C24.1 – Iron & Steel	4830	135201	70212	–6.87	–1364	39.0
D35.1 – Electr. Power	9711	0	84252	0.27	1725	22.7
T98.1 – Agriculture	53929	0	x	x	x	26.0
A1.1 – N-P Crops	30046	15392	35030	x	x	17.4
C14.1 – Apparel	8277	45675	23671	3.26	592	17.5

Notes:
a Number of employed persons, head count, 2016.
b Thousands of euros, 2016.
c Net annual wages, RSD, 2016.
d Value added at factor costs, billion RSD, 2015.
e Factor productivity, 1000 RSD, 2015.
f AAGR, 2011–2016.

Source: Adapted from Kroll et al. (2017).

of the economy, and that many are less attractive for explicit promotion as their productivity is rather low and they do not pay good wages. Finally, a few have quite obviously become unproductive beyond saving and will most probably become the subject of economic conversion rather than of promotion strategies in the future. At the same time, the differentiated analyses allows us to document that in Vojvodina, for example, wages in agriculture are higher than in a national comparison, and are even higher in the associated processing industries.

2.3.6   Step 3 of the Analysis

In a final step, the analysis juxtaposes three kinds of analysis for economic, technological and scientific specialisation along diverse indicators, synthesising them graphically in bubble charts. Figure 2.2 illustrates how specialisations were identified along different dimensions. Interestingly, the findings of this step confirmed the potential of the agricultural sector and its associated processing and equipment industries as well as that of certain light industries. Contrary to the political perception of these sectors, notable innovative activities, even patenting, could be documented in these traditionally not very dynamic areas and related industries. Figure 2.3 documents the final conclusions of the analysis for the economic, technological and scientific capacities of the four Serbian regions.

As detailed innovation survey data were available, it was possible to match economic and innovation capacities directly and to specify in which sectors industrial dynamism is accompanied by capacities for technological upgrading and innovative development. By combining these findings with that of a detailed patent analysis, it was also possible to spot emerging clusters of competence that the economic analysis alone had not revealed. Furthermore, this approach was able to specify which academic capacities remain stand-alone with no clear reference to the concrete economy of the respective regions. Figure 2.4 provides an overview of these findings.

2.4   DISCUSSION

Subsequent to the above exercise, the findings were taken up in the political discussion and confirmed as accurate by various experts in the field. Since Serbia is not yet a European Union member state, it is under no political obligation to engage in a full-fledged process to define a broad and comprehensive economic strategy with diverse priorities. However, the Serbian government did decide to further develop its policies for computer programming and, in this context, the study was used as a basis

Source: Kroll et al. (2017, pp. 29, 48, 58).

Figure 2.2 Examples of specialisation analysis across different dimensions

Economic Activities

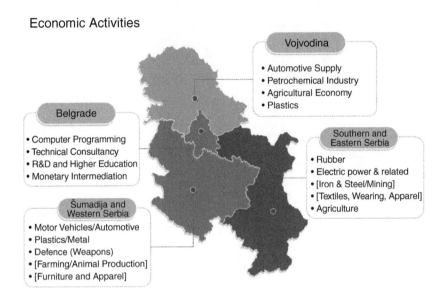

Vojvodina
- Automotive Supply
- Petrochemical Industry
- Agricultural Economy
- Plastics

Belgrade
- Computer Programming
- Technical Consultancy
- R&D and Higher Education
- Monetary Intermediation

Southern and Eastern Serbia
- Rubber
- Electric power & related
- [Iron & Steel/Mining]
- [Textiles, Wearing, Apparel]
- Agriculture

Šumadija and Western Serbia
- Motor Vehicles/Automotive
- Plastics/Metal
- Defence (Weapons)
- [Farming/Animal Production]
- [Furniture and Apparel]

Technological Activities

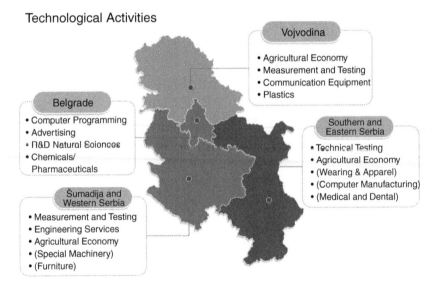

Vojvodina
- Agricultural Economy
- Measurement and Testing
- Communication Equipment
- Plastics

Belgrade
- Computer Programming
- Advertising
- R&D Natural Sciences
- Chemicals/ Pharmaceuticals

Southern and Eastern Serbia
- Technical Testing
- Agricultural Economy
- (Wearing & Apparel)
- (Computer Manufacturing)
- (Medical and Dental)

Šumadija and Western Serbia
- Measurement and Testing
- Engineering Services
- Agricultural Economy
- (Special Machinery)
- (Furniture)

Note: In leaving out Kosovo, this map follows European Union diplomatic conventions. This does not imply any positioning of the author on the Kosovo issue.

Source: Kroll et al. (2017, pp. 29, 48, 58).

Figure 2.3   Matching economic, technological and scientific specialisations of Serbia

Scientific Activities

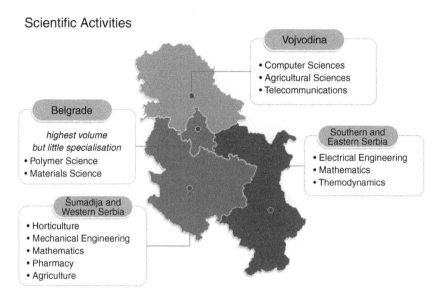

Vojvodina
- Computer Sciences
- Agricultural Sciences
- Telecommunications

Belgrade

highest volume
but little specialisation
- Polymer Science
- Materials Science

Southern and Eastern Serbia
- Electrical Engineering
- Mathematics
- Themodynamics

Šumadija and Western Serbia
- Horticulture
- Mechanical Engineering
- Mathematics
- Pharmacy
- Agriculture

Figure 2.3   (continued)

to legitimise these activities. In particular, its findings regarding the strong dynamism, high wages and visibly complementary capacities between academia and science were quoted in the discussion. At the same time, the subsequent, qualitative analysis of the information technology sector not only revealed weaknesses in the initial data (due to misclassification), but also led to a substantive qualification of the actual level of human and technological capacity (much is outsourced coding). Furthermore, those domains of activity that indeed justify the above-quoted high wages remain largely disconnected from the local economy (Kleibrink et al., 2018). The more traditional domains for which the study suggested more promising structures, in contrast, were not explored further.

The fate of this analysis confirms existing wisdom from the literature that most policy-makers only follow up analytical studies partially, and that relevant novel perspectives may be lost in the subsequent discourse (Foray et al., 2011; Iaccobucci, 2014; Kroll, 2015). In the Serbian case, aspects that would have been very relevant from a smart specialisation perspective and more focused on path renewal have not been pursued further in the end: that is, how best to modernise those industries, including agriculture, that are accountable for much employment; or how to deal with those industries, including automotive, that are well connected to international values chains, but not yet ideally positioned within them (Kroll et al., 2016).

At the same time, the study underlined how crucial it is to make this

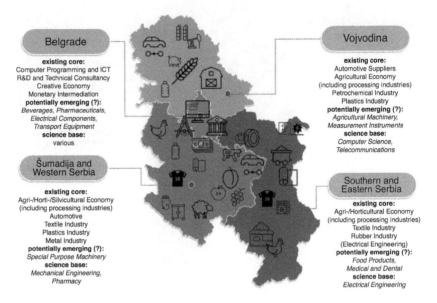

Note: In leaving out Kosovo, this map follows European Union diplomatic conventions. This does not imply any positioning of the author on the Kosovo issue.

Source: Kroll et al. (2017, p. 74).

Figure 2.4   Synthesis: potential specialisations of Serbia

distinction between scientific, technological and economic capacities. In many European areas for which smart specialisation strategies will have to be developed in the future, true localised matches between these capacities may be few and far between. Analytically, it is understandable that traditional sectors appeal less to policy-makers, as in their current state and with the very low wages that they offer, they do not provide simple solutions for economic issues. However, the analysis of the Serbian economy has underlined very graphically that smart specialisation must at least attempt to affect larger parts of the population. In the end, economic transformation can only be achieved if policy shifts its focus of support beyond the high-tech domain.

2.5   CONCLUSIONS

Having argued that there is a conceptual need to reorient future smart specialisation monitoring from one focused on science to one based on economic analysis, this chapter outlined a three-step process to implement such an analysis in practice. Reporting on a pilot case in the context of TAIEX-funded activities in Serbia, it demonstrated why and how such a monitoring approach yields different insights to a traditional, technological capacity-based one.

More precisely, it documented that economic transformation can only be achieved if working from a path renewal perspective with those sectors that are relevant in terms of employment and value added – at least as one part of the equation. Not disputing that coordinated support can be important for potential path-creating 'lighthouse sectors', it underlined that many other regions, in particular rural ones, will have other activities to work with and that, indeed, there are many different ways to distinguish them into promising and less-promising options.

If future smart specialisation efforts are to take their original ambition to drive 'economic transformation' seriously, the accompanying statistical analysis must be anchored in the economic domain as well. While the political impact of any analysis must remain *ex ante* uncertain, the above 'growth and jobs'-based approach appears to stand a good chance of resonating with regional economic policy-makers.

REFERENCES

Asheim, B. 2012. The changing role of learning regions in the globalising knowledge economy: a theoretical re-examination. *Regional Studies* **46**(3): 993–1004.

Asheim, B., and Coenen, L. 2006. Contextualising regional innovation systems in a globalising learning economy: on knowledge bases and institutional frameworks. *Journal of Technology Transfer* **31**: 163–173.

Asheim, B., and Gertler, M.S. 2005. The geography of innovation: regional innovation systems. In J. Fagerberg, D. Mowery and R. Nelson (eds), *The Oxford Handbook of Innovation*. Oxford: Oxford University Press, pp. 291–317.

Asheim, B., and Isaksen, A. 2002. Regional innovation systems: the integration of local 'sticky' and global 'ubiquitous' knowledge. *Journal of Technology Transfer* **27**(1): 77–86.

Asheim, B., Grillitsch, M., and Trippl, M. 2016. Regional innovation systems: past – present – future. In R. Shearmur, C. Carrincazeaux and D. Doloreux (eds), *Handbook on the Geographies of Innovation*. Cheltenham, UK and Northampton, MA, USA: Edward Elgar Publishing, pp. 45–62. doi: 10.43 37/9781784710774.

Bathelt, H., Malmberg, A., and Maskell, P. 2004. Clusters and knowledge: local buzz, global pipelines and the process of knowledge creation. *Progress in Human Geography* **28**(1): 31–56.

Beaudry, C., and Schiffauerova, A. 2009. Who's right, Marshall or Jacobs? The localization versus urbanization debate. *Research Policy* **38**: 318–337.

Blažek, J. 2016. Towards a typology of repositioning strategies of GVC/GPN suppliers: the case of functional upgrading and downgrading. *Journal of Economic Geography* **16**(4): 849–869.

Boschma, R. 2005. Proximity and innovation: a critical assessment. *Regional Studies* **39**(1): 61–74. doi: 10.1080/0034340052000320887.

Boschma, R. 2017. Relatedness as driver of regional diversification: a research agenda. *Regional Studies* **51**(3): 351–364. doi: 10.1080/00343404.2016.1254767.

Boschma, R., Coenen, L., Frenken, K., and Truffer, B. 2017. Towards a theory of regional diversification: combining insights from evolutionary economic geography and transition studies. *Regional Studies* **51**(1): 31–45.

Coe, N.M., and Yeung, H.W.-C. 2015. *Global Production Networks: Theorizing Economic Development in an Interconnected World*. Oxford: Oxford University Press.

Cooke, P. 1992. Regional innovation systems: competitive regulation in the new Europe. *GeoForum* **23**: 365–382.

Cooke, P. 1998. Introduction: origins of the concept. In H. Braczyk, P. Cooke and M. Heidenreich (eds), *Regional Innovation Systems*, 1st edition. London: UCL Press, pp. 2–25.

Cooke, P., Heidenreich, M., and Braczyk, H.-J. (eds). 1998. *Regional Innovation Systems: The Role of Governance in a Globalized World*. London and New York: Routledge.

Edquist, C. 1997. *Systems of Innovation: Technologies, Institutions, and Organizations*. London: Pinter.

Foray, D. (ed.). 2014. *Smart Specialization: Opportunities and Challenges for Regional Innovation Policy*. London: Routledge Taylor & Francis Group.

Foray, D., David, P.A., and Hall, B.H. 2009. Smart specialisation – the concept. Knowledge Economists Policy Brief no. 9, June. Brussels: European Commission. Available at http://ec.europa.eu/invest-in-research/pdf/download_en/kfg_policy_brief_no9.pdf (accessed 18 April 2019).

Foray, D., David, P.A., and Hall, B.H. 2011. Smart specialization – from academic idea to political instrument/the surprising career of a concept and the difficulties involved in its implementation. MTEI-WORKING_-PAPER-2011-001. Lausanne: École Polytechnique Federale de Lausanne.

Foray, D., Goddard, J., Goenaga Beldarrain, X., Landabaso, M., McCann, P., Morgan, K., et al. 2012. Guide to Research and Innovation Strategies for Smart Specialisation (RIS3). European Commission. Available at https://ec.europa.eu/regional_policy/sources/docgener/presenta/smart_specialisation/smart_ris3_2012.pdf (accessed 18 April 2019).

Freeman, C. 1987. *Technology Policy and Economic Performance: Lessons from Japan*. London: Pinter.

Frenken, K., van Oort, F.G., and Verburg, T. 2007. Related variety, unrelated variety and regional economic growth. *Regional Studies* **41**(5): 685–697.

Gianelle, C., and Kleibrink, A. 2015. Monitoring mechanisms for smart specialisation strategies. S3 Policy Brief Series, 13/2015. Seville: European Commission, Joint Research Centre.

Glaeser, E., Kallal, H., Scheinkman, J., and Shleifer, A. 1992. Growth in cities. *Journal of Political Economy* **100**(6), 1126–1152.

Grillitsch, M., Asheim, B., and Trippl, M. 2018. Unrelated knowledge combinations: the unexplored potential for regional industrial path development. *Cambridge Journal of Regions, Economy and Society* **11**(2): 257–274.

Hidalgo, C.A., Klinger, B., Barabasi, A.L., and Hausmann, R. 2007. The product space conditions the development of nations. *Science* **317**: 482–487. doi:10.1126/science.1144581.

Hollanders, H. 2017. Mapping for smart specialisation in transition countries: Moldova. The economic, innovative and scientific potential in Moldova. Seville: JRC.

Iacobucci, D. 2014. Designing and implementing a smart specialisation strategy at regional level: some open questions. *Scienze Regionali, Italian Journal of Regional Science* **13**(1): 107–126.

Isaksen, A., and Trippl, M. 2016. Path development in different regional innovation systems: a conceptual analysis. In M. Davide Parrilli, R. Dahl Fitjar and A. Rodriguez-Pose (eds), *Innovation Drivers and Regional Innovation Strategies*. London: Taylor & Francis, pp. 66–84. doi: 10.4324/9781315671475.

Isaksen, A., and Trippl, M. 2017. Exogenously led and policy-supported new path development in peripheral regions: analytical and synthetic routes. *Economic Geography* **93**(5): 436–457.

Jacobs, J., 1969. *The Economy of Cities*. New York: Random House.

Kleibrink, A., Gianelle C., and Doussineau, M. 2016. Monitoring innovation and territorial development in Europe: emergent strategic management. *European Planning Studies* **24**(8): 1438–1458. http://dx.doi.org/10.1080/09654313.2016.1181717.

Kleibrink, A., Radovanovic, N., Kroll, H., Horvat, D., Kutlaca, D., and Zivkovic, L. 2018. *The Potential of ICT in Serbia: An Emerging Industry in the European Context*. Luxembourg: Publications Office of the European Union.

Kline, S.J., and Rosenberg, N. 1986. An overview of innovation. In R. Landau and N. Rosenberg (eds), *The Positive Sum Strategy: Harnessing Technology for Economic Growth*. Washington, DC: National Academy Press, pp. 275–305.

Kroll, H. 2015. Efforts to implement smart specialisation in practice – leading unlike horses to the water. *European Planning Studies* **23**(10): 2079–2098. doi: 10.1080/09654313.2014.1003036.

Kroll, H. 2016. Policy brief on smart specialisation. Sevilla: European Commission Joint Research Centre, Smart Specialisation Platform. Available at http://s3platform.jrc.ec.europa.eu/documents/20182/196760/Policy+Brief+on+Smart+Specialisation/938913ba-040f-4d67-bb07-383e45ffaf0b (accessed 18 April 2019).

Kroll, H. 2018. Smart Specialisation Strategies, 2017 survey results. Brussels, EC Directorate-General for Regional and Urban Policy. Available at http://ec.europa.eu/regional_policy/en/information/publications/reports/2018/smart-specialisation-strategies-2017-survey-results (accessed 18 April 2019).

Kroll, H. 2019a. Eye to eye with the innovation paradox: why smart specialisation is no simple solution to policy design. *European Planning Studies* **27**(5): 932–951.

Kroll, H. 2019b. Smart specialisation in economically and institutionally less favoured regions. In I. Kristensen, A. Dubois and J. Teräs (eds), *Strategic Approaches to Regional Development: Smart Experimentation in Less-Favoured Regions*. Oxford: Routledge, pp. 36–51.

Kroll, H., Schnabl, E., and Horvat, D. 2017. Mapping of economic, innovative and scientific potential in Serbia. Seville: Joint Research Centre.

Kroll, H., Böke, I., Schiller, D., and Stahlecker, T. 2016. Bringing owls to Athens? The transformative potential of RIS3 for innovation policy in Germany's federal states. *European Planning Studies* **24**(8): 1459–1477.

Landabaso, M. 2012. What public policies can and cannot do for regional development. In P. Cooke, M.D. Parrilli and J.L. Curbelo (eds), *Innovation, Global*

Challenge and Territorial Resilience. Cheltenham, UK and Northampton, MA, USA: Edward Elgar Publishing, pp. 364–381.

Landabaso, M. 2014.Time for the real economy: the need for new forms of public entrepreneurship. *Scienze Regionali, Italian Journal of Regional Science* **13**(1): 127–140.

Lundvall, B.-Å. (ed.). 1992. *National Innovation Systems: Towards a Theory of Innovation and Interactive Learning*. London: Pinter.

Markusen, A. 1996. Sticky places in slippery space: a typology of industrial districts. *Economic Geography* **72**(3): 293–313.

Marshall, A. 1920. *Principles of Economics*. London: Macmillan.

Porter, M. 1990. *The Competitive Advantage of Nations*. New York: Free Press.

Porter, M. 1998. Clusters and the new economics of competition. *Harvard Business Review* **76**(6): 77–90.

Rodrik, D. 2004. Industrial policy for the twenty-first century. CEPR Discussion Paper Series No. 4767. London: Centre for Economic Policy Research.

Saxenian, A.L. 1994. *Regional Advantage: Culture and Competition in Silicon Valley and Route 128*. Cambridge, MA: Harvard University Press.

Vanguard Initiative. 2016. Vanguard Initiative Position Paper: Regions and future EU policies for growth and investment. Available at: https://www.s3van guardinitiative.eu/sites/default/files/docs/general/vi_position_paper_post2020_ final_7nov2016.pdf (accessed 18 April 2019).

Yeung, H.W.-C. 2009. Regional development and the competitive dynamics of global production networks: an East Asian perspective. *Regional Studies* **43**(3): 325–351.

3. Mapping relatedness in European regions

Frank van Oort, Nicola Cortinovis, Teodora Dogaru and Jeroen van Haaren

3.1 INTRODUCTION

The spatial heterogeneity of European regions becomes theoretically and policy-wise ever more important when looking at regions through the lenses of innovation policy and smart specialisation. The smart specialisation strategies, that become important and popular in regional economic development planning in Europe, build heavily upon the concepts of related variety and relatedness introduced in the recent evolutionary economic geography discourse.

The entrepreneurial discovery process calls for the mapping of related industrial and innovative development trajectories; given the present specialisation of individual regions. In particular, this connects directly to the innovation and structural change features of the related variety conceptualisation. Frenken et al. (2007) first introduced this typology, where sectoral diversity is split into related variety and unrelated variety, in order to discriminate between sectors where physical and functional proximity allows knowledge to move from one sector to another (related variety), and sectors where ideas and skills are unlikely to spill over, or only in cases of breakthrough technologies (unrelated variety). Within-sector related variety and between-sector unrelated variety are commonly measured by sectoral decomposition. By using entropy measurement, employment or production in detailed four-digit industries is considered to be functionally related to their two-digit aggregates, while the two-digit sectors themselves are mutually unrelated. In its basic meaning, related variety is conceptually linked to innovative renewal, new market exploration and employment growth, while unrelated variety is linked to a portfolio effect that protects a region against unemployment. Regional specialisation and clustering remain traditionally hypothesised to be attached to productivity growth (Frenken et al., 2007).

When European regional economic policy becomes increasingly place-based in character, the need for comparative information on agglomeration externalities in European regions (Barca et al., 2012) is fuelled. This case is ever more obvious in relation to the opportunities for entrepreneurial discovery, related variety and structural change branching into new, yet related industries, and forms the core of the regional smart specialisation processes. In the heterogeneous regional setting of European regions, the mapping process of economic opportunities is highlighted by distinguishing characteristics in structural change. The regionally varying degrees of industrial organisation and institutional development are crucially attached to different levels of technological progress in Europe. The effects of specialisation and related or unrelated variety on regional economic growth should therefore be assessed in light of different levels of technological progress of European regions.

This chapter introduces the concepts of related variety and skill-relatedness in the European Union, and discusses how this links to the entrepreneurial search process and innovative structural change in regional contexts. The concept of relatedness is central, and it encompasses more than sectoral branching because it also captures various other important forms of proximity and regional relatedness in Europe. These include input–output and global value chain linkages, institutional proximity, technological and cognitive relatedness, knowledge transfer mechanisms and infrastructural relatedness. The core literature concerning these concepts is summarised in section 3.2 of this chapter. Section 3.3 provides an outlook on recent empirical work on mapping related variety and relatedness on the European Union (EU) regional level. Throughout the chapter, we argue that although relatedness is a key element for supporting place-based innovation processes and policies, their interdependence and functioning, one versus the other, requires more attention in both scientific and policy circles. We illustrate this by presenting new empirical research (section 3.4) which puts skill-relatedness on the local (sub-regional) map of the Netherlands. We link the patterns of mapped relatedness to policy implications at the local and regional level, and show that diversification strategies may be more complex to actively pursue when they have to comply with existing entrepreneurial, educational, industrial organisation, and infrastructural and social network conditions. Section 3.5 concludes, and presents a research agenda on how relatedness in Europe may be integrated more effectively in economic and geographical research and policy.

3.2 SPECIALISATION, DIVERSITY AND RELATED VARIETY

3.2.1 Specialisation and Scale Economies

Many regions in Europe are specialised in certain sectoral activities: Rotterdam and Antwerp in port activities and related industrial sectors (for example, chemicals), London and Frankfurt in business and financial services, Eindhoven and Munich in high-tech systems, Birmingham and Toulouse in automotive and aerospace industries, Cambridge and Wageningen in life science and health-related sectors, and Andalucía and South Holland in horticulture (Combes and Overman, 2004). The conceptual approach to clusters traditionally stresses the importance of such specialisations (Fornahl et al., 2010). Specialisation provides a basis for in-depth investment in infrastructure, the labour market, knowledge and institutions (Duranton and Puga, 2004). In these cases, economies of scale are possible, and when these are bound to urban environments, we speak of agglomeration economies. These are typically generative (of productivity, innovation or growth) and not just distributional in character. In the current global economy, in-depth investment has become almost a precondition for effective competition with other regions, allowing clusters to contribute to the competitiveness and economic growth of a region (Thissen et al., 2013; Capello, 2017). However, a specialised economy is also vulnerable. Specialisation limits the number of economic activities a region can engage in, and reduces the opportunities for cross-fertilisation and renewal (Frenken et al., 2007). As the economist Schumpeter observed at the beginning of the previous century, creating new combinations of existing ideas is often crucial to innovation. Regions should therefore ideally be diversified as well as specialised. Pure specialisation makes a region vulnerable, while too much diversity in economic activities hinders the focus needed to compete successfully on world markets (Van Oort, 2013). This suggests that only the largest economic regions can be economically viable, since small regions cannot possibly specialise in a large number of activities at the same time (Mewes, 2019a).

There may be various ways to overcome urban and regional fragmentation which is characteristic of Europe. One way is hypothesised to be related to urban structure. Within the discipline of urban economics, an extensive stream of work has been devoted to examining the benefits associated with agglomeration economies, arising when larger urban size and density enable productive clustering of firms and people. Thereby, the profits come from the micro mechanisms of learning through the interaction and diffusion of ideas between proximate firms, the improved matching between a concentrated population of numerous firms and the inputs they require, and the sharing of indivisible facilities, large labour pools or gains from variety and the individual specialisation of firms located in the agglomeration (Duranton and Puga, 2004). Simultaneously, the negative consequences, namely agglomeration diseconomies, have received an increasing amount of attention as well. A regional over-reliance on the infrastructure and capacity of a single city could risk disadvantages such as congestion, pollution and surging land rents and prices for localised labour. Instead, second-tier or smaller cities could attempt to attain the same agglomeration advantages while mitigating the above-mentioned risks through a different spatial structure in which their efforts and sizes are bundled. Together, multiple cities – that is, multiple sources of agglomeration economies – may interact and exchange production factors in order to attain higher levels of production. Although this concept of polycentricity has been received with enthusiasm among policy-makers and academic researchers, the wide variety of definitions, scales and other operationalisations applied to different settings and contexts currently makes the clear delineation of a polycentricity study almost as important as its empirical components for a useful interpretation of its results. In a recent study, Ouwehand et al. (2019) analysed the relation between polycentricity and productivity for European regions using an econometric identification strategy. They find that significant effects exist for both urban size and structure. While confirming, within the literature, the general finding that larger urban size positively affects regional productivity, they also observe that several well-connected smaller cities or regions may have equivalently more agglomeration effects than larger cities. Yet, their research also suggests the inability of smaller cities in substituting the economic urbanisation externalities associated with a single large city when that larger city is located nearby (the 'agglomeration shadow').

Another way of overcoming 'smallness' in a European setting may be smart specialisation: the idea that regions may evolve (diversify) into new specialisations, in which regions can build competitive advantages that link to existing strengths of regions while reflecting innovative new crossovers and market opportunities (Foray, 2015). Diversification is not new to the agglomeration or cluster discussion. Sector-specific localisation or specialised-cluster economies are generally counterbalanced by general urbanisation economies, and enhanced by economic diversity instead of specialisation. Diversity advantages may be related to endogenous growth potentials, but also to diversifying foreign direct investment (FDI) and input–output relations, human capital externalities and knowledge spillovers (Dogaru et al., 2017; Caragliu and Nijkamp, 2016). In particular,

Jane Jacobs (1969) initiated the idea that variety in regional industry or its technological base may positively affect economic growth. In empirical studies, the relation between agglomeration and growth is ambiguous and indecisive in regard to whether specialisation or diversity is contextually facilitated by (sheer) urbanisation (Melo et al., 2009). However, this dichotomy between specialisation and diversity ignores the synergies that are possible between particular economic activities, regardless of the existent specialisation degree. Medium-sized regions can combine economic cohesion with a high level of diversification by making skilful use of these synergies. These synergy effects are at the core of the smart specialisation conceptualisation and policy aims, and they are rooted in the evolutionary economic concepts of related variety and relatedness (Van Oort and Lambooy, 2020).

3.2.2 Related Variety

The key in 'solving' the specialisation–diversity controversy may be in what has recently been introduced as related variety (Frenken et al., 2007; Van Oort, 2013), since the largest opportunities for knowledge transfer exist between companies that belong not to the same but to related branches of industry. Much research underlines that knowledge and growth potentials are neither equally accessible nor equally relevant for economic actors. Among other forms of proximity (Boschma, 2005), scholars have focused on the importance of cognitive proximity, for the transmission of knowledge across an economy. In this sense, the more related the knowledge bases of different actors are, the easier it is for ideas, capabilities and knowledge to be profitably exchanged and applied. In contrast, when the cognitive distance is significant and actors do not 'speak the same language', knowledge spillovers are less likely to take place. Companies from related branches of industry have overlapping knowledge bases. This overlap facilitates intercompany communication. Shared knowledge, frames of reference and applied technology make it easier for them to understand one another. The fact that this overlap is only partial means that there is room for them to learn from one another. The presence of a high volume of related economic activities in a region thus potentially facilitates the generation of new combinations of existing technologies. The diversity of activities spreads the risk, so that the region is not dependent on only a handful of branches of industry. In Frenken et al. (2007), related variety is measured by industry-classification membership, with more detailed industries being part of broader industries by administrative classification. Cortinovis and Van Oort (2015) apply this to European regions.

Hence, according to the conceptualisation of related variety, regions benefit from an industrial structure consisting of a large number of different but related branches of industry. A study of long-term diversification in various regions of Sweden provided empirical proof of this hypothesis (Neffke et al., 2011). This study showed that it is easiest for regions to attract new branches of industry that are related to existing ones. Conversely, companies in certain branches of industry are more likely to leave a region if no related activity is present there. Thus, branches of industry related to those already present in the region fit the region's industrial profile better than those for which this is not the case. The identification of such branches of industry is thus vital for the potential economic policy of a region, as is the case in smart specialisation. Therefore, it is important to determine which branches of industry are related to which.

3.2.3   Relatedness

In recent research, relatedness is more broadly conceptualised than related variety originally was. The concept of relatedness still aims at capturing how knowledge, technologies and assets already present in a (local) economy influence the possibility of diversification over time (Hidalgo et al., 2007). In other words, the opportunities for an economy to diversify and operate in a new (for the region) sector depend on the industries already present in the economy. The more two sectors are cognitively related, the easier it is for firms to redeploy their assets, acquire new capabilities and move from one sector to the other (Hidalgo et al., 2007; Cortinovis et al., 2017). The concept of relatedness synthesises the different dimensions in which two industries can be proximate, be it because of similar technologies, skills or production processes, input–output relations, or similar institutional arrangements. Empirical studies have confirmed the predominance of this process of related diversification for productivity and employment gains (Cortinovis et al., 2019) at both national and regional scale (Neffke et al., 2011). Unrelated diversification is rarer, yet has large growth and innovation potential in breakthrough technologies in regions (Castaldi et al., 2015).

Over time, the measurement of relatedness between industries, technologies and regions has been more sophisticated than the original one of related variety. Studies on European regions have recently focused on trade vis-à-vis knowledge relations between European regions (Cortinovis and Van Oort, 2018), and their extrapolation to FDI investments and subsequent employment growth in receiving countries (Cortinovis et al., 2019). In these studies, co-location of industries was used for measuring relatedness. Other studies focus on labour mobility and its recombination capacities, or the absence of it and its locking-in consequences, as has been studied in a proximity approach in Csáfordi et al. (2018) and Eriksson (2011). Mewes (2019b) focuses on the quality dimension of knowledge relation between regions in Europe. In principle, any regionalised and interregional set of network relations on a European scale is interesting for testing hypotheses on diversification and smart specialisation.

3.3 MAPPING RELATED VARIETY AND RELATEDNESS IN EUROPE

This section summarises a couple of previous studies where related variety (Cortinovis and Van Oort, 2015) and relatedness (Cortinovis et al., 2017; Dogaru et al., 2017) were mapped in detail. We particularly focus on the mapping of concepts, but also discuss its main implications for regional policy.

In calculating related and unrelated variety, as introduced above, Cortinovis and Van Oort (2015, pp. 16–17) apply the same approach as in Frenken et al. (2007). They use two entropy measures calculated on employment shares in 260 regions in Europe for nine years in a panel setting (N = 2340). Detailed sectoral information on the regions is needed to calculate these measures (obtained and aggregated from the firm-level Orbis database collected by Bureau Van Dijk). Using the progressive structure of the Statistical Classification of Economic Activities in the European Community (NACE) of this employment data, from broader to finer groupings, we consider to be unrelated those sectors that belong to each of the 21 different sections of the classification (variation between sections). Simultaneously, detailed industries within each of these sections are considered to be related to one another, precisely because they belong to the same section (and presumably share consumer and producer markets and production technologies). The choice of using sections as cut-off for between and within level variation is made to capture the greatest possible amount of relatedness among sub-sectors. For instance, firms manufacturing textile products and those producing apparel belong to the same section ('C') but to different NACE sub-sectors (divisions 13 and 14, respectively). An approach using divisions to compute related and unrelated variety would have considered these two sub-sectors to be unrelated, while they are actually rather similar.

The method introduced by Frenken et al. (2007) accounts for the entropy in the distribution of employment shares within each level of the industrial classification. Unrelated variety ($UVar_{it}$) is therefore the measure of entropy among the 21 NACE sections and can be calculated as:

$$UVAR_{it} = \sum_{s=1}^{S} P_s log_2 \left(\frac{1}{P_s} \right),$$

where P_s represents the share of employment in section S over total employment in region i at time t. In a similar fashion, related variety $(RVar_{it})$ is measured as the weighted sum of entropy within each of the S sections in the classification. Specifically:

$$RVAR_{it} = \sum_{s=1}^{S} P_s H_s,$$

with:

$$H_s = \sum_{d \in S_s} \frac{p_d}{P_s} log_2 \left(\frac{1}{p_d / P_s} \right),$$

where p_d represents the employment share of division d over the total. Figure 3.1 depicts the spatial distribution of related and unrelated variety across the sample in 2004 used in Cortinovis and Van Oort (2015). As the map clearly indicates, variety at high levels of aggregation exhibits no strong resemblance to variety at low levels, strongly suggesting that the choice of sector aggregation is not trivial. Related variety appears to be a somewhat more urban regional feature than unrelated variety (cf. Frenken et al., 2007), with higher scores in Lombardy, Catalonia, Paris, Hamburg, Munich and Eastern European urban regions. Figure 3.2 maps unrelated variety, and we notice that this pattern is not the reciprocal of the pattern of related variety. Southern European regions generally score higher on the unrelated variety indicator.

Cortinovis and Van Oort (2015) introduced technological regional regimes (see Figure 3.3), which turned out to be extremely important for the interpretation of the modeling outcomes. European regions are ranked according to their capacities in terms of knowledge accessibility, knowledge absorption and knowledge diffusion. Building on this, we assign the regions in our sample into three technological regimes ('high-technological regime', 'medium-technological regime' and 'low-technological regime'). For regions in the top technological regime, higher related variety is associated with higher employment growth, lower unemployment growth and higher productivity growth. For these same regions, unrelated variety was also positively related to productivity growth. In the other two regimes, the results are less clear: low-tech regions only benefit from related variety in terms of productivity growth; conversely, for the medium-technology regime, we obtained generally insignificant results.

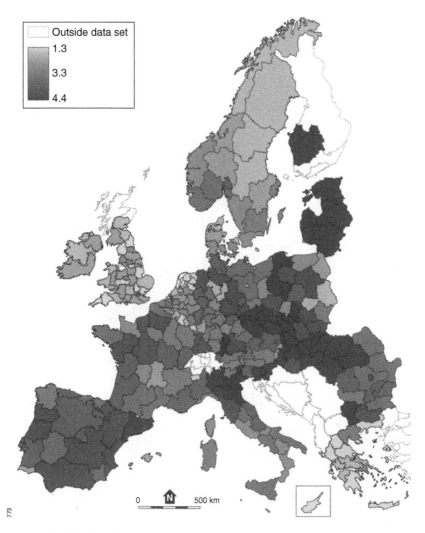

Source: Cortinovis and Van Oort (2015, p. 17).

Figure 3.1   Related variety in European NUTS 2 regions (2004)

We concluded in Cortinovis and Van Oort (2015, pp. 25–27) that diversity, and especially related variety, can have a positive effect on growth, but predominantly when the technological and knowledge endowment of the region is high. In other words, agglomeration economies have differential effects across regions in different regimes. The reason may be obvious: externalities associated with knowledge flows only 'pay off' in economies

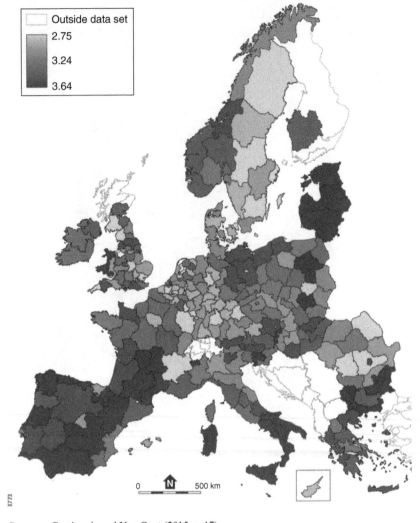

Legend:
- Outside data set
- 2.75
- 3.24
- 3.64

0   N   500 km

Source: Cortinovis and Van Oort (2015, p. 17).

Figure 3.2   Unrelated variety in European NUTS 2 regions (2004)

that have a high stock of knowledge and technology. Prior research on
the impact of related and unrelated variety was unable to longitudinally
analyse this on a pan-European scale. These results support the notion
that, to be effective, policies must consider the context and the features,
such as the knowledge and technological endowment, of any (targeted)
region.

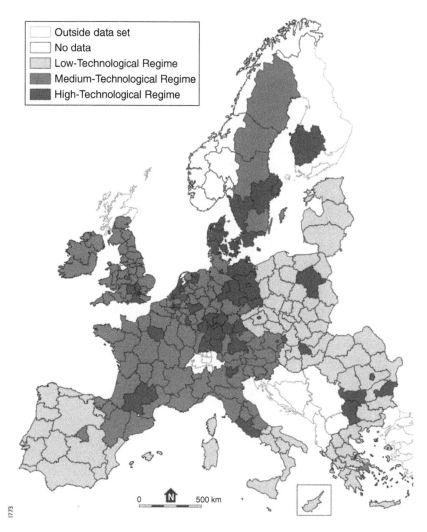

Source: Cortinovis and Van Oort (2015, p. 18).

Figure 3.3 Technological regimes in Europe

The filtering role of absorptive capacity of regions and of regional (formal and informal) institutions was confirmed in later work on the role of relatedness in European regions (Cortinovis et al., 2017; Dogaru et al., 2017). This argues that little attention has been given in the literature to the intermediate function of economic diversification processes regarding the impact of institutions on economic performance. Cortinovis et al.

(2017) explore the interplay between sectoral proximity (relatedness) and the quality of institutions to better understand their effects on diversification dynamics and their potential consequences for regional development. Following up on the challenge to distinguish formal from relatively under-investigated informal institutions, an econometric analysis is applied to a European regional setting. Given the significant differences across regions in formal and informal institutional arrangements, the regional dimension is considered particularly relevant for Europe: 'The EU is a prime example of how an international territorial system emerges out of increasing economic integration among nation states with relatively similar levels of development but with different social, institutional, and technological features in regions' (Barca et al., 2012, p. 143). Cortinovis et al. (2017) first investigate whether the hypothesis of sectoral relatedness and proximity driving diversification holds for EU regions. When this is confirmed, their analysis takes a closer look at the role of formal and informal institutions. They focus both on the direct effects of institutions over the acquisition of new industrial specialisations ('entrepreneurial discovery') and on the interaction between regional institutional endowments and the levels of relatedness among different sectors in the economy. They find that formal institutions (quality of governance) are indirectly impacting on diversification by enlarging the density of related industries. In addition, informal institutions that relate to norms and values (for example, religious organisations, trade unions, voluntary work and societal organisations) take over the role of formal institutions in the diversification process when formal institutions are actually less developed in Europe.

Uniquely, in respect to informal institutions and social capital, Cortinovis et al. (2017) introduce the level of trust and involvement of people in associational life within EU regions using the European Values Study database. This dataset contains survey data on the social attitudes and values of people at regional level. In Cortinovis et al. (2017), both formal institutions and informal institutions are found to be essential in relation to the capacity of European regions to economically diversify over time, and to the related growth and creation of new (innovative) market niches. Figure 3.4 shows the maps of formal institutions (formal regulation, quality of government), and patterns of indicators for informal institutions (trust, social capital). Consequently, we learn that Central and Eastern European regions score particularly low on many of the indicators regarding growth-enhancing institutions (for example, 'trust' and 'bridging social capital'), which magnifies and causes the limited endogenous diversification and growth potentials of these regions (Dogaru et al., 2017).

Dogaru et al. (2017, pp. 161–162) remark that institutional arrangements in knowledge creation and organisation influence the effectiveness

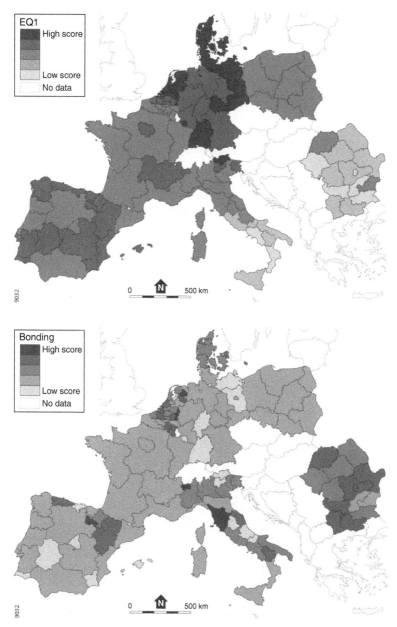

Note: Regional patterns of quality of governance (EQ1), level of trust (Trust), bonding social capital (Bonding) and bridging social capital (Bridging) as applied in Dogaru et al. (2017).

Figure 3.4   European regional scores of indicators of institutional quality

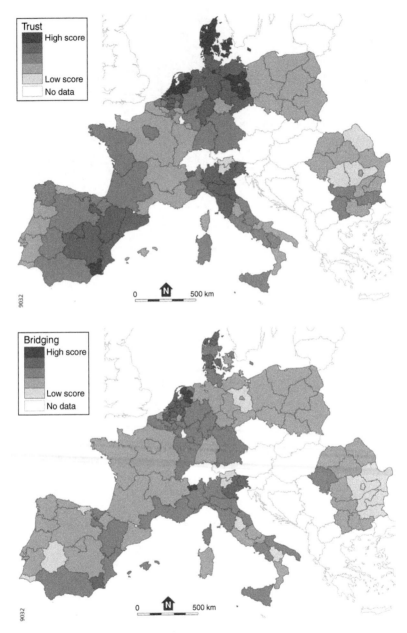

Figure 3.4   (continued)

of governance instruments applicable in European regions as well. If in the past governments supported a handful of strategic sectors and cities, modern times require identification of various groups of resources, provision of a knowledge framework and flexible innovative policies for long-term growth to create and develop competitive local businesses. The next section focuses on this regional complexity in more detail.

3.4 MAPPING SKILL-RELATEDNESS IN THE NETHERLANDS

3.4.1 Skill-Relatedness

In a nationwide empirical study, Van Oort et al. (2015) considered relatedness in terms of employee skills; that is, in terms of the human capital deployed by companies. Human capital is by far the most important production factor in today's knowledge economy. Companies compete not only for customers, but also and in particular for talent and skill-educated people. As a result, regions where people with the right skills and work experience are to be found are much sought after by the international business world. Branches of industry are said to be skill-related if they need employees with the same kind of skills. Skill-relatedness can be measured on the basis of work mobility between different branches of industry. People prefer to work in branches of industry that are skill-related to the one where they were employed previously. Employers prefer recruiting human capital (resources) from skill-related branches of industry, since such employees only require low investment for further training and adapt to their new job faster than those from unrelated sub-sectors.

Thus, the national Dutch study that we introduce here as a mapping example used labour flows between companies from different branches of industry as a measure of skill-relatedness. The presence of skill-related branches of industry in a region has three main advantages. Firstly, good embedding in the local labour market offers a branch of industry access to a labour force with the relevant skills. The fact that they share this labour force with other branches of industry yields scale benefits in the training of employees. Secondly, growth in skill-related branches of industry can compensate for economic downturn in a given branch of industry. The interchange ability of employees allows growing branches of industry to hire workers who were dismissed elsewhere, thus avoiding a major loss of human capital. Thirdly, there is wide scope for exchange of knowledge between related branches of industry. As a result, skill-related branches of industry often complement one another (cross over) in innovation processes. The face-to-face communication that is essential in innovative joint ventures is easier to coordinate at a local level than at a distance. Using labour market areas, within the Netherlands and potentially across the borders, crossover potentials are determined for the strong regional clusters in the Netherlands. In line with the conceptual and measurement arguments introduced in this chapter, skill-relatedness of these strong and potentially promising sectors can then be considered as the regional 'DNA' that may foster and embed future new specialisations (smart diversification and specialisation).

In this section, we present a novel method of mapping skill-relatedness on the local level in the Netherlands. We first explain how skill-relatedness is defined in the case study of the Netherlands, and why it is indicative for economic renewal and innovation in regions. For broad sectors assigned as most important clusters by the Dutch government (so-called 'top sectors'), specialisation patterns are then drawn on the maps.

Also drawn on the maps are then concentrations of firms in skill-related industries; meaning industries where employees in key industries of the top sectors[1] can also work because these industries require similar employee-level skill sets and competences. Identification of skill-related industries is by labour mobility: employees frequently change jobs between skill-related industries. Since this mapping exercise is highly helpful to local policy-makers, the policy implications of this procedure will be discussed as well.

3.4.2   Mapping Skill-Relatedness

In this sub-section, we present patterns of skill-related economic activities plotted on detailed maps of the Netherlands. Skill-relatedness is a measure for innovation potential (Neffke et al., 2011) since economic renewal and innovation are not implicit. Often, existing knowledge in firms is combined with new knowledge, leading to crossovers that eventually can lead to economic growth. One of the most important ingredients for regional anchoring of such growth trajectories concerns skills of employees that are present in cities and regions. This determines what a local population can produce, which occupations the population has, and to which industries this contributes. In terms of the conceptualisation of related variety and its implication for renewal, regions have to find a balance between specialisations and variety. Thus, regional strategies revolve around diversification.

---

[1]   See Appendix Table 3A.1 for the definition of these key industries of top sectors.

In this human capital view of economic renewal, regions are central, as skills of people are to a large extent bounded by labour market regions where people live and work (Diodato and Weterings, 2015; Glaeser et al., 2014). Not all skills are equally important for innovation and renewal. High-skilled occupations and industries are more important than low-skilled ones (Burger et al., 2018). Skills are not equal to educational level: high-skilled employees can also learn on the job or develop through creativity.

Empirically, it is almost impossible to determine exactly which knowledge and skills are needed for regional economic growth trajectories. Following Neffke and Henning (2013), the study of Van Oort et al. (2015) looked at labour mobility (job switches) and not the skills of employees directly. Most productive labour mobility takes place between jobs of similar or related skill levels, where employers demand the same kind of skills for vacancies. Industries are labelled skill-related when many employees change jobs between these industries. For instance, a chemical engineer starts working in a biotechnology firm, or a biochemistry expert starts working in life science and health sectors. It is those forms of skill-relatedness that are particularly interesting for the search of crossover and growth opportunities. This analysis used statistical micro data between 2009 and 2011 – the Social Statistical database (SSB) at Statistics Netherlands – to measure labour mobility between industries, using 277 detailed industries (3–4 digit level) that encompass the whole national economy. In Van Oort et al. (2015), more labour flows than expected were determined on the basis of expected mobility patterns and their comparison to the actual ones. Employees with more generic skills (for example, secretarial), can be expected to switch jobs across many industries. In the case of people with specific skills, some job switches will occur more often than others. This way, chance or random movements can be ruled out. When mobility is greater than expected, it is concluded that industries are skill-related. Skill-related industries can be visualised in so-called industry spaces: diagrams with plotted industries where skill-related ones are plotted closer to each other than skill-unrelated ones (Figure 3.5). The density of this network and the position of industries in it partly describe the potential of economic renewal. If we know that five industries are characterised by skill-relatedness on a national scale, and at least four of them are present (specialised) in a certain region, then the fifth can be expected to enter the regional economy ('opportunity'). Likewise, when the industries in a region are not skill-related at all, these may be at risk of disappearing ('threat').

It is important to keep in mind that skill-related industries may lead to growth only on certain conditions because, as Michael Porter (2000, p. 88)

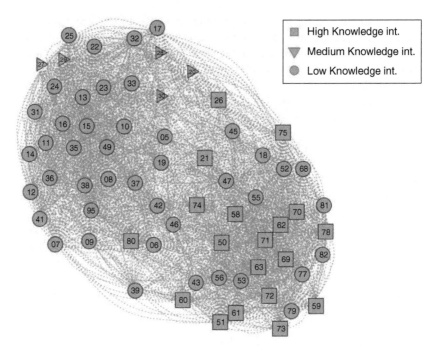

Source: Cortinovis et al. (2019, p. 15).

*Figure 3.5   A network representation of relatedness based on
co-occurrence (industry space for Europe)*

has stated: 'the mere co-location of companies, suppliers, and institutions
creates the *potential* for economic value; it does not necessarily ensure
its realization'. Outside industrial organisation, location factors such as
accessibility, entrepreneurship and high-educated labour are important
for the realisation of potential. These can be argued to be correlated with
the embedding conceptualisation of relatedness (Neffke et al., 2011),
although this is not always to be taken for granted.

The industry-space visualisation of Figure 3.5 is something different
than a geographical mapping of opportunities and threats. For five
top sectors in the Netherlands, this translation into geographical space
(mapping) is presented in Figures 3.6–3.10. Every symbol on the map
represents a geo-coded, individual firm establishment (for overview,
only firms with more than ten employees are visualised). We used the
Landelijk Informatiesysteem Arbeidsplaatsen/National Labour Force
Registration (LISA) database for this micro data mapping, having all
individual establishments with paid work (including micro-firms, although

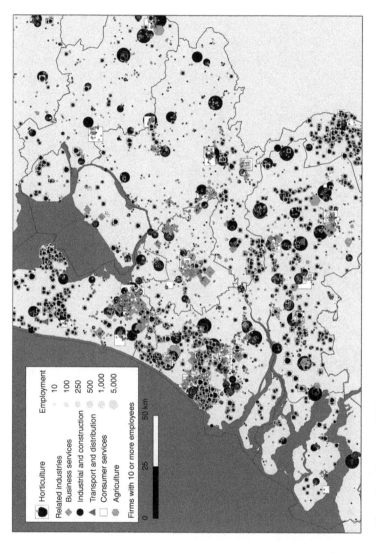

Legend:
Horticulture
Related industries
Business services
Industrial and construction
Transport and distribution
Consumer services
Agriculture

Employment
10
100
250
500
1,000
5,000

Firms with 10 or more employees

0   25   50 km

Source: Adapted from Van Oort et al. (2015, p. 117, Figure 2.21b).

Figure 3.6   Spatial distribution of horticulture firms and skill-related firms (Central Netherlands, skill-related firms ≥ 10 employees)

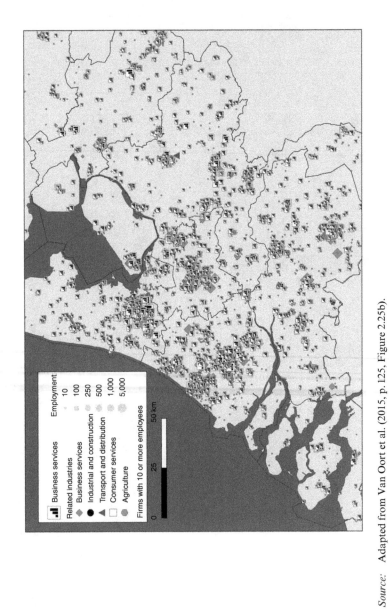

Source: Adapted from Van Oort et al. (2015, p. 125, Figure 2.25b).

Figure 3.7 Spatial distribution of business service firms and skill-related firms (Central Netherlands, skill-related firms ≥ 10 employees)

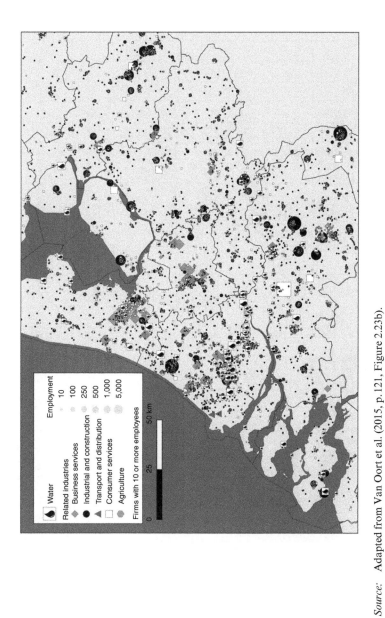

Source: Adapted from Van Oort et al. (2015, p. 121, Figure 2.23b).

Figure 3.8   Spatial distribution of water construction and management firms and skill-related firms (Central Netherlands, skill-related firms ≥ 10 employees)

65

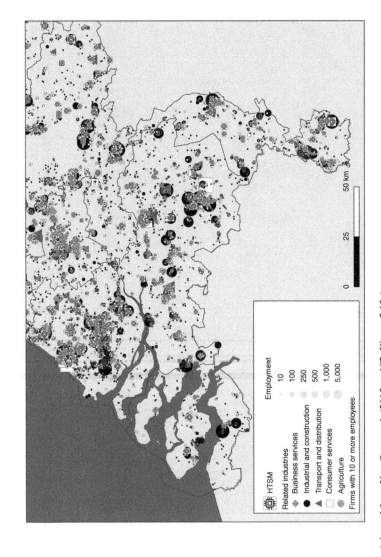

Source: Adapted from Van Oort et al. (2015, p. 102, Figure 2.13c).

Figure 3.9   Spatial distribution of high-tech systems and materials firms and skill-related firms (South Netherlands, skill-related firms ≥ 10 employees)

66

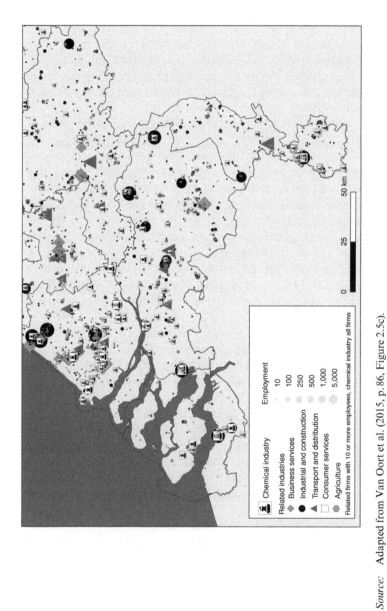

Source: Adapted from Van Oort et al. (2015, p. 86, Figure 2.5c).

Figure 3.10 Spatial distribution of chemical production firms and skill-related firms (South Netherlands, skill-related firms ≥ 10 employees)

not visualised) incorporated in the Netherlands (see Van Haaren et al., forthcoming). The iconic symbols represent individual firms in a certain top sector: horticulture in Figure 3.6, business services in Figure 3.7, water construction and management firms in Figure 3.8, high-tech systems and materials firms in Figure 3.9, and chemical production firms in Figure 3.10 (see Appendix Table 3A.1 for definitions). Skill-related industries, determined as explained above, are then visualised on the maps when having ten or more employees, and grouped into shaded symbols according to broad sectors (black circles for manufacturing firms, grey triangles for distribution firms, and so on). All symbols of firms are scaled with their employment size in 2015.

Figure 3.6 presents all firms and establishments in horticulture – production of vegetables, flowers and green genetics (see Appendix Table 3A.1) – as indicated by the icons. The horticulture cluster in the Netherlands is strongly concentrated in the Westland region (the greenhouse area near Delft), the flower area of Bollenstreek near Leiden, and the north of Limburg and Brabant. Around the Westland region, but also in the north of Limburg, skill-related establishments are in the direct vicinity of the concentrations of top-sector firms. Crossovers with university research (Leiden, Wageningen, Utrecht), specialised services in Amsterdam, and manufacturing firms in Rotterdam come to the fore in Figure 3.6. Not all skill-related firms are located in close proximity of the top sector firms, leaving room for network organisations of learning and cooperation.

Figure 3.7 maps the business service establishments targeted in the top sector policy of the national government in a similar fashion. Part of this sector is accountancy and management consulting (Appendix Table 3A.1). Large concentrations are visible in the wider urban agglomerations of Amsterdam, Rotterdam and Utrecht. Skill-related industries are in research and development, market research, information and communication technology (ICT) activities and financial services; all of which concentrate in the same urban environments. Although many manufacturing firms have input–output relations with business service firms, there is hardly any skill-relatedness between manufacturing and servicing firms. Accessibility and quality of life are important location factors for business firms.

The top sector of water construction and management focuses on delta technology (protection), ship building and water sports equipment – all uniquely Dutch economic specialisations (Figure 3.8). It is especially concentrated in Rotterdam and around Dordrecht in the province of Zuid-Holland. Skill-related industries are machinery, construction, transport and rental activities. There are almost no higher education facilities in water construction and management in the cluster region, which may be a threat in the long run.

The top sector of high-tech systems and materials (HTSM) concentrates on high-tech industries, such as optical and medical instruments, and fibre production (Figure 3.9). This is the largest top sector of the Netherlands in terms of added value, employment and international competitiveness. There are skill relations especially in the areas of machinery, electro technical engineering, aerospace and automotive industries, and research and development in public and private institutes. The regions of Brainport Eindhoven in Noord-Brabant and Zuid-Holland show the largest concentration of HTSM firms, and also in skill-related firms.

Finally, the chemical industry top sector (Figure 3.10) concentrates in the Rotterdam port area and in Zuid-Limburg, with large skill-related concentrations of firms in the various industries' surroundings.

3.4.3 Policy Instruments for (Skill-)Relatedness

In focus group sessions in all regions assigned by national policy (Randstad, Groningen, Twente, Arnhem-Nijmegen, Brainport Eindhoven, Limburg and South-West Brabant), regional stakeholders were confronted with the research outcomes on skill-relatedness as presented above. Following up on research questions that are important for smart specialisation (McCann et al., 2017), multi-level governance, regional innovation systems, crossovers and diversification opportunities, interregional connectedness and regional development strategies were discussed extensively. In all sessions, there was large commitment to the presented analyses. The specialisations as well as some of the crossovers were identified, while many potential diversification opportunities were regarded as new, and the method of skill-relatedness in itself as innovative. The important issue for most local policy-makers was the bridge from the mapped skill-relatedness and smart diversification (new specialisations) to policy instruments. In this view, 'economic' policy instruments were envisioned as potentially more important than 'spatial' ones. In the following, we discuss this briefly.

In the regional innovation system literature there is a general belief in (market) system functioning and system regulation. This can come under pressure when there is market failure (there are external effects, or growth opportunities are missed), system failure (there is insufficient cooperation and interaction between market parties, government, knowledge institutions and society) or government failure (larger societal goals are not reached). Governments can, in this vision, act themselves as 'brokers' in the regional economy. A precondition for this is that the local DNA or entrepreneurial ecosystem should be known (Stam, 2015). Our empirical research on the mapping of skill-relatedness contributes to this understanding. But while knowing (more) about this DNA and entrepreneurial search system, there seems to be a lack of such insight on many levels of governance. Despite this lack of information, policy-makers have pronounced opinions and thoughts about what should be done to help innovation and regional development prosper.

In line with the conceptualisation of relatedness, the empirical analyses suggest that economic renewal and growth on short and medium-long term in the cities and regions of the Netherlands will not be completely unrelated to present specialisations: a strategy must use the strengths of the region. Clusters should be envisioned to grow in close connection to common labour market opportunities, since these are the most fruitful human capital conditions for crossovers. Aiming at clusters and themes that do not align with any of the regional skill strengths or opportunities may turn out to be useless. It was also remarked that cluster conditions may be bettered for embedding industries that currently are not interwoven in the region's production structure. This will be considerably more expensive to realise than branching the economy in line with plausible diversification paths (Neffke et al., 2011).

The analyses in van Oort et al. (2015) also suggest paying attention to declining clusters. The education of workers should be geared towards employment elsewhere in the region, as this will foster resilience. When taking skill-relatedness seriously, either as a source for crossovers and innovation or as a portfolio concept in resilient economies, there should be a good matching of skills, labour demand and supply, and education. Local and regional labour market policies are important, but they are heavily determined by national institutional settings (for example, minimum wages, collective wage agreements in sectors and industries, technological innovation subsidies on employment in research and development). Regional human capital agendas may be a step towards tailored policies, although there is a long way to go for such a government role. This government role concerns educational matching in line with the region's skill opportunities, knowledge transfer (valorisation) and cooperation between firms and knowledge institutes, life-long learning opportunities, and high-skilled labour market matching. The government could have a stronger coordinating role. If governments are to have brokerage roles in the regional innovation and economic performance arena, then they should also have more knowledge of the processes at hand. At the same time, governments cannot explicitly impose upon firm or university behaviours. A real-life case of multi-level governance was presented to all participants in the focus group sessions. The participants concluded that this case challenges their own strategies as put down in policy documents. The participants especially stress that knowledge of the region's entrepreneurial and skills DNA is essential for identifying and interpreting best practices for governance implementation. Custom fit and niche market development aiming at innovative knowledge, and focusing on local cluster expertise, backed up by regional education and policy initiatives, is required from governments. Policy-makers participating in the regional workshops agreed that on the short term this is impossible to establish, although working towards such a larger coordinating role will be achieved.

The coordination role of governments is emphasised both in the literature and in practice. Economic policy aiming at labour market matching, valorisation and education is at the heart of these processes. Spatially, this can be accompanied by 'hot spots' policies in engineering (private-led), or science (public-led) or urban (creativity-led) campuses and clusters (Van Haaren et al., forthcoming). Despite the fact that spatial conditions are then essential, it is only in combination with the economic conditions that these may be sufficient to foster crossovers, diversification and renewal.

3.5 CONCLUSIONS AND REFLECTION

This chapter has mapped related variety and relatedness at European regional level and skill-relatedness at Dutch local level. Although related variety and skill-relatedness are rather new concepts and methods in identifying crossovers in regional economic development, they have not been intensively and empirically researched in a quantitative manner. We show that economic relatedness can be applied to analyses that inform place-based and network-based approaches of policy. In addition, our analyses also show complementary needs for policies. Skill measurement and skill-matching are top priorities on national and regional policy scales.

Regardless of how firms will find their labour matching needs, higher structural issues at the regional level need to be addressed. In this respect, the region of Dordrecht excels in water construction and management firms in its top sector cluster, yet fails to have local knowledge institutions and education related to this important concentration in the Netherlands. Therefore, skill-relatedness as a standard for renewal and innovation in European regions needs to be complemented by other factors and networks. Mapping relatedness in Europe and skill-relatedness in the Netherlands reveals that interregional relations have larger regional footprints than often suggested (larger than cities or even labour market regions). While interregional competition is more often the common ground (McCann et al., 2017), interregional coordination surfaces as another basic ingredient.

Depending on the position of industries and products in their stage of the life cycle (more mature industries have a stronger urge for adaptation, renewal and transition), strong clusters are exposed to diversification opportunities as well. Policy can actively focus on such diversification ('smart specialisation') processes. Unrelated diversification is another option, since it may be necessary for future development into transitions. Yet, transitions are usually not met with evolutionary diversification approaches alone. Mapping related variety and relatedness potentially fuels many multilevel policy discussions and evaluations. Links between relatedness and regional resilience remain important research avenues. They concern network governance and place-based strategies, alongside firm-level impacts of relatedness, particularly their survival, growth and innovative performance. At European scale, related diversification is at the core of the development of the regional smart specialisation paradigm. Despite burgeoning evidence on governance efforts and best practices in policy initiatives, *ex post* and *ex ante* quantitative evaluations are scarce. This chapter shows that given the emergence of micro data and mapping techniques, there are more possibilities in this respect.

The institutional embedding of smart specialisation strategies poses challenges for our analysing framework. The European Union distinguishes itself from other global economic structures, as a union of member states with a single market and free movement of goods, services and people. Twenty-eight nations share a dynamic geo-cultural and socio-economic space defined by intertwined historical roots and evolutionary development paths, multilayered societal structures and trade relations. This institutional proximity fosters the European translation of the values of the United Nations: prosperity, peace and partnership. The territorial histories of most member states' position the region as a central unit in national geo-historical structures. Besides national identities, regional cultural backgrounds become relevant in looking at institutional frameworks as part of regional profiles.

Zooming in on European growth resources and beyond national frameworks, the region is a symbiosis of cultural heritage, community and lifestyle as a basis for the development of economic systems. Moreover, regional synergy within and beyond the constituent nations has become part of the core values of sustainable development and long-term European growth. This argument reveals itself in the light of regional inequalities, a European heterogeneous pool of competitive advantages, uneven technological development paths and capitalisation capacities upon knowledge spillovers, trade networks and privileged positions in global value chains. Our mapping exercise shows that such challenges are complex and often path-dependent (evolutionary) in nature. Local and regional specificities combined with interactions brought by trade led to the formation of regional and national identities which merged into one European culture and similar lifestyles. High-skilled human capital, brain drain and increased levels of innovation are expected to turn the tables on former regional monopolies and mass production, by creating new scale and scope economies and agglomeration economies.

The mapping exercise also reveals that some regions structurally lag behind in recombination, crossover and prosperity prospects. In the context of globalisation, institutional proximity and knowledge spillovers, Europe developed growth patterns of regional profiles. Some groups of regions (mostly in Western countries) have sustained long-term growth through increased levels of employment supported by diversified economies in tertiary sectors. Central Eastern European (CEE) regions reflect increased productivity levels by being highly specialised in medium- and low-tech industries (Dogaru et al., 2017). As an extrapolated result, their convergence rate towards other regional economies based on knowledge-intensive business sectors is reduced. In order to remap the future of European regions, constant attention to the structuring effects of specialisation, diversification and forms of relatedness is needed.

REFERENCES

Barca, F., P. McCann and A. Rodríguez-Pose (2012), 'The case for regional development intervention: place-based versus place-neutral approaches'. *Journal of Regional Science* **52**: 134–152.

Boschma, R. (2005), 'Proximity and innovation: a critical assessment'. *Regional Studies* **39**: 61–74.

Burger, M., S. Stavropoulos, S. Ramkumar, J. Dufourmont and F. van Oort (2018), 'The heterogeneous skill-base of circular economy employment'. *Research Policy* **48**: 248–261.

Capello, R. (ed.) (2017), *Seminal Studies in Regional and Urban Economics*. Berlin: Springer.

Caragliu, A. and P. Nijkamp (2016), 'Space and knowledge spillovers in European regions: the impact of different forms of proximity on spatial knowledge diffusion'. *Journal of Economic Geography* **16**: 749–774.

Castaldi, C., K. Frenken and B. Los (2015), 'Related variety, unrelated variety and technological breakthroughs: an analysis of US state-level patenting'. *Regional Studies* **49**: 767–781.

Combes, P.P. and H. Overman (2004), 'The spatial distribution of economic activities in the European Union'. In: J.V. Henderson and J.F. Thisse (eds), *Handbook of Regional and Urban Economics*. Amsterdam: Elsevier, pp. 2845–2909.

Cortinovis, N. and F.G. van Oort (2015), 'Variety, economic growth and knowledge-intensity of European regions: a spatial panel analysis'. *Annals of Regional Science* **55**: 7–32.

Cortinovis, N. and F.G. van Oort (2018), 'Between spilling over and boiling down: network-mediated spillovers, local knowledge base and productivity in European regions'. *Journal of Economic Geography* **19**(6): 1233–1260. DOI: 10.1093/lby058.

Cortinovis, N., F.G. van Oort and R. Crescenzi (2019), 'Multinational enterprises, industrial relatedness and employment in European regions'. Working paper, Erasmus University Rotterdam.

Cortinovis, N., J. Xiao, R. Boschma and F.G. van Oort (2017), 'Quality of government and social capital as drivers of regional diversification in Europe'. *Journal of Economic Geography* **17**: 1179–1208.

Csáfordi, Z., L. Lőrincz and B. Lengyel (2018), 'Productivity spillovers through labor flows: productivity gap, multinational experience and industry relatedness'. *Journal of Technological Transfer* **45**: 86–121.

Diodato, D. and A. Weterings (2015), 'The resilience of regional labour markets to economic shocks: exploring the role of interactions among firms and workers'. *Journal of Economic Geography* **15**: 723–742.

Dogaru, T., F. van Oort and N. Cortinovis (2017), 'Smart specialisation and local economic development in Eastern Europe'. In: P. McCann, F. van Oort and J. Goddard (eds), *The Empirical and Institutional Dimensions of Smart Specialisation*. London: Routledge, pp. 145–164.

Duranton, G. and D. Puga (2004), 'Micro-foundation of urban agglomeration economies'. In: J.V. Henderson and J.F. Thisse (eds), *Handbook of Regional and Urban Economics*. Amsterdam: Elsevier, pp. 2063–2117.

Eriksson, R. (2011), 'Localized spillovers and knowledge flows: how does proximity influence the performance of plants?' *Economic Geography* **87**: 127–154.

Foray, D. (2015), *Smart Specialisation: Opportunities and Challenges for Regional Innovation Policy*. London: Routledge.

Fornahl, D., S. Henn and M.P. Mensel (2010), *Emerging Clusters: Theoretical, Empirical and Political Perspectives on the Initial Stage of Cluster Evolution*. Cheltenham, UK and Northampton, MA, USA: Edward Elgar Publishing.

Frenken, K., F.G. van Oort and T. Verburg (2007), 'Related variety, unrelated variety and regional economic growth'. *Regional Studies* **41**: 685–697.

Glaeser, E.L, A. Giacomo, M. Ponzetti and K. Tobio (2014), 'Cities, skills and regional change'. *Regional Studies* **48**: 7–43.

Hidalgo, C.A., B. Klinger, A.L. Barabàsi and R. Hausmann (2007), 'The product space conditions the development of nations'. *Science* **317**: 482–487.

Jacobs, J. (1969), *The Economy of Cities*. New York: Random House.

McCann, P., F. van Oort and J. Goddard (eds) (2017), *The Empirical and Institutional Dimensions of Smart Specialisation*. London: Routledge.

Melo, P.C., D.J. Graham and R.B. Noland (2009), 'A meta-analysis of estimates of agglomeration economies'. *Regional Science and Urban Economics* **39**: 332–342.

Mewes, L. (2019a), 'Scaling of atypical knowledge combinations in American metropolitan areas from 1836 to 2010'. *Economic Geography* **95**: 341–361.

Mewes, L. (2019b), 'Quality dimensions of knowledge and regional development. Relatedness, complexity, novelty, and impact of knowledge'. PhD thesis, Utrecht University.

Neffke, F. and M. Henning (2013), 'Skill relatedness and firm diversification'. *Strategic Management Journal* **34**: 297–316.

Neffke, F.M.H., M. Henning and R. Boschma (2011), 'How do regions diversify over time? Industry relatedness and the development of new growth paths in regions'. *Economic Geography* **87**: 237–265.

Ouwehand, W., F.G. van Oort and N. Cortinovis (2019), 'Spatial structure and productivity in European regions'. Working paper, Erasmus University Rotterdam.

Porter, M. (2000), 'Location, competition and economic development: local clusters in a global economy'. *Economic Development Quarterly* **14**: 15–34.

Stam, E. (2015), 'Entrepreneurial ecosystems and regional policy: a sympathetic critique'. Utrecht: USE Discussion Paper 1507.

Thissen, M., F. van Oort, D. Diodato and A. Ruijs (2013), *Regional Competitiveness and Smart Specialisation in Europe: Place-Based Development in International Economic Networks*. Cheltenham, UK and Northampton, MA, USA: Edward Elgar Publishing.

Van Haaren, J., F.G. van Oort and J.D. Maasland (forthcoming), 'Local cluster strategies and firm performance in the Netherlands'. In: D. Fornahl and N.Grashof (eds), *Regional Clusters in a Global World*. Cheltenham, UK and Northampton, MA, USA: Edward Elgar Publishing.

Van Oort, F.G. (2013), 'Unity in variety? Agglomeration economics beyond the specialization–diversity controversy'. In: C. Karlsson, M. Andersson and T. Norman (eds), *Handbook of Research Methods and Applications in Economic Geography*. Cheltenham, UK and Northampton, MA, USA: Edward Elgar Publishing, pp. 259–271.

Van Oort, F.G. and J.G. Lambooy (2020), 'Cities, knowledge and innovation'. In: M.M. Fischer and P. Nijkamp (eds), *Handbook of Regional Science*. Berlin: Springer, pp. 475–488.

Van Oort, F.G., A. Weterings, L. Nedelkoska and F. Neffke (2015), 'Ruimte geven aan economische vernieuwing. Een onderzoek naar arbeidsmobiliteit en skill-gerelateerdheid in Nederlandse regio's'. Den Haag: Ministry of Infrastructure and Environment.

APPENDIX

Table 3A.1   The definition of clusters and auxiliary key industries in Van Oort et al. (2015)

Cluster	SBI08	Description
Core industries		
1a Agro-food production	103	Production of vegetables and fruit
	105	Dairy production
	106	Production of wheat
	1081	Production of sugar
1b Agro-food services	0161	Business services for horticulture and agriculture
2 Chemicals	192	Oil refinery and applications
	201	Production of chemical products
3 Creative industry and services	631	Websites
	582	Software publishing
	591	Film and TV
4 Energy	062	Natural gas extraction
	352	Production of gas
	091	Services for oil and gas extraction
	3511	Electricity production
5 High-tech systems and materials (HTSM)	265	Production of measurement equipment
	267	Production of optical instruments
	2731	Production of (optical) fibres
	325	Production of medical instruments
6 Life sciences and health	212	Pharmaceutical industry
	72112	R&D biotechnology
	72193	R&D health
	266	Radiation equipment
7 Logistics	5221	Land transport services
	494	Land transport
	5222	Water transport services
	5223	Air transport services
8 Horticulture	0113	Vegetable production
	0119	Young crops production
	013	Flowers and plants
	0164	Green genetics
9 Water	4291	Delta technology: waterway construction
	3011	Shipbuilding
	3012	Sport and recreation ships

Table 3A.1   (continued)

Cluster		Core industries	
		SBI08	Description
10	Information and	6201	Software/programming
	communication	6202	ICT consultancy
	technology (ICT)	6209	IT advice
11	Financial services	641	Banks
		643	Stock experts
		649	Financial intermediates
		651	Insurance
12	Business services	7022	Management consultancy
		692	Accountancy

Source: Translated from Van Oort et al. (2015).

4. Mapping global value chains

Giovanni Mandras and Andrea Conte

4.1 INTRODUCTION

In recent years, global value chains (GVCs) have become the new paradigm for the production of goods and services. Indeed, production is increasingly internationally fragmented, and parts and components of final goods can be produced in different countries and regions, and subsequently assembled along their value chains.

One of the consequences of this fragmentation of production at the international level is the difficulty in identifying the country or region of origin of a final product. Moreover, official (and aggregate) trade statistics seem to have partially lost their ability to correctly describe product flows between countries/regions and, in particular, to identify where the value added is generated at each stage of the supply chain. For example, a region/country could export a product limiting itself exclusively to assembling intermediate goods produced in other regions. In this scenario, economic agents, firms, industries and regions are both importers and exporters of intermediate goods which can be exchanged many times before being resold as final goods, thus leading to a substantial double counting in gross trade statistics as they record trade every time a product crosses the country borders.[1]

This phenomenon involves not only an increase in the number and the value of international transactions, but also new forms of interdependence between the actors, requiring a deeper assessment of commercial relations both from a bilateral point of view and in their systemic form. Therefore, the increasing complexity of the organization of production along global value chains requires new approaches to the analysis of international trade flows. Accounting frameworks should focus more on the characteristics and the interconnections of the global production network, especially in

---

[1] UNCTAD (2013) gives a very rough estimation of the double counting at global level (estimated as the total amount of foreign value added content in global exports) at around 28 per cent.

a free and highly integrated market such as the single market within the European Union. Furthermore, according to the related GVCs literature, an important implication of this new paradigm is to go beyond industries when analysing trade, production and innovation patterns, moving towards a business functional approach.

The basic data that provide a description of such an interdependent production structure are collected in the make (supply) and use tables and/or input–output tables. The challenge in constructing such datasets is to have consistently defined data in a coherent framework using the same product and industry classifications. Each country/region requires a table describing: (1) its within-region, or intra-regional production; (2) its export of commodities to industries and final use in the other regions; and (3) its imports from the other regions. A number of recently created global multi-region input–output (MRIO) tables and new analytical modelling frameworks (Koopman et al., 2010; Johnson and Noguera, 2012; Wang et al., 2013; Koopman et al., 2014; Los et al., 2016) have helped to develop a more precise breakdown of a country's exports with information on the origin and final absorption of value added. However, almost all existing MRIO databases are at country level, meaning that the national economies are treated as homogeneous blocks, hiding the differences among their sub-national level entities.[2]

The regional dimension matters, as production processes can be distributed across regions and not only across countries; research and development (R&D) activity might take place in one region while manufacturing takes place in another region within the same country. This could lead to a different regional specialisation in different business functions, requiring different place-based innovation policies focused on the increase of local know-how and innovation capabilities. This means that policy-makers need a deep knowledge of the economic environment in terms of location-specific factors that might attract investments leading to a maximisation of the regional value added (OECD, 2018).

For the purposes of this work, focused on European Union (EU) regions, we use a novel and unique database that includes all EU Nomenclature of Territorial Units for Statistics (NUTS) 2 regions and thus allows us to measure linkages with respect to European value chains (EVCs)[3] by means of these interregional input–output tables. In order to

---

[2] The usefulness of this geographically averaged attribute may be limited when the differences between parts of the country under consideration are very significant (Miller and Blair, 2009).

[3] Thissen et al. (2019) describe the construction of the multi-region input–output (MRIO) table for the EU28 at the NUTS 2 regional level. Although the

do so, we provide the technical description of the methodology adopted to trace where and how value added is created and distributed in both domestic and international segments of the supply chains, defined as a system of value added sources and destinations (Koopman et al., 2014; KWW hereafter).

The remainder of the chapter is organised as follows. In section 4.2 we illustrate the concepts and measurement in gross-export accounting, including the basic data needed and some insights from the Leontief model highlighting its various potential uses. Section 4.3 focuses on gross exports and value added trade patterns within the European Union at NUTS 2 level. Section 4.4 proposes an illustrative example by analysing the contribution of the European Union single market to the EU region's gross domestic product (GDP) using the Italian regions. Section 4.5 briefly summarises policy implications and recommendations on how to benefit more from expanding GVCs.

4.2   ACCOUNTING FOR GROSS EXPORTS: CONCEPTS AND MEASUREMENT

Final goods and services are composed of intermediate inputs coming from different production stages (raw material extraction, processing, manufacturing, and so on) and from different countries/regions around the world. However, conventional trade statistics seem unable to describe the product flows between countries/regions and to identify where the value added is generated at each stage of the supply chain. Following the Organisation for Economic Co-operation and Development (OECD) definition, the trade in value added (TiVA) concept addresses this issue by measuring trade as value added generated by countries/regions along the supply chain of the final goods and services production. The indicators derived from this approach provide new insights and deeper knowledge into the commercial relations between nations/regions for researchers and policy-makers.

Figure 4.1 illustrates, in a simplified way, the TiVA principle. In this example, we have a generic final good produced in three countries (A, B and C) and sold for consumption in a fourth country (D). Using conventional trade statistics, the total value of gross export would be €100 (exports values are recorded each time the intermediate inputs cross the

main purpose of such data is the base-year calibration of the spatial computable general equilibrium (CGE) model RHOMOLO (Lecca et al., 2018), the dataset itself can be exploited for additional uses.

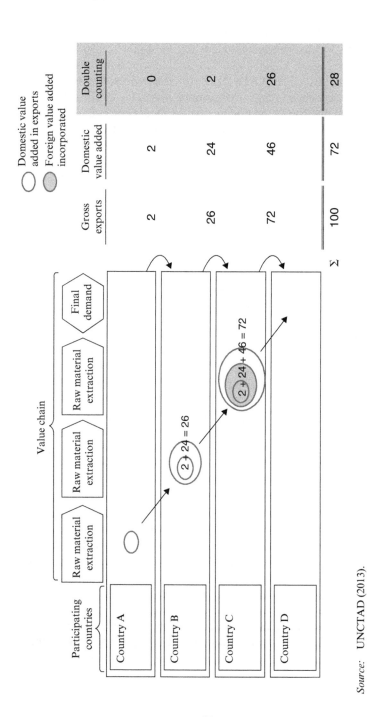

	Gross exports	Domestic value added	Double counting
	2	2	0
	26	24	2
	72	46	26
Σ	100	72	28

Domestic value added in exports

Foreign value added incorporated

Source: UNCTAD (2013).

Figure 4.1 Trade in value added concept

borders), while the adoption of the TiVA approach (using the domestic value added to measure exports) leads to an estimate of gross exports of €72. The difference of €28 is defined as double counting, or foreign value added incorporated (UNCTAD, 2013). In other words, the basic principle of the TiVA approach is that, for instance, the value of the raw material exported by A (or the value added derived from the processing stage in B) should only be counted once as a GDP contribution in the original country, and not multiple times as in the case of gross trade statistics.

The indicators we use are the most commonly used indicators in the TiVA analysis and, furthermore, constitute the basis of gross export decomposition in value added terms (IMF, 2017):

- DVA is the domestic value added embodied in a region's gross exports is the direct and indirect (DVX) value added generates (domestically) in producing exported goods and services. Following the KWW (2014) decomposition, DVA includes two main components: value added exports (VAX; Johnson and Noguera, 2012) and the domestic content in intermediate exports that finally returns home (VS1; Hummels et al., 2001).
- FVA is the foreign value added embodied in gross exports is the value added content of intermediate imports used in a region to produce goods and services for export. FVA indicator is similar to the vertical specialisation measure (VS) proposed by Hummels et al. (2001).

The rest of this section, mainly based on the decomposition proposed by KWW (2014), Borin and Mancini (2015) and IMF (2017), presents and formalises all the necessary steps involved in the gross exports decomposition to provide the reader with a comprehensive technical background to perform value added trade analysis. In particular, the next paragraphs illustrate how applying the Leontief (1941, 1986) input–output modelling framework allows us to assess the degree of interdependency of the economic activities and thus to produce indicators of interest for both researchers and policy-makers. In order to do so, numerical examples are provided to help the reader develop the intuition behind this approach.

4.2.1   Organisation of Basic Data: Input–Output Tables

Supply and use tables (SUTs) represent the starting point of the analysis. SUTs provide data on commodities groups (along the rows), and on the branches of economic activity and industries (along the columns). By means of these rectangular matrices, SUTs show in a very detailed manner all the production processes in a national or regional economy linking industries, products and sectors. More specifically, a supply table describes the supply formation of goods and services, both domestic and imported; while a use table shows the use of goods and services both as intermediate inputs and as final goods, plus the generation of value added by the economic sectors (Eurostat, 2008). Thus, SUTs combine in a single framework the information included in the balance account for goods and services (by product and by industry), in the production account (by industry), and in the primary income distribution account.

Input–output (IO) tables are derived from a transformation of the SUTs and are defined as a set of sectorally disaggregated economic accounts.[4] The IO tables represent a snapshot of the flows of products and services produced and consumed in the economy in a single year. The basic principle relies on the identification and disaggregation of all the monetary flows between industries (inter-industry expenditure flows), consumers and suppliers of production factors in the economy.

A stylized IO table is shown in Table 4.1, where we can distinguish three main blocks: (1) the inter-industry transaction matrix; (2) the domestic value added matrix disaggregated into the main components; and (3) the final demand matrix disaggregated for different categories of consumers. IO tables are symmetric, meaning that there can be either industries or products on their rows and columns, but not both as in the SUTs. Moreover, by reading the table along its rows, we can observe the distribution of each sector's output (sales to other sectors or to final consumers); the columns give information on the inputs required in the production process by each sector. Three accounting identities must hold: in each sector the value of gross input is equal to the value of gross output, total intermediate demand is equal to total intermediate sales, and total primary demand is equal to the total final expenditure.

A simple IO table provides us with all the necessary information to analyse the economic structure of a given region/country but it does not allow for a complete trade analysis because information on the sources of imports or export destination for each economic sector is not provided. Additional data on bilateral trade are needed to move from an IO table to a system of interregional IO tables where all the countries/regions represented are linked by trade (OECD–WTO, 2012). Figure 4.2 shows a simplified MRIO table representing two countries and one industry linked by trade. Such inclusion of imports and exports disaggregated by origin and destination allows us to perform value added trade analysis.

---

[4] See the 'Eurostat Manual of Supply, Use and Input–Output Tables' (Eurostat, 2008) for a complete and detailed description of the different approaches used in the transformation of SUTs in IO tables.

Table 4.1 Stylized IO table

		Producers as consumers								Final demand			
		Agriculture	Mining	Const.	Manuf.	Trade	Transp.	Services	Other	Personal consumption expenditures	Gross private domestic investment	Gov't purchases of goods and services	Net exports of goods and services
Producers	Agriculture												
	Mining												
	Const.												
	Manuf.												
	Trade												
	Transp.												
	Services												
	Other												
Value added	Employees	Employee compensation								Gross domestic product			
	Business Owners and Capital	Profit-type income and capital consumption allowance											
	Government	Indirect business taxes											

Source: Miller and Blair (2009).

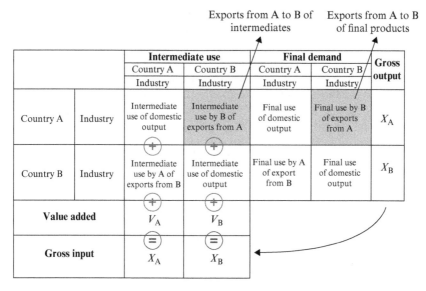

Source: UNCTAD (2013).

Figure 4.2 Simplified MRIO table: two countries, one industry

IO and MRIO tables can be used as the basis for an economic model where exogenous final demand drives total output (Leontief, 1986; Miller and Blair, 2009). The transmission mechanisms linking changes in exogenous demands to changes in aggregate and sectoral activities are called multipliers. These multipliers quantify the knock-on effects throughout the economy generated by an exogenous change in final demand. In other words, IO multipliers allow us to measure to what extent an increase (decrease) in final demand of one sector entails expansionary (contractionary) effects in the output of all sectors, including the perturbed sector. By using a global MRIO system we can compute the interregional multipliers to quantify not only the domestic, but also the foreign economic impact of a demand-side policy or programme implementation. In terms of trade integration, the higher the trade-related component of the multiplier, the higher the interdependence between regional economies.

4.2.2 The Classical Leontief Model

The key element behind the Leontief model is the representation of sectoral interdependence, which in the case of an MRIO table extends to interregional dependence via trade flows of goods and services among regions (Isard, 1951; Moses, 1955, 1960; Miller, 1966). This type of model has been mainly used in the field of environmental economics (see, e.g., Yazan et al., 2017; De Koning et al., 2016), but alternative applications are numerous in fields such as international trade, economic growth (Jones, 2011) and the business cycle (Acemoglu et al., 2012).

In order to represent formally the IO model, let us start by characterising sectoral output as follows:

$$x_i = \sum_{j=1}^{n} z_{ij} + y_i \qquad (4.1)$$

where x_i is the output of sector i; z_{ij} stands for transactions from sector i to sector j; y_i stands for sales from sector i to final demand users. Equation (4.1) simply means that output is given by the sum of intermediate sales and final demand. We could rewrite equation (4.1) as follows:

$$x_i = \sum_{n=1}^{n} a_{in} x_n + y_i \qquad (4.2)$$

$\sum_{n=1}^{n} a_{in} x_n$ stands for intermediate sales (equivalently to $\sum_{j=1}^{n} z_{ij}$) expressed as output multiplying the technical coefficients a_{in}. The latter express the quantity of input i used to produce output x and are defined as the ratio between intermediate transactions divided by output:

$$a_{in} = z_{in}/x_n \qquad (4.2.1)$$

These coefficients are fixed, meaning that constant returns to scale are assumed, and it is a way to represent the available production technology in the economy. In matrix notation, we can rewrite equation (4.2) as follows:

$$X = Ax + Y \qquad (4.3)$$

where, X is the vector of gross outputs, Y is the vector of final demands, and A is the matrix of technical coefficients (also called IO coefficients).

Equation (4.3) can be solved for X, and pre-multiplying both sides of equation (4.3) by $[I - A]^{-1}$ we obtain the following:

$$X = [I - A]^{-1}Y \qquad (4.4)$$

where, $[I - A]^{-1}$ is called either the Leontief inverse or the total requirements matrix. Y is assumed to be completely exogenous, which means that demand does not relate to production. Equation (4.4) can be used to calculate the multipliers, as by modifying the exogenous demand vector one can calculate the output necessary to sustain such alternative demands. This analysis relies on three assumptions: (1) the supply side of the economy is entirely passive; (2) there are no supply constraints, nor unused capacity; and (3) the production technology for all sectors is represented by fixed coefficients (meaning that an increase in the production of any sector's output means a proportional increase in that sector's input requirements). Point (3) means that inputs substitutability is neglected.

In terms of trade analysis, if a MRIO system is not available for a particular country/region, we will show (in section 4.5) that the classical single-region model can be used in order to compute the direct DVA in exports and, in turn, FVA can be obtained subtracting DVA from gross exports (Los et al., 2016).

The multi-region IO framework
If we consider a two regions, one sector accounting framework, gross output in region S and sector i, $X_s(i)$, is given by the sum of intermediate and final demand goods consumed locally or traded. Formally, and rewriting (4.1), in equilibrium we have the following relationship:

$$X_s(i) = \sum_r \sum_j z_{s,r}(i,j) + \sum_s y_{s,r}(i) \qquad (4.5)$$

where, $z_{s,r}(i,j)$ is the intermediate inputs matrix that contains the intermediate goods produced in region s and sold in destination r that we are able to map by sectors of origin and destination (i and j, respectively); $y_{s,r}(i)$ represents the total final demand goods i produced in region s and consumed in region r.

If both regions trade intermediate and final goods, it follows that gross output of each region is such that $x_s = \sum_r y_{s,r}$ where $x_1 = x_{11} + x_{12}$ and $x_2 = x_{21} + x_{22}$ (for $s,r = 1,2$). The output produced in region 1 is therefore divided into the output used in the same region x_{11}, and the output needed to satisfy the demand of good and services of region 2, x_{12}. The accounting relationship is such that $x_s = a_{ss}x_s + a_{sr}x_r + y_{ss} + y_{sr}$, where the elements on the right-hand side represent the domestic intermediate input purchased domestically, the intermediate input purchase abroad, the domestic final demand goods, and the final demand goods imported from abroad, respectively.

Generalization to G-country (one industry) case   Moving to a general case of G regions producing N goods (internationally traded both as intermediate inputs and as final good), we have that:

$$X_s = \sum_r^G (A_{sr}X_r + Y_{sr}) \tag{4.6}$$

where, A_{sr} is the NxN matrix of coefficients for intermediate inputs produced in s and processed further in r:

$$A_{sr} = \begin{bmatrix} a_{1,1}^{sr} & a_{1,2}^{sr} & \cdots & a_{1,N}^{sr} \\ a_{2,1}^{sr} & a_{2,2}^{sr} & \cdots & a_{1,N}^{sr} \\ \vdots & \vdots & \ddots & \vdots \\ a_{N,1}^{sr} & a_{N,2}^{sr} & \cdots & a_{1,N}^{sr} \end{bmatrix} \tag{4.7}$$

Using the block matrix notation, the general setting of production and trade between G regions and N goods (equation 4.6) can be defined as follows:

$$
\begin{bmatrix} X_1 \\ X_2 \\ \vdots \\ X_G \end{bmatrix} = \begin{bmatrix} A_{11} & A_{12} & \cdots & A_{1G} \\ A_{21} & A_{22} & \cdots & A_{2G} \\ \vdots & \vdots & \ddots & \vdots \\ A_{G1} & A_{G2} & \cdots & A_{GG} \end{bmatrix} \begin{bmatrix} X_1 \\ X_2 \\ \vdots \\ X_G \end{bmatrix}
$$
$$
+ \begin{bmatrix} Y_{11} & Y_{12} & \cdots & Y_{1G} \\ Y_{21} & Y_{22} & \cdots & Y_{2G} \\ \vdots & \vdots & \ddots & \vdots \\ Y_{G1} & Y_{G2} & \cdots & Y_{GG} \end{bmatrix} \begin{bmatrix} 1 \\ 1 \\ \vdots \\ 1 \end{bmatrix} \tag{4.8}
$$

From (4.8) we can derive the relationship linking gross output and final demand as:

$$
\begin{bmatrix} X_1 \\ X_2 \\ \vdots \\ X_G \end{bmatrix} = \begin{bmatrix} I - A_{11} & -A_{12} & \cdots & -A_{1G} \\ -A_{21} & I - A_{22} & \cdots & -A_{2G} \\ \vdots & \vdots & \ddots & \vdots \\ -A_{G1} & -A_{G2} & \cdots & I - A_{GG} \end{bmatrix}^{-1} \begin{bmatrix} \sum_r^G Y_{1r} \\ \sum_r^G Y_{2r} \\ \vdots \\ \sum_r^G Y_{1G} \end{bmatrix}
$$

$$= \begin{bmatrix} B_{11} & B_{12} & \cdots & B_{1N} \\ B_{21} & B_{22} & \cdots & B_{2N} \\ \vdots & \vdots & \ddots & \vdots \\ B_{G1} & B_{G2} & \cdots & B_{GG} \end{bmatrix} \begin{bmatrix} \sum_r^G Y_{1r} \\ \sum_r^G Y_{2r} \\ \vdots \\ \sum_r^G Y_{1G} \end{bmatrix} \qquad (4.9)$$

where B_{sr} denotes the NxN block of the multiplier matrix (the Leontief inverse, $[I - A]^{-1}$) in a global IO setting. It provides indication on how much of region's s gross output of a good is required to produce one unit of region r's final production.

4.2.3 Estimating Trade in Value Added (TiVA) and Value Added Trade[5]

Once the generalized equation (4.9) linking the final demand and output for G-regions has been defined, the next step is to calculate the direct value added share in each unit of gross output produced by region s. The share of value added per unit of output by region s (defined as the region s value added divided by the total output of region s), is equal to one minus the direct intermediate input share of all the supplier regions, domestic and foreign:

$$V_s = u_N \left(I - \sum_r^G A_{rs} \right) \qquad (4.10)$$

where u_N is the $1xN$ unit row vector. Placing the value added regional shares as diagonal element in a $GxGN$ matrix, the direct domestic value added matrix for all regions (note that we are considering only one sector per region) is defined as follows:

$$V = \begin{bmatrix} V_1 & 0 & \cdots & 0 \\ 0 & V_2 & \cdots & 0 \\ \vdots & \vdots & \ddots & \vdots \\ 0 & 0 & \cdots & V_G \end{bmatrix} \qquad (4.10.1)$$

[5] The estimation process presented and the notation used in this section are derived from Koopman et al. (2014), OECD-WTO (2014) and Borin and Mancini (2015).

The overall *GxGN* value added share matrix is obtained by multiplying V by the Leontief inverse B:

$$
VB = \begin{bmatrix}
V_1B_{11} & V_1B_{12} & \cdots & V_1B_{1G} \\
V_2B_{21} & V_1B_{22} & \cdots & V_1B_{2G} \\
\vdots & \vdots & \ddots & \vdots \\
V_GB_{G1} & V_GB_{G2} & \cdots & V_GB_{GG}
\end{bmatrix}
\tag{4.11}
$$

The VB matrix allow us to quantify (in proportional terms) how much value added each region needs from itself and from the others (rest of the EU regions in our case) to reach its actual level of gross output. Note that the diagonal elements represent the domestic value added share of internally produced goods, while the off-diagonal elements the foreign share for the production of the same goods.

The final steps consist in the estimation of two matrixes; VBE to determine the domestic and foreign value added embodied in gross export, which is independent of how value added is used by importers' regions; and VBY, which depends on how region's exports are used by importers. In order to formalise VBE we need to define the aggregate gross exports matrix, *E*, where the diagonal elements give the total exports for the corresponding region (or sectors), as follows:

$$
E = \begin{bmatrix}
E_1 & 0 & \cdots & 0 \\
0 & E_2 & \cdots & 0 \\
\vdots & \vdots & \ddots & \vdots \\
0 & 0 & \cdots & E_G
\end{bmatrix}
\tag{4.12}
$$

Thus, the TiVA matrix is defined as:

$$
TiVA = VBE = \begin{bmatrix}
V_1 & 0 & \cdots & 0 \\
0 & V_2 & \cdots & 0 \\
\vdots & \vdots & \ddots & \vdots \\
0 & 0 & \cdots & V_G
\end{bmatrix}
\begin{bmatrix}
B_{11} & B_{12} & \cdots & B_{1G} \\
B_{21} & B_{22} & \cdots & B_{2G} \\
\vdots & \vdots & \ddots & \vdots \\
B_{G1} & B_{G2} & \cdots & B_{GG}
\end{bmatrix}
$$
$$
\begin{bmatrix}
E_1 & 0 & \cdots & 0 \\
0 & E_2 & \cdots & 0 \\
\vdots & \vdots & \ddots & \vdots \\
0 & 0 & \cdots & E_G
\end{bmatrix}
\tag{4.13}
$$

where:

- the diagonal elements show the domestic valued added embodied in exports (DVA);
- the off-diagonal row elements show the indirect value added in exports (DVX);
- the off-diagonal column elements show the foreign valued added embodied in exports (FVA).

Furthermore, the TiVA matrix is used to compute indexes able to quantify the position and the participation of a region/sector along the value chain, thus providing useful insights from a policy-maker perspective (KWW, 2014).

Finally, defining the VBY matrix substituting in (4.13) the gross export matrix E with the final demand matrix, Y:

$$
Y = \begin{bmatrix} Y_1 & 0 & \cdots & 0 \\ 0 & Y_2 & \cdots & 0 \\ \vdots & \vdots & \ddots & \vdots \\ 0 & 0 & \cdots & Y_G \end{bmatrix}
\tag{4.14}
$$

we can derive the value added matrix by pairs of source-absorption regions as:

$$
VBY = \begin{bmatrix} V_1 & 0 & \cdots & 0 \\ 0 & V_2 & \cdots & 0 \\ \vdots & \vdots & \ddots & \vdots \\ 0 & 0 & \cdots & V_G \end{bmatrix} \begin{bmatrix} B_{11} & B_{12} & \cdots & B_{1G} \\ B_{21} & B_{22} & \cdots & B_{2G} \\ \vdots & \vdots & \ddots & \vdots \\ B_{G1} & B_{G2} & \cdots & B_{GG} \end{bmatrix}
$$
$$
\begin{bmatrix} Y_1 & 0 & \cdots & 0 \\ 0 & Y_2 & \cdots & 0 \\ \vdots & \vdots & \ddots & \vdots \\ 0 & 0 & \cdots & Y_G \end{bmatrix}
\tag{4.15}
$$

From the matrix above:

- summing up the matrix along the rows, we derive information on how each region's domestic value added is used by the region itself and all its downstream regions;

- summing up the matrix along the columns, we derive information on the region sources of value added in each region's final demand, accounting for all upstream regions' value added contributions to a specific region final goods output.

The supply-side perspective (the second point) decomposes how each region's value added is used, directly or indirectly, to satisfy internal or external final demand; while the user-side prospective (first point) decomposes a region's final goods and services into its original region sources (KWW, 2014). The following section provides some numerical examples to better clarify the intuitions of this approach.

4.2.4 A Numerical Example: Two Regions, Two Sectors

Consider the hypothetical MRIO table in Box 4.1, table (A), where two regions (R1, R2), two sectors (s1, s2), value added (VA) and final demand (FR1, FR2) are shown.[6]

The first step is to compute the A matrix (as in section 4.2.1)[7] and, once the Identity matrix (C) is defined and subtracted from A (D), we can compute B, the $[I - A]^{-1}$ matrix (the Leontief inverse). These multipliers (E) provide some preliminary intuitions on the economic structure of the two regions considered; the total output multiplier of R2-s1 (obtained summing up the correspondent rows) is 4.4, meaning that €1 invested in the sector 1 of R2 is able to generate €4.4 (€1 is the direct effect, while 3.40 is the indirect effect). However, from a trade analysis perspective, we can see that only €2.88 are generated in R2 (2.2 + 0.67) while the other 1.52 (0.88 + 0.65) will be generated in R1 which is benefiting from the investment made in R2 because of the trade link (spillover effect). Thus, already from the MRIO multipliers we can draw some preliminary information on the degree of interdependence between regions: the higher the trade component of the MRIO multiplier, the higher the interconnections between regional economies.

Tables (G), (J) and (K) reflect the matrixes VB, VBE (or Tiva matrix) and VBY formalised in (4.11), (4.13) and (4.15), respectively (section 4.2.3). In detail, the VB matrix (where V stands for the value added coefficient matrix F)[8] is the basic measure of value added share by source

---

6   See Table 4.1 in section 4.2.1 for a description of each element in (A).

7   Each element of the A matrix is given by the intermediate transactions and output ratio (25/121 for R1-s1, 50/135 for R2-s1 and so on).

8   Value added coefficients are computed as the ratio between VA and total output: for R2-s2 the coefficient is 30/121 = 0.30.

BOX 4.1 TIVA: A NUMERICAL EXAMPLE

(A)

		R1			R2			
		s1	s2	FR1	s1	s2	FR2	Total
R1	s1	25	30	5	25	25	11	121
	s2	50	50	30	2	2	1	135
	VA	30	40					
R2	s1	10	5	5	50	50	15	135
	s2	6	10	25	25	30	20	116
	VA				33	9		
Total		121	135		135	116		

(B)

A		R1		R2	
		s1	s2	s1	s2
R1	s1	0.21	0.22	0.19	0.22
	s2	0.41	0.37	0.01	0.02
R2	s1	0.08	0.04	0.37	0.43
	s2	0.05	0.07	0.19	0.26

(C)

I		R1		R2	
		s1	s2	s1	s2
R1	s1	1	0	0	0
	s2	0	1	0	0
R2	s1	0	0	1	0
	s2	0	0	0	1

(D)

I − A		R1		R2	
		s1	s2	s1	s2
R1	s1	0.79	−0.22	−0.19	−0.22
	s2	−0.41	0.63	−0.01	−0.02
R2	s1	−0.08	−0.04	0.63	−0.43
	s2	−0.05	−0.07	−0.19	0.74

(E)

B		R1		R2	
		s1	s2	s1	s2
R1	s1	1.85	0.83	0.88	1.07
	s2	1.24	2.16	0.65	0.79
R2	s1	0.59	0.51	2.20	1.46
	s2	0.39	0.40	0.67	1.86

(F)

V		R1		R2	
		s1	s2	s1	s2
R1	s1	0.25	0	0	0
	s2	0	0.30	0	0
R2	s1	0	0	0.24	0
	s2	0	0	0	0.08

(G)

VB		R1		R2	
		s1	s2	s1	s2
R1	s1	0.46	0.21	0.22	0.26
	s2	0.37	0.64	0.19	0.23
R2	s1	0.14	0.12	0.54	0.36
	s2	0.03	0.03	0.05	0.14

(H)

E		R1		R2	
		s1	s2	s1	s2
R1	s1	61	0	0	0
	s2	0	5	0	0
R2	s1	0	0	20	0
	s2	0	0	0	41

(I)

Y		R1		R2	
		s1	s2	s1	s2
R1	s1	16	0	0	0
	s2	0	31	0	0
R2	s1	0	0	20	0
	s2	0	0	0	45

(J)

VBE		R1		R2	
		s1	s2	s1	s2
R1	s1	28	1	4	11
	s2	22	3	4	10
R2	s1	9	1	11	15
	s2	2	0	1	6

(K)

VBY		R1		R2	
		s1	s2	s1	s2
R1	s1	7	6	4	12
	s2	6	20	4	10
R2	s1	2	4	11	16
	s2	0	1	1	7

of production. It reflects the underlying production embedded in the MRIO model specified in (4.8). It is important to recall that the diagonal elements represent the DVA share of internally produced goods, while the off-diagonal elements represent the FVA share for the production of the same goods. In our example, considering R1, the DVA content of s1 and s2 is 46 per cent and 64 per cent and the FVA is 54 per cent and 36 per cent, respectively.[9]

The VBE or Tiva matrix (where E stands for the total exports matrix H) decomposes gross exports in their DVA, FVA and DVX content and allows us to calculate the degree of integration in terms of the region participation in a GVC. Furthermore, the matrix provides insights to characterise a regional economy's position in GVCs, quantifying its upstream and downstream component. The VBY matrix (where Y stands for the global final demand matrix I) provides information both from the supply side (rows) and user side perspective (columns). From the supply side perspective we derive information on how each region's domestic value added is used by the region itself and all its downstream regions. Looking at R1-s1, from the MRIO table (A) we know that the total value added is 30 and, from the VBY matrix we can see that 7 units are used directly by R1-s1 (24 per cent) and 6 by the R1-s2 (21 per cent), meaning

---

[9]   Note that because all the value added must be either domestic or foreign, the sum along each column is unity (KWW, 2014).

that the remaining 16 units (55 per cent) of the R1-s1's value added is used by the downstream region R2. From the user side perspective, this matrix decomposes a region's final goods and services into its original region sources. For example, looking at the R2-s2, from the MRIO table (A) we have a total final demand of good and services of 45 (25+20) of which 7 come from the s2's production (14 per cent), while 22 (50 per cent) of the R2-s2 final consumption come from R1.

4.3 EU REGIONS: GROSS EXPORTS AND MAIN VALUE ADDED TRADE PATTERNS

This section presents a general overview in terms of gross exports and imports, trade and internal backward linkages (IO multipliers), and some preliminary results in terms of value added trade patterns within the EU single market, by means of a novel database described as follows.

4.3.1 Data

This novel dataset covers 267 NUTS 2 regions with a ten-sector disaggregation, and it is obtained from a complex procedure which can be briefly summarised as follows (the full procedure is explained in Thissen et al., 2019):

1. Eurostat data are used to construct national supply and use tables (SUTs) for all the member states of the EU28 with NACE rev. 2 sectors to the latest available year.
2. National SUTs are linked with trade flows of goods and services (BACI and United Nations datasets).
3. SUTs are regionalised using regional data on production and consumption and applying the commodity balance approach (Miller and Blair, 2009).
4. Inter-regional IO tables for all NUTS 2 regions of the EU28 are created with 65 NACE rev. 2 sectors.
5. Transport data are used as a proxy for interregional trade estimation. The regional trade matrices accompanying these tables are consistent not only with national SUTs, but also with the main European transport data, taking into account multimodal transport with endogenously determined transhipment locations. This makes it possible to analyse the role of transhipment locations in regional trade and to relate actual transport costs to multiregional trade flows.

4.3.2   EU Regional Trade

As an example of potential applications of these data, we provide an overview of the trade links between NUTS 2 regions by distinguishing exports and imports (as a share of GDP) to other EU regions within country and between different EU member states. Figures 4.3 and 4.4 depict trade (as a share of GDP) to other EU member states. On average, regions with the highest export shares are found to be predominantly in Central and Eastern Europe. This confirms the importance of exports for these economies and their role in pushing the relatively high growth rates experienced by many of these regions since their integration into the European single market.

Moreover, most Central and Eastern European regions have a share of exports well above 100 per cent. In turn, this means that consumption and investments in locally produced final goods and services are less than the total imports of intermediate goods. As confirmed by Figure 4.4, where imports are reported, these regions import a lot of non-final goods to turn them into final products which are then exported rather than consumed locally.

Conversely, the lower export share in many rich EU regions, on average, reflects lower intermediate inputs trade, reflecting a relatively (compared to GDP) lower degree of economic integration along the production processes within the EU. Notice that gross trade should be used only as a first intuition on the economic integration of an economy, since the value added content in exports is a better indicator to analyse value chains.

Figures 4.5 and 4.6 depict regional trade (as a share of GDP) within each EU member state. Trade patterns for within-country trade are quite similar to those emerging for between-country trade. In turn, this emphasises the existing trade links for intermediate inputs, especially between Central and Eastern EU regions. The cases of the United Kingdom (UK) and Greek regions are particularly interesting with regard to within-country trade, showing very big differences in import and export ratios compared to those of other EU member states. Finally, looking at the case of Italy, our estimations confirm that Southern regions import more than they export to Northern regions.

4.3.3   Quantifying the Economic Interdependence: The IO Multiplier

As mentioned in section 4.2.1, the analysis of IO multipliers is useful to assess not only the domestic, but also the foreign economic impact of a demand-side policy. Indeed, interregional multipliers provide a first

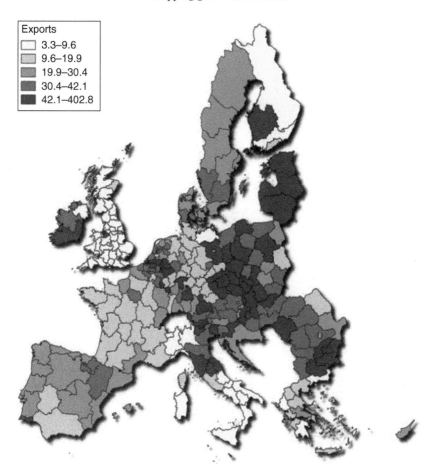

Figure 4.3   Exports to other EU member states as a share of GDP (%)

intuition on the degree of trade-related integration. Figure 4.7 plots domestic backward linkages (x-axis) and trade backward linkages (y-axis) derived from the Leontief multiplier.[10] The two lines show the computed domestic (internal) and trade backward linkages. On average, we see that €1 invested in a region is able to generate an additional €0.33 outside the region and €1.22 in the region itself.

---

[10]   The domestic backward linkages obtained in each region are represented by the diagonal of the Leontief matrix, the B_{sr} matrix in equation (4.9). The trade backward linkages are instead the sum in each row of the Leontief matrix except the region involved.

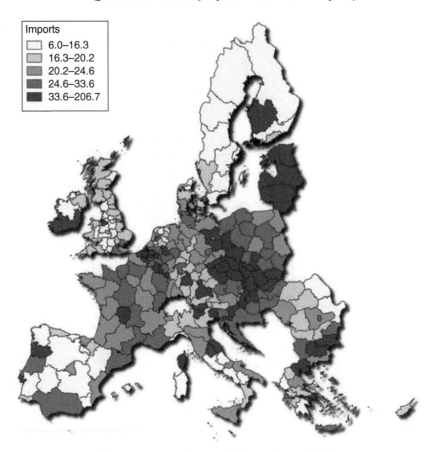

Figure 4.4   Import from other EU member states as a share of GDP (%)

Looking at the top-right quadrant we have regions that generate greater
internal multipliers and also high spillovers at the benefit of the rest of the
EU. Conversely, the bottom-left quadrant shows those regions with lower
trade and internal linkages.

4.3.4   Value Added Trade Patterns

In order to assess EU regions' trade in value added, we adopt the
indicators described in section 4.2 as a starting point in gross export
decomposition (IMF, 2017). Figures 4.8 and 4.9 plot the DVA and
FVA indicators derived from the TiVA approach formalised in (4.13).
Based on our trade data, where exports have been corrected for

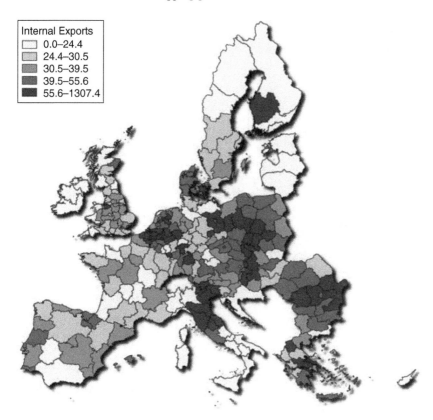

Figure 4.5 Exports (within each EU member state) as a share of GDP (%)

re-exports,[11] and considering only interregional trade within the EU, the computed average DVA embedded in the gross exports of the EU regions is around 74 per cent, and thus 26 per cent of FVA is in exports. The latter provides a very rough estimation of the double counting coming from standard trade statistics on gross exports (UNCTAD, 2013). DVA content seems to vary widely across regions (see Figure 4.8) and, in particular, for those regions belonging to the same country. This within-country heterogeneity underlines the importance of taking into account the regional dimension in TiVA analysis.

Looking at the FVA share of exports (Figure 4.9) we have a first rough

---

[11] For a full description on the methodology used to clean official trade statistics for re-exports, see Thissen et al. (2019).

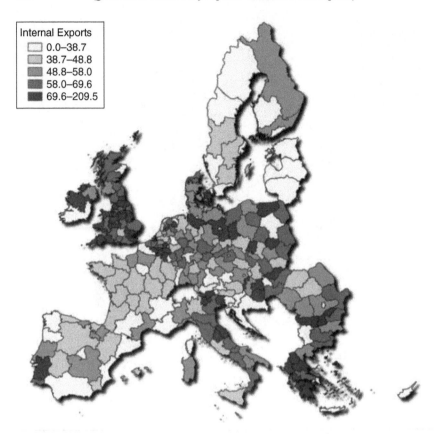

*Figure 4.6   Imports (within each EU member state) as a share of GDP
(%)*

indication of the regions with the most segmented value chains, as it is used as a proxy to quantify how many times intermediate inputs (goods and services) cross regional borders in the process of final goods and services production. Our results suggest, not surprisingly, that Central and Eastern regions seem to have the more fragmented supply chains due to the strong delocalisation processes in the automotive and electronics sectors.

DVA and FVA shares in exports confirm that both the highly integrated single market and shared institutional settings boosted the rise and development of strong regional value chains within the EU. Moreover, as pointed out by UNCTAD (2018), it is the EU as a whole that drives the high average of FVA content at global level for developed economies. Indeed, United States and Japan show a more limited share of FVA since they are able to capture a large part of value added generated internally.

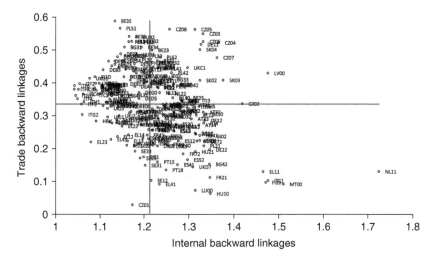

Figure 4.7 The IO multipliers: trade and internal backward linkages

4.4   AN ALTERNATIVE APPROACH: THE HYPOTHETICAL EXTRACTION METHOD

Los et al. (2017) have used such IO methodology to quantify the level of integration of UK regions on EU final demand by adopting the following procedure. In order to quantify the level of integration of a certain region *y*, it is sufficient to modify the *A* matrix of equation (4.7) by setting to zero all trade links of region *y* to the rest of the EU and then to calculate the inverse of this new matrix. In addition, all trade links between *y* and the rest of the EU from the final demand vector should be set to zero.[12]

The new matrix and vector should be used to calculate the new production X^{y*} in region *y*, which can then be used to quantify the level of integration of such region as $1 - \frac{X^{y*}}{X^y}$. This indicator can be calculated for a single region, for entire countries, as well as for groups of regions and countries, and can also be sector-specific.

As an illustrative example, we conduct a similar exercise on Italian regions. Figure 4.10 illustrates the necessary modification to the MRIO data in order to carry out the analysis (Panel A), and the cells that have to be set to zero in the A matrix (Panel B) in order to quantify the degree of integration of the Italian regions within the EU market.

---

[12]   Notice that Los et al. (2017) only do the latter due to the different focus of their analysis.

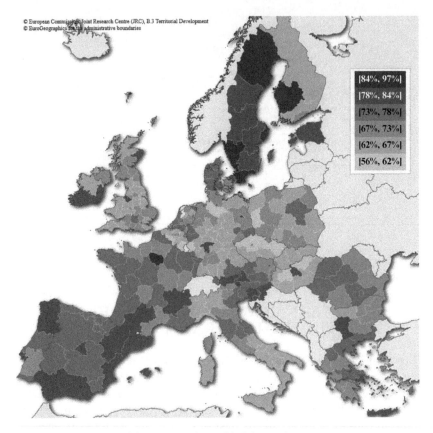

Figure 4.8   Share of domestic value added (DVA) content in exports

This methodology allows the MRIO framework to quantify the level of interdependencies of regions and countries with a higher degree of precision with respect to standard trade statistics which make use of imports and exports data, and put them in relation with GDP such as the standard openness index calculated as: $\frac{(imp + exp)}{GDP}$.

Such an analysis applied to the regions of Italy (used here as a mere representative example) and calculated over GDP rather than output yields the results contained in Figure 4.11 for the Italian economy as a whole, and in Figure 4.12 for the regional detail. Regarding the sector disaggregation contained in Figure 4.11, the lowest dependence on the rest of the EU is recorded for services related to public administration, education and health, as well as in the construction sector, which relies on domestic markets rather than international ones. Four of the ten

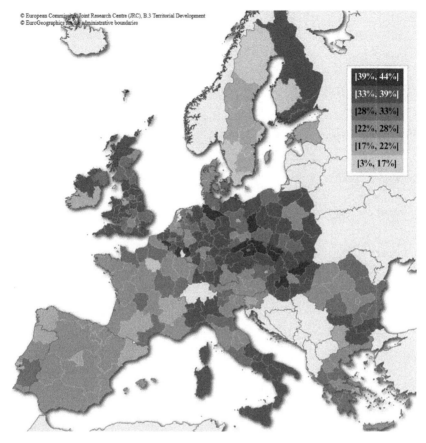

Figure 4.9   Share of foreign value added (FVA) content in exports

sectors are characterised by values above the Italian level of integration: agriculture and forestry, information and communication, professional and administrative activities, and manufacturing, with the manufacturing unsurprisingly being the sector most dependent on the rest of the EU.

Results contained in Figure 4.12 suggest that the GDP of the regions of central and Northern Italy is the most dependent on trade of both intermediate and final goods with the rest of the EU, with values above the 11.01 per cent recorded for Italy as a whole. Southern regions, with the exception of Calabria (due to the presence of the important port of Gioia Tauro, the largest Italian port for container shipping), are characterised by a lower dependence on the rest of the EU.

	Regions in other EU28 countries	**Regions in ITALY**	Countries outside the EU28	Regions in other EU28 countries **Final Demand**	Regions in ITALY **Final Demand**	Countries outside the EU28 Final Demand **Final Demand**	***Gross Output***
Regions in other EU28 countries	Z^{EU_EU}	Z^{EU_IT}	Z^{EU_row}	F^{EU_EU}	F^{EU_IT}	F^{EU_row}	X^{EU}
Regions in ITALY	Z^{IT_EU}	Z^{IT_IT}	Z^{IT_Row}	F^{IT_EU}	F^{IT_IT}	F^{IT_Row}	X^{IT}
Countries outside the EU28	Z^{Row_EU}	Z^{Row_IT}	Z^{Row_Row}	F^{Row_EU}	F^{Row_IT}	F^{Row_Row}	X^{Row}
Value Added	W^{EU}	W^{IT}	W^{Row}				
Gross Output	X^{EU}	X^{IT}	X^{Row}				

Panel A

	Regions in other EU28 countries	**Regions in ITALY**	Countries outside the EU28	Regions in other EU28 countries **Final Demand**	Regions in ITALY **Final Demand**	Countries outside the EU28 Final Demand **Final Demand**	***Gross Output***
Regions in other EU28 countries	Z^{EU_EU}	0	Z^{EU_row}	F^{EU_EU}	0	F^{EU_row}	X^{EU}
Regions in ITALY	0	Z^{IT_IT}	Z^{IT_Row}	0	F^{IT_IT}	F^{IT_Row}	X^{IT}
Countries outside the EU28	Z^{Row_EU}	Z^{Row_IT}	Z^{Row_Row}	F^{Row_EU}	F^{Row_IT}	F^{Row_Row}	X^{Row}
Value Added	W^{EU}	W^{IT}	W^{Row}				
Gross Output	X^{EU}	X^{IT}	X^{Row}				

Panel B

Figure 4.10 Stylised MRIO table with a disaggregation of Italian regions

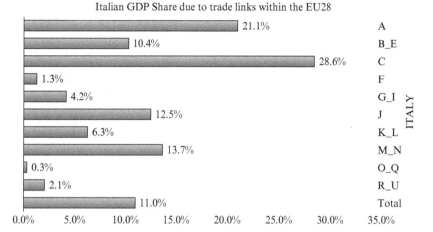

*Figure 4.11   Trade-related GDP of Italian sectors (NACE rev. 2)
dependent on the rest of the EU*

4.5   CONCLUSIONS

In this chapter, after formalising all the main steps needed to map GVCs in value added terms, we started to explore their role at regional (subnational) level; often neglected in the GVC literature, where the focus is mainly on country-level analysis. Moreover, in a context of place-based innovation processes, the mapping of value added is complementary to the pure industrial specialisation approach, allowing a better understanding of the innovation process itself and, consequently, a better design of more effective innovation policies for different level of governments, as well as analysis of the territorial implications of these policies when made operational. Since regions tend to specialise in specific business activities rather than specific industries (OECD, 2018), their effective participation into GVCs depends on the local know-how, R&D and innovation capabilities.

Using a system of inter-regional IO tables for 267 NUTS 2 regions, we derived the distribution of VA trade by regions decomposing gross exports in terms of DVA (the ability of a region to add value to its exports) and FVA (an indicator that provides a first estimation of the vertical specialisation). Furthermore, using an alternative approach we analysed trade contribution to regional GDP formation using Italian regions as an example.

Based on our trade data, the computed average DVA embedded in the gross exports of the EU regions is around 74 per cent and, thus, 26 per cent of FVA is in exports. DVA content varies widely across regions and,

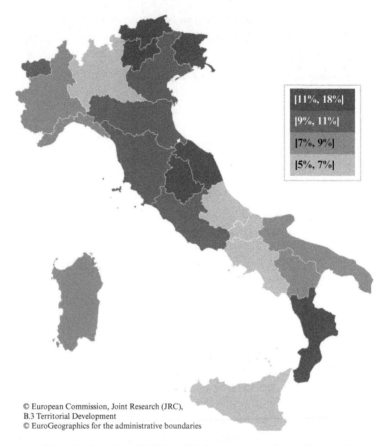

[11%, 18%]
[9%, 11%]
[7%, 9%]
[5%, 7%]

© European Commission, Joint Research (JRC),
B.3 Territorial Development
© EuroGeographics for the administrative boundaries

*Figure 4.12   Trade-related GDP of Italian regions dependent on the rest of
the EU market*

in particular, among those regions belonging to the same country. This
within-country heterogeneity reflects the different regional capabilities and
underlines the importance of taking into account the regional dimension
in the policy-making process. Considering the FVA share of exports, we
found that Central and Eastern regions seem to have the more fragmented
supply chains, mainly because of their specialisation in the automotive and
electronics sectors.

Finally, DVA and FVA shares in exports confirm that both the highly
integrated single market and shared institutional settings boosted the rise
and development of strong regional value chains within the EU.

This type of analysis opens up several avenues of research on the importance of trade links both within the EU, and between EU regions and

countries and the rest of the world, which in turn could provide a quantification of the economic importance of EU integration and of the EU single market. Moreover, this framework is useful for evaluating the impact of a wide range of territorial policies, their spatial economic spillovers, and thus the role that coordination could play for economic policy-makers at different levels of policy governance and for different policy areas.

REFERENCES

Acemoglu, D., Carvalho, V.M., Ozdaglar, A., and Tahbaz-Salehi, A. (2012). The Network Origins of Aggregate Fluctuations. *Econometrica* **80**(5), 1977–2016.

Borin, A., and Mancini, M. (2015). Follow the Value Added: Bilateral Gross Export Accounting. Temi di Discussione (Working Papers), 1026, Banca d'Italia.

De Koning, A., Huppes, G., Deetman, S., and Tukker, A. (2016). Scenarios for a 2°C World: A World Trade-Linked Input–Output Model with High Sector Detail. *Climate Policy* **16**(3), 301–317.

Eurostat (2008). Eurostat Manual of Supply, Use and Input–Output Tables. Eurostat Methodologies and Working Papers, Luxembourg.

Hummels, D., Ishii, J., and Yi, K.M. (2001). The Nature and Growth of Vertical Specialization in World Trade. *Journal of International Economics* **54**, 75–96.

International Monetary Fund (IMF) (2017). Calculating Trade in Value Added. Washington, DC: International Monetary Fund.

Isard, W. (1951). Interregional and Regional Input–Output Analysis: A Model of Space Economy. *Review of Economics and Statistics* **33**, 318–328.

Johnson, R.C., and Noguera, G. (2012). Accounting for Intermediates: Production Sharing and Trade in Value Added. *Journal of International Economics* **86**(2), 224–236.

Jones, C.I. (2011). Misallocation, Economic Growth, and Input–Output Economics. NBER Working Papers No. w16742, National Bureau of Economic Research.

Koopman, R., Wang, Z., and Wei, S.-J. (2014). Tracing Value-Added and Double Counting in Gross Exports. *American Economic Review* **104**(2), 459–494.

Koopman, R., Powers, W., Wang, Z., and Wei, S.-J. (KWW) (2010). Give Credit Where Credit Is Due: Tracing Value Added in Global Production Chains. NBER Working Paper No. 16426. Cambridge, MA: National Bureau of Economic Research.

Lecca, P., Barbero, J., Christensen, M., Conte, A., Di Comite, F., Diaz-Lanchas, J., et al. (2018). RHOMOLO V3: A Spatial Modelling Framework. EUR 29229 EN. Luxembourg: Publications Office of the European Union. doi: 10.2760/671622, JRC118661.

Leontief, W. (1941). *The Structure of American Economy, 1919–1929*. Cambridge, MA: Harvard University Press.

Leontief, W. (1986). *Input–Output Economics*. Oxford: Oxford University Press.

Los, B., Timmer, M.P., and de Vries, G.J. (2016). Tracing Value-Added and Double Counting in Gross Exports: Comment. *American Economic Review* **106**(7), 1958–1966.

Los, B., McCann, P., Springford, J., and Thissen, M. (2017). The Mismatch between Local Voting and the Local Economic Consequences of Brexit. *Regional Studies* **51**(5), 786–799.

Miller, R. (1966). Interregional Feedback Effects in Input–Output Models: Some Preliminary Results. *Papers in Regional Science* **17**(1), 105–125.

Miller, R.E., and Blair, P.D. (2009). *Input–Output Analysis: Foundations and Extensions*. Cambridge: Cambridge University Press.

Moses, L. (1955). The Stability of Interregional Trading Patterns and Input–Output Analysis. *American Economic Review* **45**, 803–826.

Moses, L. (1960). A General Equilibrium Model of Production, Interregional Trade, and Location of Industry. *Review of Economics and Statistics* **42**, 373–397.

OECD (2018). *Productivity and Jobs in a Globalised World: (How) Can All Regions Benefit?* Paris: OECD Publishing.

Organisation for Economic Co-operation and Development and World Trade Organization (OECD–WTO) (2012). Trade in Value-Added: Concepts, Methodologies and Challenges (Joint OECD–WTO Note).

Organisation for Economic Co-operation and Development and World Trade Organization (OECD–WTO) (2013). OECD–WTO Trade in Value Added (TiVA) database, FAQs: Background Note.

Thissen, M., Ivanova, O., Mandras, G., and Husby, T. (2019). European NUTS 2 Regions: Construction of Interregional Trade-Linked Supply and Use Tables with Consistent Transport Flows. JRC Working Papers on Territorial Modelling and Analysis No. 01/2019, JRC115439. Seville: European Commission.

United Nations Conference on Trade and Development (UNCTAD) (2013). Global Value Chains and Development: Investment and Value Added Trade in the Global Economy. Advance unedited version.

United Nations Conference on Trade and Development (UNCTAD) (2018). World Investment Report: Investment and New Industrial Policies. United Nation Publication.

Wang, Z., Wei, S.-J., and Kunfu, Z. (2013). Quantifying International Production Sharing at the Bilateral and Sector Levels. NBER Working Papers 19677, National Bureau of Economic Research.

Yazan, D.M., Mandras, G., and Garau, G. (2017). Environmental and Economic Sustainability of Integrated Production in Bio-Refineries: The Thistle Case in Sardinia. *Renewable Energy* **102**, 349–360.

PART II

Understanding the Territorial Dimension of Innovation

5. Mapping regional innovation patterns and their evolution

Roberta Capello and Camilla Lenzi

5.1 INTRODUCTION

The place-based approach to development policies has achieved full acceptance in the academic and policy debate and has driven profound changes in the conceptualization, foundations and goals of the European Union (EU) Cohesion Policy (CP) in the programming period 2014–2020 and in the upcoming one 2021–2027. Just a decade ago, however, this perspective was far from dominant. In fact, the place-based approach to regional development policy has been the outcome of a wider debate on the nature and the conceptual underpinnings of regional development interventions. This debate revolved, to a large extent, around the dichotomy between place-based versus place-neutral approaches to regional development and attracted the attention of both scholars in the EU (McCann and Ortega-Argilés, 2015) and nowadays also in the United States (Austin et al., 2019), and representatives from important international organizations such as the World Bank and the Organisation for Economic Co-operation and Development (OECD) (Barca, 2009; Barca et al., 2012; OECD, 2009a, 2009b; World Bank, 2009).

The conceptual appeal and strength of the place-based approach have been so powerful that this perspective has also been gaining momentum in recent times in the fields of competitiveness, industrial and innovation policies, and has been fully ascribed in the Smart Specialization Strategy (S3) framework, the dominant regional innovation policy common across all EU territories (Camagni and Capello, 2013; Camagni et al., 2014; McCann and Ortega-Argilés, 2015). Indeed, the theoretical pillars of S3 are fully consistent with the place-based approach adopted in the reformed 2014–2020 CP; in fact, the ideas of embeddedness, connectedness and diversification, at the basis of the spatial application of S3, are all meant to valorise primarily the existing (underexploited) local assets, which are, by definition, specific of each single place. Despite the difficulties and delays in the implementation of S3 in reality, especially in the initial phase of take-off, the attractiveness and logical stringency of S3 are such that its application is now also being experimented with outside the EU borders (Matusiak and Kleibrink, 2018).

S3 is essentially a fully decentralised policy approach aimed at exploiting untapped local potentials in the field of innovation. However, the emerging literature on the early assessment of S3 in EU regions highlights multiple and substantial risks associated with decentralised approaches such as S3 (see, for overviews, Capello and Kroll, 2016; Landabaso, 2014). These risks include, among others, the duplication or fragmentation of efforts, the misallocation of public spending to inappropriate local policies, and the misalignment of interventions aimed at industrial renewal with respect to existing local (underexploited) assets.

Awareness of the myopia of fully aspatial, centralised, approaches, as well as of the risks of fully decentralised ones, suggests that an alternative, intermediate perspective can be useful to mitigate the negative consequences stemming from the adoption of these two opposite views. This intermediate, meso-level perspective advocates the relevance of developing common innovation strategies for similar types (that is, groups) of (problematic) regions within which to frame and identify place-specific (that is, place-based) innovation actions, consistent with the multi-level policy approach of the reformed CP. For each group of regions, then, it is possible to define innovation pathways with the highest probability of success, and to prevent unlikely local strategies and undue use of public resources (Camagni and Capello, 2013).

By grouping regions on the basis of similarities in innovation processes, a taxonomy of innovative regions can operationally serve this purpose and, by complementing the place-based perspective, can help to mitigating its potential risks and weaknesses (Camagni et al., 2014). A similar approach is also helpful in sustaining and reinforcing the constitutive pillars of any regional S3. In fact, a taxonomy of innovative regions allows regions to identify the most promising territorial assets, tangible as well as intangible, to be leveraged upon in order to achieve innovation, industrial renewal and, more broadly, regional development. This step is fundamental to sustain and to reinforce the embeddedness pillar (and the successful implementation) of any regional S3. Moreover, a taxonomy of innovative regions allows regions to benchmark themselves, to identify similar regions to cooperate with and to learn from their experience; a fundamental step to sustain and to reinforce the connectedness pillar (and the successful implementation) of any regional S3.

All this having been said, the main problem is to develop the most effective tool with which to group regions according to their innovative capacities and needs. This chapter, then, critically analyses the available existing taxonomies and, on the basis of their limitations, proposes the regional innovation pattern taxonomy as the most recent scientific effort to develop a regional innovation taxonomy. The main aim of the taxonomy is that it has to be a useful policy tool to suggest innovation strategies specific to each group of innovative regions, aimed at the reinforcement and upgrading of the existing regional innovation mode.

The chapter is organised as follows. After presenting a critical review of existing regional innovation taxonomies (section 5.2), the chapter presents the conceptual underpinnings at the basis of the regional innovation pattern taxonomy, and its extension from an evolutionary perspective (section 5.3). The empirical mapping and verification of this taxonomy (also from a dynamic perspective) in the case of EU regions is presented next (section 5.4), leading to the suggestion of regional innovation policies specific for each type of innovation pattern; that is, smart innovation policies (section 5.5). Conclusions end the chapter (section 5.6).

5.2   A CRITICAL REVIEW OF EXISTING REGIONAL INNOVATION TAXONOMIES

The usefulness of ranking and benchmarking regions according to their innovation potential has been fully recognised in institutional and policy-making circles as well as in the scientific literature a long time ago, and several attempts have been developed to identify regional taxonomies so as to monitor the innovative performance of territories, on the basis of both qualitative and quantitative approaches.

Qualitative approaches are generally centred on highly detailed and deep knowledge of single case studies (Ajmone Marsan and Maguire, 2011). In this regard, the regional innovation system (RIS) approach figures prominently, not only in the scientific domain but also in the policy-making debate (Asheim and Gertler, 2005). Regional innovation systems have been classified according to multiple dimensions. A first typology has been obtained by distinguishing RISs according to the existence and localization of knowledge organizations, the type of knowledge interactions among local actors, and the source and stimuli of the interactions among them, thus identifying three main types of regional innovation systems: territorially embedded, regionally networked and regionalised national innovation systems (Asheim and Isaksen, 2002; Asheim and Gertler, 2005; Trippl et al., 2018).

Moreover, regional innovation systems have been distinguished according to their capacity to develop high-tech dynamic sectors, that is, institutional versus entrepreneurial (Cooke, 2004); as well as according to the types of problems and barriers faced to develop and to become a fully functioning regional innovation system, that is, fragmented (metropolitan), locked in (old industrial region) and thin (peripheral) ones (Todling and Trippl, 2005). More recently, the classification of RISs has been enriched with the knowledge bases typologies; that is, analytical, synthetic and symbolic knowledge (Asheim and Gertler, 2005; Asheim, 2007).

Notwithstanding the merits of each typology, an important weakness of any qualitative approach such as the regional innovation system one resides in is that single cases are not amenable to produce comparable quantitative benchmarks of regions according to their innovation and economic performance; an exercise that institutions in charge of regional innovation policies are increasingly concerned with (Ajmone Marsan and Maguire, 2011). Quantitative approaches may have received greater attention in the scientific and policy-oriented debate, because of the possibility they offer to consider and to compare a larger number of regions. In this respect, several efforts exist in the literature.

Verspagen (2010) developed a 'spatial hierarchy' of innovative regions in Europe (EU25) that are grouped according to both their innovative (that is, patenting) and economic performance and sectoral specialisation. Accordingly, four groups of regions are identified, namely South Europe, East Europe, West Europe and North Europe. Nevertheless, the mix among (local and external) knowledge inputs, territorially embedded elements that facilitate the creation of knowledge and innovation, and economic performance indicators prevented any great progress in departing from the pattern of a strong core (West and North Europe) and a periphery (South and East Europe).

In a similar vein, Navarro et al. (2009) identified seven groups of regions in the EU25 on the basis of 21 indicators, including knowledge-generating inputs (for example, R&D indicators), regional structural characteristics (for example, agglomeration economies, population educational level, sectoral employment), innovative outputs (for example, patents) and economic outputs (for example, GDP per capita). The seven groups were further aggregated into three blocs corresponding to different levels of technological and economic development: low, for regions classified as peripheral, agricultural and under industrial restructuring; medium, for central, service-oriented and industrially restructured regions; high for technologically advanced, specialized, service-oriented and capital regions. In this case, also, not much progress was achieved in superseding a core–periphery dichotomy.

Wintjes and Hollanders (2010) identified seven groups of regions on the basis of 20 indicators spanning several domains: employment indicators capturing regional sectoral structure and specialisation in high-tech and knowledge-intensive industries; human capital indicators capturing the level of education of the population and the workforce; technology and research activities intensity indicators; indicators of the characteristics of the labour market; and of the productivity and investments in the local economy. Despite the richness of the data and the statistical analysis, the arising spatial patterns confirmed the usual West–North to East–South divide, with some nuances depending on the regional sectoral specialisation.

The OECD also developed a regional innovation taxonomy, extending the analysis beyond the EU context to include the United States, Canada and Korea, based on the work by Ajmone Marsan and Maguire (2011). Three groups of regions have been identified: knowledge hub regions, industrial production zones, non-science and technology-driven regions, on the basis of the following indicators: gross domestic product (GDP) per capita, population density, unemployment rate, tertiary-educated labour force, regional employment sectoral structure (including employment in high-tech), research and development (R&D) and patent intensity. Ajmone Marsan and Maguire (2011) themselves acknowledged the strong similarities of the results obtained for EU countries with existing taxonomies (e.g., Wintjes and Hollanders, 2010; Navarro et al., 2009; the Regional Innovation Scoreboard 2006 and 2009).

The Regional Innovation Scoreboard (RIS) (2002, 2003, 2006, 2009, 2012, 2014, 2016, 2017, 2019), developed by the EU Commission Directorate-General for Internal Market, Industry, Entrepreneurship and SMEs (DG GROW), is perhaps the best-known taxonomy, which has enjoyed widespread success and has been repeated constantly over time, including an increasing number of countries and indicators. RIS is the regional application of the European Innovation Scoreboard and closely follows its methodology by partitioning the EU space into four groups of regions (innovation leaders, strong innovators, moderate innovators, modest innovators) based on 27 indicators spanning several dimensions (employment in high-tech and knowledge-intensive industries, education, publications, R&D, intellectual property rights, innovation and cooperation for innovation at the firm level). An important novelty introduced by the RIS, with respect to previous taxonomies, was the use of indicators of firm-level innovation at the regional level (derived from Community Innovation Surveys, CISs). Despite this important novelty, the categorisation of regions obtained is confined to the four groups used in the European Innovation Scoreboard at the national level, which prevents the highlighting of underlining spatial patterns in innovative behaviours (Hollanders et al., 2009).

Closely related to the RIS, there are additional initiatives from the EU

Commission, which have produced interesting regional innovation groupings. The first initiative is the Regional Competitiveness Index (RCI), launched in 2010 and published every three years (2010, 2013, 2016, 2018) by the Directorate General for Regional and Urban Policy (DG REGIO). One of the sub-pillars of this multidimensional index is the innovation sub-pillar, which is the output of the combination of three composite indicators at the regional and national levels accounting for technological readiness, business sophistication and innovation (Annoni and Dijkstra, 2017). Interestingly, the set of variables used to build the innovation sub-pillar includes indicators of the use of information and communication technologies (ICTs) across the population (measured at the regional level) and across firms (measured at the national level) to account for technological readiness; of the regional employment sectoral structure and the cooperative attitude of firms (both measured at the regional level) to account for business sophistication; and of research expenditures, publications, patents, human resources dedicated to science, high-tech and creative occupations, high-tech exports and new product sales (all measured at the regional level) to account for innovation. The RCI and RIS share important similarities in the dimensions and indicators considered. The advantage of the RCI, being freed from reproducing the four categories identified by RIS, is that it allows spatial patterns in regional innovation to be better described.

The second initiative is the European Service Innovation Scoreboard (ESIS) developed by DG GROW in two editions, 2014 and 2015 (Hollanders et al., 2014). ESIS represents a novel approach to monitor the transformation and upgrading of traditional economic sectors and industries into more productive, competitive and high-value-added businesses based on service innovation, intended as innovation taking place in service or manufacturing industries that add further value and contribute significantly to overall productivity and profitability. ESIS builds upon the RCI and RSI, enriched with new indicators such innovation expenditures in networking, connecting and brokerage services, utilities and infrastructure services; knowledge-intensive business services (KIBS); and the regional share of companies that introduced a service and/or product, process, marketing or organizational innovation. ESIS includes scorecards for more than 270 regions on a broad array of variables, grouped along five main dimensions (framework conditions, service innovation inputs, service innovation throughputs, service innovation outputs, and outcomes), with the final aim to compare each region with the EU and the respective national average, and not to cluster regions according to specific variables.

Existing taxonomies present undeniable merits and progress has been made over time to provide a more nuanced accounting of territorial trends in innovation. As an example, the use of innovation data at the regional level is indeed a novelty introduced by the score-boarding exercises promoted by DG GROW and DG REGIO, and interesting results have been achieved by empirically departing from the knowledge–innovation equivalence typical of the previous taxonomies using knowledge indicators such as R&D or patent intensity as proxies for innovation outputs. Most of previous taxonomies, in fact, grouped European regions only on the basis of their intensities of knowledge production, taking for granted that knowledge equates with innovation, and neglecting the more complex and heterogeneous ways in which knowledge may be created, acquired, utilised and transformed into innovation at the regional level, depending on heterogeneous territorial conditions behind local innovation modes.

Yet, even when elements other than pure knowledge intensity indicators have been considered, the methodology used to identify the groups of regions has been that of mixing together (local) knowledge inputs (for example, gross domestic R&D expenditure as a share of GDP, business R&D expenditure as a share of total R&D expenditure, patent applications per million inhabitants, scientific publications per million inhabitants), territorially embedded elements that facilitate the creation of knowledge and innovation (for example, tertiary education as a share of the labour force, population density), and economic performance indicators (for example, GDP per capita, unemployment rate, regional shares of employment by sector). The rather simplistic theoretical approach underlying these exercises is that of linking knowledge to innovation and economic growth through some enabling factors, following the idea that regional growth is the straightforward outcome of any knowledge creation activity and learning process taking place at the local level, with the support of innovation-prone local conditions supposed to be the same in each region regardless of their knowledge intensity and innovation development stage.

However, for a taxonomy to guide regionally focused innovation policy, consistent with smart specialisation strategy, it requires the identification of context-specificities in the knowledge-to-innovation process, in a way similar to how a place-based approach is postulated for a renewed EU regional development policy (Barca, 2009): that is, it must be a conceptually driven taxonomy consistent with a specific view of how knowledge and innovation take place and mix at the local level and which, accordingly, emphasises the context (pre-)conditions supporting local innovation processes and their different stages.

The existing taxonomies are unsatisfactory precisely in this regard because they are mostly data-driven rather than conceptually driven. By merging together indicators as diverse as innovation performance, knowledge inputs such as R&D, sectoral structure and specialisation, presence of spatial innovation enablers, existing taxonomies do not advance clear expectations on the conceptual relationships among the variables used. They mix innovation input and output indicators, as well as local conditions for knowledge and innovation to occur, without any conceptual expectations on the outcome of the mix, so that the groupings obtained tend to be mostly driven by statistical relationships among variables (patents are strongly correlated with R&D and human capital) rather than interpreted through conceptual expectations. Moreover, none of the above-mentioned taxonomies has deep and rich territorial roots. Regional groupings, in fact, are obtained mostly on the basis of economic structural indicators (for example, industrial specialization and labour market characteristics) and research propensity indicators, while little effort is made to link the resulting partition of the European space to specific contextual conditions enabling knowledge and innovation processes to take place at the local level. Instead, the context conditions are those upon which policy-makers should act in order to stimulate innovation and knowledge creation to occur; they have to be clearly identified and highlighted in each grouping, so that policy-makers know what the local 'capacity' to innovate and the mode to acquire new knowledge are in each group of regions, in order to properly act on them.

An additional limitation of existing taxonomies refers to their static nature. Most of them have been produced for single periods of time, and when they are available in multiple editions over the years (for example, RIS, RCI, ESIS), results are simply compared over time, signalling progress, stability or regression, but without clear explanations of (and expectations related to) why such changes took place.

The regional innovation patterns taxonomy proposed in this chapter (and fully presented in the next sections) introduces some conceptual novelties that help in taking a step forward in the elaboration of a sound and conceptually grounded taxonomy of innovative regions, and overcoming the limitations mentioned above. First, the regional innovation patterns framework applies a spatially diversified linear model of innovation that separates out the different stages of the innovation process and breaks the knowledge-to-innovation chain inspiring most of previous taxonomies. As convincingly argued in the literature (Capello and Lenzi, 2014), in fact, innovation can successfully emerge from externally sourced knowledge, and not only because of the availability at the local level of knowledge and research-intensive activities. Second, by building upon the vast literature on knowledge and innovation processes at the local level, it posits clear expectations about the importance of specific regional characteristics in the different phases of the innovation process, giving rise to a specific local innovation pattern. Third, it develops clear conceptual arguments as to explain changes in regional innovation patterns and the emergence of new (more complex) ones.

These conceptual premises have important implications from the empirical point of view, in that a taxonomy fully consistent with such a standpoint requires:

1. Separating empirically the knowledge and innovation stages, and grouping regions according to both dimensions. Therefore, focusing on knowledge-related variables alone is somewhat partial, and the availability of original innovation regional data is extremely helpful in this regard.
2. Linking (and reading) the partitioning of the European space in the light of specific regional characteristics.
3. Distinguishing the knowledge and innovation stages from their impact on a region's economic performance and, differently from previous taxonomies, keeping knowledge and innovation variables separate from economic performance indicators. This latter point is crucial for assessing the efficiency and effectiveness of each pattern of innovation for economic performance.
4. Identifying specific regional characteristics favouring changes in existing regional innovation patterns.

The next sections outline the conceptual underpinnings of the regional innovation patterns framework, also in a dynamic perspective (section 5.3), and their empirical measurement and mapping in European regions (section 5.4).

5.3 REGIONAL INNOVATION PATTERNS AND THEIR DYNAMICS: THE CONCEPTUALISATION

Regional innovation patterns are defined as 'alternative spatial combinations of context conditions and of specific modes of performing and linking the different phases of the innovation process' (Capello and Lenzi, 2013a). Behind this synthetic definition is the idea that the presence/absence of some context conditions within a region is at the basis of the creation of knowledge and innovation and/or its adoption from outside the region; the spatially heterogeneous mix of context conditions and of specific types of innovative activities gives rise to alternative regional innovation patterns. In short, regional patterns of innovation are obtained as different variants of the linear knowledge–invention–innovation model, once the different stages are broken down, separated, differently allocated in time and space, and finally recomposed following a relational logic of interregional cooperation and exchange (Camagni, 2015). Three main 'archetypal' innovation patterns have been conceptualized, namely:[1] a science-based pattern, a creative application pattern and an imitative innovation pattern.

The differences between regional innovation patterns depend not simply on the intensity as well as the mix of knowledge and innovation activities in the region, but are also manifested in terms of the functional characteristics and the relational structure supporting knowledge and innovation creation and acquisition (see Figures 5.1–5.3). Two main components play a founding role in the identification of regional innovation patterns. First, knowledge and innovation-creating functions (that is, the functional characteristics), in the form of institutions and organizations (for example, universities, research centres and local firms) internal to and available in a region. Second, the different learning and innovation processes, linked to alternative relational structures supporting knowledge and innovation creation and acquisition (that is, the relational structure). Different types of relationships are considered: informal relations (within the region) aimed to generate knowledge (for example, informal exchange of knowledge that gives rise to local collective learning processes) as well as long-distance relationships that take place between local actors and selected extra-regional partners, strongly intertwined with the functional elements.

In particular, in the science-based pattern, (scientific) knowledge is mostly created locally, typically by universities, R&D centres and large firms. Knowledge is exchanged not only within the region among local actors, but also on a bilateral basis across regions (for example, across research centres and technology-intensive firms based in other regions), meaning that local relationships are complemented and enriched by interregional cooperation with selected partners (Jensen et al., 2007). Depending on the nature of scientific knowledge being produced, the science-based pattern can give rise to a basic or an applied science-based pattern. Basic scientific knowledge is produced through research activities and tends to have wider technological applications and commercial value, to be more original, recombinatorial and radical, and to be oriented to general-purpose technologies (GPT) such as biotechnology, ICT and

---

[1] For a fuller discussion, see Capello and Lenzi (2013a).

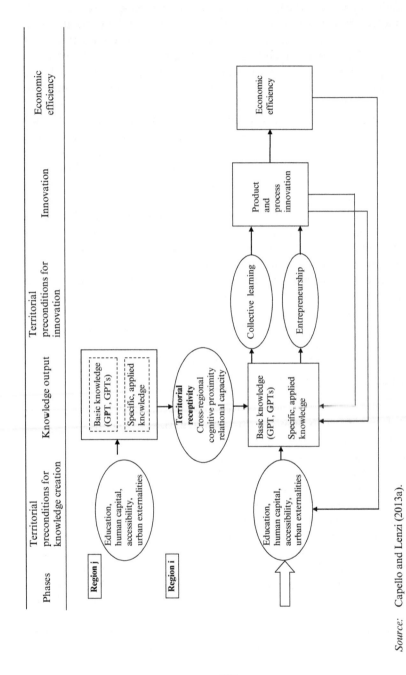

Source: Capello and Lenzi (2013a).

Figure 5.1 Science-based innovation pattern

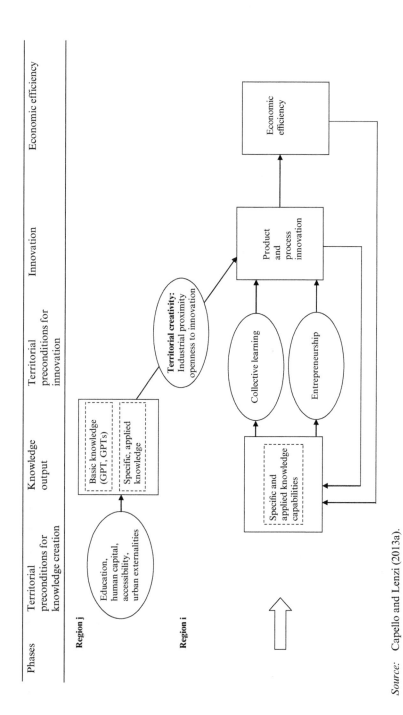

Source: Capello and Lenzi (2013a).

Figure 5.2 Creative application pattern

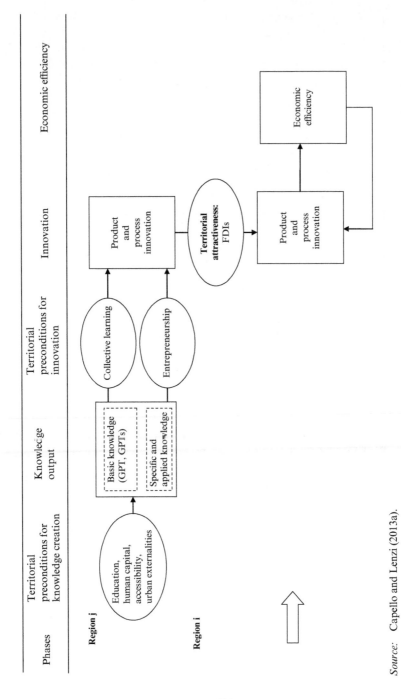

Source: Capello and Lenzi (2013a).

Figure 5.3 Imitative innovation pattern

nanotechnology. The opposite applies to the applied scientific knowledge (Capello and Lenzi, 2013a).

In the application-based pattern, external relations are essential to access locally weak or unavailable (formal or informal) knowledge to be used for local innovation needs (Foray, 2009; Licht, 2009). In fact, local firms source technology and knowledge from externally based economic actors; this process is particularly favoured by the presence of creative entrepreneurs and collective learning mechanisms within the region, which allow for local knowledge circulation. Knowledge exchanges are nourished more by cognitive and sectoral proximity (that is, shared cognitive maps) than by belonging to the same local community (Asheim and Isaksen, 2002). Depending on the nature of external knowledge being exchanged, the application-based pattern can give rise to a formal or an informal application-based pattern. Formal knowledge refers to codified technological, engineering-based knowledge; and informal knowledge refers to knowledge that is uncodified, tacit, embedded in professional capabilities, and based on professional practices and experience (Capello and Lenzi, 2013a).

In the imitation pattern, instead, local firms acquire external knowledge and innovation by imitating those developed by actors based in other regions; that is, external knowledge is acquired as embedded in innovations developed elsewhere, and then replicated and, possibly, adapted locally. This is typically the case of regions with weak local knowledge creation sources, in which relationships involve local firms and dominant firms – namely, multinationals – and are aimed at the adoption of innovations new for the area (Pavlínek, 2002; Varga and Schalk, 2004). Depending on the nature of the imitation process at place, the imitation pattern can give rise to an active or a passive imitation pattern. Active imitation indicates a certain degree of adaptation and creativity in the imitation process; passive imitation, instead, refers to pure replication of what already exists.

Interestingly, regional innovation patterns, despite representing structural characteristics, can change over time. In particular, the purposeful (and deviant) behaviour of local actors can push a region to move away from the existing and prevailing innovation pattern towards a new and more complex one. Three main pathways, highlighted in the literature (Martin and Sunley, 2006; Martin, 2010; Simmie, 2012), have been identified as the most promising in leading to a change of a regional innovation pattern (Capello and Lenzi, 2018):

- Creation: when new knowledge field, function and relationship opportunities become dominant with respect to existing ones.

- Diversification: when knowledge field, function and relationship opportunities new to what already exist are added to existing ones.
- Upgrading: when existing knowledge field, function and relationship opportunities are reoriented towards more advanced ones.

Due to the path-dependent nature of all the constitutive elements defining regional innovation patterns, changes have to be expected to be rare and incremental; yet, regions better equipped with local preconditions to implement creation, diversification and upgrading strategies are more likely to change their innovation pattern. Importantly, this conceptual approach (also in its dynamic extension) has been operationalised and has inspired the empirical analysis developed to identify the taxonomy of regional innovation patterns in the case of European regions, as discussed in the next section.

5.4   MAPPING REGIONAL INNOVATION PATTERNS AND THEIR EVOLUTION IN EUROPEAN REGIONS

As discussed in section 5.2, quantitative approaches are most often used in order to develop taxonomies of innovative regions. Quantitative approaches generally take two forms: scoreboard indices, and groupings developed by means of statistical cluster analyses. Score-boarding involves the collection and comparison of innovation-related indicators across regions in order to rank them. In this respect, as already noted in section 5.2, the best-known example in the EU context is the RIS. The ensuing overall ranking results in a grouping of regions into four categories: innovation leaders, strong innovators, moderate innovators and modest innovators. Regions are grouped according to three sub-categories: enablers, firm activities and outputs. Other ranking exercises based on composite indices exist, also outside the European context. For example, the Annual Report of Regional Innovation Capability of China includes an overall index based on five composite indices for knowledge creation, knowledge attainment, enterprise innovation capacity, innovation environment and economic impact (Ajmone Marsan and Maguire, 2011).

In order to group regions on the basis of innovation-related variables, the alternative approach to score-boarding is cluster analysis. Cluster analysis is a statistical method that uses a set of variables (for example, a selection of socio-economic, structural and innovation-related indicators) to obtain groups (that is, clusters) of regions that are most similar. The advantage of cluster analysis is that it enables the identification of meaningful commonalities among regions, on the basis of the variables considered, without neglecting their single specificities. The groupings obtained by means of cluster analysis facilitate benchmarking, also among regions with the greatest degree of commonality. Cluster analysis also presents an important advantage over score-boarding. Scoreboards, in fact, exhibit an important drawback, notably that the overall rankings tend to imply a single model or standard to which all regions must conform, reflected in high values on the composite variables on which scoreboards are based (Ajmone Marsan and Maguire, 2011). This approach clearly conflicts with the idea of regional innovation patterns in which innovation is conceived as a relative concept: regions have to be considered as innovative if local firms are able to do something new with respect to their past, and not with respect to a dominant paradigm present worldwide (Camagni, 2015).

Therefore, in order to identify empirically regional innovation patterns, a k-means cluster analysis was performed on three variables accounting for the degree of knowledge and innovation produced by a region. Considering variables accounting for both elements has a conceptual foundation; in fact, by emphasising the role of endogenous capabilities for knowledge and innovation creation, it is possible to derive a taxonomy of regions in terms of their knowledge and innovation potentials to then be read in the light of specific territorial elements. In the regional innovation patterns framework, in fact, knowledge and innovation can take place at different stages and places, and thus can mix in a variety of ways in regions.

Specifically, the cluster analysis was run on two innovation variables and one knowledge intensity variable. As to the innovation variables, the share of firms introducing product and/or process innovation and the share of firms introducing marketing and/or organisational innovations were chosen, since they encompass the largest category of innovators and can thus take different innovation typologies into account. Used for the intensity of knowledge production was the indicator of the region's knowledge base size (that is, the share of EU total patents) (see Capello and Lenzi, 2013a for additional details).

The identification of the appropriate number of clusters to be retained was based on conceptual and statistical criteria, such as the relationship between within-cluster and between-cluster variance, but also the number of regions in each group. By balancing the information advantages provided by expanding the number of clusters and the interpretability of the results in terms of innovation patterns, six clusters were finally retained, each including a reasonable portion of observations, so that they could be plausibly interpreted as patterns of innovation. Importantly, the six groups of regions differ statistically and significantly in terms of the main variables used for the clustering exercise, as well as of several other variables characterising each of them (see Capello and Lenzi, 2013a for additional details).

The taxonomy of innovative regions obtained confirms two important aspects. First, each conceptual pattern can show distinct processes of knowledge accumulation and knowledge acquisition channels for innovation discovery, depending on different cognitive bases, and each variant can be actually mapped in real data; the six groups of regions obtained, in fact, map into the conceptual patterns outlined in section 5.3. Second, regional innovation patterns can evolve over time. Regional innovation patterns have been identified empirically in European regions – that is, 262 EU Nomenclature of Territorial Units for Statistics (NUTS) 2 regions of 27 EU countries – for both the period 2002–2004 and the period 2004–2006 (Capello and Lenzi, 2013a, 2018; Figures 5.4 and 5.5). In particular:

- The science-based pattern is subdivided into:
  - a basic science pattern, conceptually referring to the first conceptual innovation pattern, which comprises regions with a strong knowledge and innovation creation capacity, specialised in GPTs, and very well connected to other regions in terms of scientific knowledge acquisition and exchange;
  - an applied science pattern, which is distinguished from the former in that regions in this group are different in terms of their cognitive bases, made of applied scientific knowledge.
- The creative application pattern is subdivided into:
  - a formal application pattern, which groups regions characterised by a lower knowledge intensity than in the previous two cases, although not negligible, and a high level of entrepreneurial creativity, which enables the translation of applied and formal knowledge (sourced outside the region) into local innovation;
  - an informal application pattern, which differs from the former in terms of the prevailing knowledge base; regions in this group have a low degree of local formal knowledge in the form of patents and R&D but they have a high degree of local capabilities (that is, non-scientific and tacit knowledge embedded in professionals), and a high degree of entrepreneurial creativity which enables the acquisition of informal knowledge, embedded in professional capabilities, external to the region and its translation into local innovation.
- The imitative innovation pattern is subdivided into:
  - the active imitation pattern, which includes regions with a relatively weak knowledge and innovation intensity but relatively

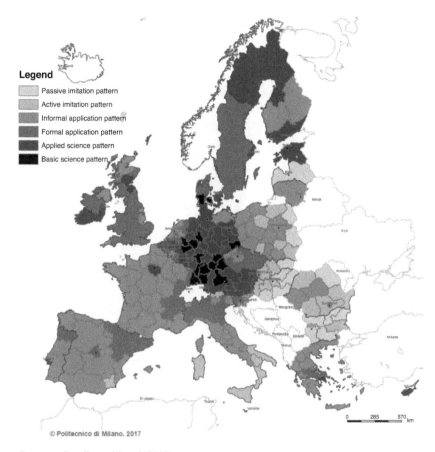

Legend

Passive imitation pattern
Active imitation pattern
Informal application pattern
Formal application pattern
Applied science pattern
Basic science pattern

© Politecnico di Milano. 2017

Source: Capello and Lenzi (2018).

Figure 5.4   Regional innovation patterns (2002–2004)

higher entrepreneurship, collective learning and innovation potentials, representing favourable conditions to initiate an imitation process characterised by some degree of creativity and adaptation of already existing innovations developed elsewhere;

– the passive imitation pattern, which comprises the regions with the lowest knowledge and innovation intensity and, unfortunately, also the lowest endowment of those preconditions (for example, creative entrepreneurship, collective learning) that may open the regions to virtuous imitation and innovation catching-up processes.

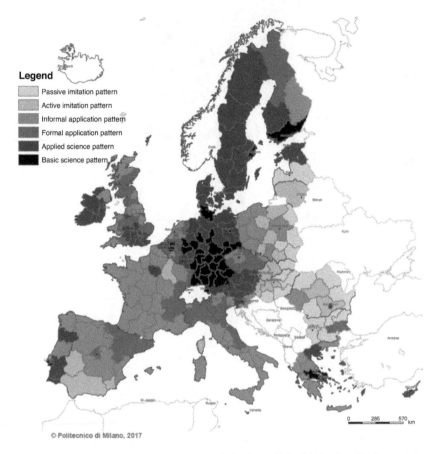

Source: Capello and Lenzi (2018).

Figure 5.5   Regional innovation patterns (2004–2006)

The comparison of Figures 5.4 and 5.5, representing the innovative patterns in two different periods of time, suggests, as expected, a remarkable
persistence in regional innovation patterns, with some islands of change.
Most of the regions maintained their innovation pattern, with only 23
per cent of regions able to change towards a more complex pattern of
innovation in the examined period. Persistence is predominant especially
in regions in the least complex patterns, highlighting the difficulties in
escaping and unlocking backwardness conditions. When changes take
place, they are generally incremental rather than radical, and mostly
occur in close proximity to the prevailing pattern, that is, changes are
gradual and not abrupt. Finally, the most complex patterns experience

the highest degree of turbulence; both science-based patterns expanded, and especially the basic science pattern (which almost doubles in terms of number of regions).

Importantly, it has been proved that the ranking in terms of formal knowledge and innovation performance characterising regional innovation patterns does not necessarily translate into a ranking in terms of economic performance or efficiency, meaning that each innovation pattern can produce economic efficiency gains (Capello and Lenzi, 2013b). Yet, a change towards a more complex innovation pattern is beneficial to sustain growth (Capello and Lenzi, 2019).

The main research and policy questions, then, become how to reinforce the existing innovation patterns, how to promote changes in order to achieve a more advanced pattern, and under what conditions such progress is reasonably conceivable and feasible. Regional innovation policies, specific to each pattern, can play an important role in this respect, and the next section presents the idea of smart innovation policies, recently proposed by Camagni and Capello (2013), as those regional innovation policies aimed at both helping regions to sustain and to valorise the existing innovation pattern and its efficiency for growth, but also to improve it and to move towards a more complex pattern.

5.5 REGIONAL INNOVATION PATTERNS AND SMART SPECIALISATION: SMART INNOVATION POLICIES

Smart innovation policies have been conceived and elaborated in an effort to offer a spatially sound inclusion of S3 into an appropriate regional innovation policy framework, in the general spirit of the place-based approach of the EU CP 2014–2020 and the general goal of turning the priorities of the Europe 2020 Flagship Initiative – Innovation Union into real practical actions (Camagni et al., 2014). Smart innovation policies are aimed at increasing the innovation capability of an area by maximising the effectiveness of accumulated knowledge and by fostering territorial applications and diversification, on the basis of local specificities and the characteristics of the prevailing innovation pattern in each region.

In a relatively recent work (Camagni and Capello, 2013), a way has been suggested to adapt the two policy concepts of S3 – embeddedness and connectedness – to the specificities of each single regional pattern of innovation with the aim to valorise the virtuous aspects and to maximise the efficiency of each pattern. Each pattern, in fact, calls for a setting of different policy goals, in terms of both embeddedness and connectedness.

In terms of policy goals aimed at reinforcing local knowledge creation capabilities (that is, embeddedness), maximising the returns from R&D investments can be the right option for regions with a sufficient critical mass of R&D investments already present in the area, that is, regions in the basic and applied science patterns. These regions, in fact, can exploit the indivisibilities associated with research activity and take advantage of additional R&D funding coming from joint and integrated efforts of regional, national and EU bodies, especially by taking into consideration their different research specialisations; that is, GPT and basic science in one case, and applied science in the other.

Differently, support to basic research does not represent the most appropriate policy goal for the application patterns, regardless of their respective knowledge specialisation. The relatively weaker technological and scientific knowledge endowment prevents the achievement of a critical mass of R&D investments and the possibilities to exploit economies of scale in knowledge production; in these cases, the returns to R&D from these kinds of policies are deemed to be modest. More promising and rewarding are, instead, innovation policies aimed at sustaining new applications and interregional cooperation in applications, by boosting regional capabilities to rapidly respond to external stimuli (such as the emergence of a new technology) and to realise creative search processes concerning product and market diversification. With the goal of maximising the returns from the co-invention of applications, the right policy tools can be aimed at supporting creative application, the capacity to quickly shift from old to new uses, the increase of productivity in existing uses either by incentivising technological projects that foresee new and creative uses of existing scientific knowledge (formal application pattern) or by incentivising entrepreneurial creativity and search in products and markets diversification (informal application pattern).

Maximising the returns from imitation, finally, is an appropriate policy goal for regions in the active and passive imitation patterns, and can be achieved by favouring fast diffusion of existing innovations, by strengthening local openness to change and to innovation (for example, by reducing economic, social or institutional barriers and frictions to change) and by supporting favourable negotiations between local firms and local branches of multinationals. Policy interventions should target not simply embeddedness but also connectedness, that is, knowledge acquisition from outside the region, with varying specificities according to the different patterns of innovation.

In the science-based patterns, attraction and mobility of scientists and inventors and joint research cooperation projects can work as appropriate policy tools. The EU has already developed experience in this respect through the setup of the European Research Area (ERA) put forward by the European Commission, an area composed of all research and development activities, programmes and policies in Europe which involve a transnational perspective. Again, attention has to be paid to the specificities and specialisation of each region's knowledge base.

Incentives for the acquisition of external knowledge to be exploited into new creative applications can represent an important tool in the case of the application patterns. Examples include cooperative technological activities in those regions where an applied technological base exists, though modest, especially in the case of regions in the formal application pattern; for regions in the informal application pattern, instead, participation of local actors in specialised international fairs, attraction of star researchers even for short periods of time, or support for work experience in best-practice knowledge-creation firms, can represent valuable innovation policy tools.

Lastly, in the case of the imitation patterns, more traditional incentives can still represent efficient tools to attract new knowledge in areas with a very limited – formal or informal, scientific or technical – knowledge base, including incentives to attract multinationals. These traditional instruments, however, could be pursued with a renewed attention to the local context; for example, with enhanced attention to cooperation in specialised subcontracting with multinationals.

Moreover, patterns differ in terms of the main beneficiaries of these policy recommendations: universities, research centres and R&D-intensive firms in the science-based patterns; local firms, especially entrepreneurs, and small firms in the others. Importantly, the regional innovation pattern taxonomy provides a precise rationale and operationality to the above-mentioned policy goals, and differentiated priorities can be assigned to the different groups of regions depending on their positioning in the knowledge-to-innovation process.

This general (and novel) policy approach can be subject to doubts and criticisms; in fact, regions may risk deepening their traditional specialisations and become exposed to lock-in effects and to becoming less flexible (and resilient) in a fast-changing economic environment. Yet, the application of the smart specialisation and innovation strategy to the regional innovation pattern setting requires an evolutionary attitude. This evolutionary attitude will translate into actions aimed at targeting, suggesting and supporting local learning processes towards the detection of new needs, new creative applications and diversification of established technologies, new forms of blending knowledge advancements and local specialisation, and the discovery, and possibly the orientation, of future technological trends. Moreover, the valorisation of this evolutionary attitude can lead to jumps from one pattern to another and more complex one.

Even if such jumps may occur in a limited number of cases (as highlighted in section 5.4), and given the responsibility in the management of public money, policy-makers would do best to stick to promoting such changes in the least risky and the most likely successful cases, while strengthening the upgrading and diversification processes within each single innovation pattern. Therefore, while in general smart innovation policies are aimed at increasing the efficiency and effectiveness of innovation processes within each single pattern, 'evolutionary innovation policies' can be conceived and implemented for the most advanced regions within each pattern, which are best positioned to move towards a more complex one because of a greater endowment of those regional context conditions characterising the targeted destination pattern (Capello and Lenzi, 2018).

Because of the gradual and path-dependent nature of changes in innovation patterns, the most advanced regions in the imitation patterns could jump to the application ones through the creation of new local competences and an entrepreneurial spirit, adding local value to external knowledge. Similarly, regions could shift from the informal to the formal application pattern by reinforcing local applied science and development research. Efficient regions in the formal application pattern could try to limit the existing low returns of R&D activities, limited to some tiny specialisation sectors, through diversification into technological fields in which to invest and innovate, thus approaching the characteristics of the applied science pattern. Moreover, the most advanced regions in the applied science pattern could strengthen their science base in GPT fields so as to move towards the basic science pattern; differently, regions in the basic science pattern could be stimulated to avoid the possible risks of decreasing returns of R&D activities in terms of knowledge creation by diversifying research into new application fields in new industries, merging aspects of the applied science pattern.

As discussed in Camagni et al. (2014), 'evolutionary' strategies and policies of this kind are not easy, nor are they immediate in nature. Instead, they should be the outcome of careful assessment and monitoring, in order to avoid misallocation of public resources in backing impossible local dreams. Any possible engagement in such policies, therefore, requires several conditions to be met to guarantee the existence of fertile ground upon which evolutionary policies can deliver virtuous effects. The first step for the implementation of these policies is the identification of the most advanced regions within each pattern, intended as those with the greatest endowment of the context conditions specific to the targeted destination pattern, and in particular of a sufficient critical mass in existing specific innovation activities (R&D, technological knowledge, production know-how, managerial competences). Moreover, regions able to change their innovation pattern should rely on the presence of reliable (new) local actors capable of managing new crucial innovative functions and, finally, the presentation of credible and well-assessed research and innovation projects. Only under these conditions can evolutionary policies find fertile ground upon which to produce virtuous effects.

Even if it is not possible to exclude innovation being the outcome of unforeseeable events, of totally unexpected creative 'jumps' and the breaking-up of existing technological and innovation trajectories, the bulk of innovation processes do have a systemic, complex and incremental nature, based on necessary slow, smooth and localised learning processes. Therefore, as argued in Camagni et al. (2014), it is rational to claim that regional innovation policies, depending on public funds, should mainly adhere to the existing innovation trajectories and patterns, based on specific and well-defined context conditions and capabilities, presenting reasonable risks and the highest expected returns for the entire regional economy.

5.6   CONCLUSIONS

This chapter has proposed the development and application of regional innovation taxonomies as a useful policy tool to complement decentralised regional innovation policy approaches (that is, S3) and to mitigate the multiple risks arising from their implementation, as highlighted in the early assessment of the first stage of the implementation of S3 (Landabaso, 2014; Capello and Kroll, 2016).

After discussing a critical review of existing regional innovation taxonomies available in the scientific literature and in the policy field, the chapter introduced the conceptual underpinnings of the regional innovation pattern taxonomy, and its extension from an evolutionary perspective, which is one of the most recent efforts in the existing literature to develop a regional innovation taxonomy overcoming several of the limitations characterising previous ones (Capello and Lenzi, 2013a, 2018). The regional innovation pattern taxonomy represents a sound territorially and conceptually based taxonomy of innovative regions, and a useful tool to identify common strategies and approaches for similar (problematic) regions and operationality to differentiated policy goals and priorities depending on the positioning of the different groups of regions in the knowledge-to-innovation process. Applied to the case of EU regions, in two periods of time (2002–2004 and 2004–2006), this taxonomy not only helps regions to identify the existing territorial (underexploited) assets on which to relaunch innovation, competitiveness and renewal, but it also helps to identify those regions that are the best candidates to progress up the innovation ladder, and which territorial assets are more likely to deliver change and through which strategy.

Smart innovation policy strategies have been suggested as a way to offer a spatially sound inclusion of the S3 into an appropriate regional innovation policy framework, and to adapt the two policy concepts of S3 – embeddedness and connectedness – to the specificities of each single regional pattern of innovation with the aim to valorise the virtuous aspects of each pattern and to maximise its efficiency; that is, by setting different policy goals (in terms of both embeddedness and connectedness) for each pattern. Evolutionary innovation policies, specific to each pattern, have been identified as those policies targeting the most advanced regions in each pattern and those most likely to move to a more complex pattern.

For both smart innovation policies and their evolutionary variant, warnings have been raised to prevent their inappropriate application. First, innovation policies, in both their static and dynamic version, have to target the specificities of each pattern in terms of goals and recipients, if they are expected to deliver the desired outcomes. This is the most promising approach to reinforce the efficiency and effectiveness of each innovation pattern. Second, caution has to be applied in devising and implementing evolutionary innovation policies. While attractive, these policies should avoid backing impossible local dreams and generating misallocation and mismanagement of public funds. Because of the very nature of innovation processes and innovation patterns, changes in innovation patterns are rare, incremental and path-dependent, and require a multidimensional approach. Pursuing a change of the current innovation pattern is therefore not always, and not universally across space, the superior option; sometimes, if local conditions are not completely favourable, the reinforcement of the existing innovation pattern can represent a more promising option and development strategies should be adapted accordingly.

REFERENCES

Ajmone Marsan, G. and Maguire, K. (2011), 'Categorisation of OECD regions using innovation-related variables', OECD Regional Development Working Papers, 2011/03, Paris: OECD Publishing.

Annoni, P. and Dijkstra, L. (2017), 'Measuring and monitoring regional competitiveness in the European Union', in Huggins, R. (ed.), *Handbook of Regions and Competitiveness: Contemporary Theories and Perspectives on Economic*

Development, Cheltenham, UK and Northampton, MA, USA: Edward Elgar Publishing, pp. 49–79.

Asheim, B.T. (2007), 'Differentiated knowledge bases and varieties of regional innovation systems', *Innovation: The European Journal of Social Science Research* **20**: 223–241.

Asheim, B.T. and Gertler, M. (2005), 'The geography of innovation', in Fagerberg, J., Mowery, D. and Nelson, R. (eds), *The Oxford Handbook of Innovation*, Oxford: Oxford University Press, pp. 291–317.

Asheim, B.T. and Isaksen, A. (2002), 'Regional innovation systems: the integration of local "sticky" and global "ubiquitous" knowledge', *Journal of Technology Transfer* **27**(1): 77–86.

Austin, B., Glaeser, E. and Summers, L.H. (2019), 'Saving the heartland: place-based policies in 21st century America', *Brookings Papers on Economic Activity*. https://www.brookings.edu/wp-content/uploads/2018/03/3_austinetal.pdf (accessed 22 July 2019).

Barca, F. (2009), 'An agenda for a reformed cohesion policy: a place-based approach to meeting European Union challenges and expectations', Independent Report prepared at the request of the European Commissioner for Regional Policy, Danuta Hübner, European Commission, Brussels.

Barca, F., McCann, P. and Rodríguez-Pose, A. (2012), 'The case for regional development intervention: place-based versus place-neutral approaches', *Journal of Regional Science* **52**(1): 134–152.

Camagni, R. (2015), 'Towards creativity-oriented innovation policies based on a hermeneutic approach to the knowledge-space nexus', in Cusinato, A. and Philippopoulos-Mihalopoulos, A. (eds), *Knowledge-Creating Milieus in Europe: Firms, Cities, Territories*, Berlin: Springer Verlag, pp. 341–358.

Camagni, R. and Capello, R. (2013), 'Regional innovation patterns and the EU regional policy reform: towards smart innovation policies', *Growth and Change* **44**(2): 355–389.

Camagni, R., Capello, R. and Lenzi, C. (2014), 'A territorial taxonomy of innovative regions and the European regional policy reform: smart innovation policies', *Scienze Regionali – Italian Journal of Regional Science* **13**(1): 69–106.

Capello, R. and Kroll, H. (2016), 'From theory to practice in smart specialization strategy: emerging limits and possible future trajectories', *European Planning Studies* **24**(9): 1393–1406.

Capello, R. and Lenzi, C. (2013a), 'Territorial patterns of innovation in Europe: a taxonomy of innovative regions', *Annals of Regional Science* **51**(1): 119–154.

Capello, R. and Lenzi, C. (2013b), 'Territorial patterns of innovation and economic growth in European regions', *Growth and Change* **44**(2): 195–227.

Capello, R. and Lenzi, C. (2014), 'Spatial heterogeneity in the knowledge, innovation and economic growth nexus: conceptual reflections and empirical evidence', *Journal of Regional Science* **54**(2): 186–214.

Capello, R. and Lenzi, C. (2018), 'Regional innovation patterns from an evolutionary perspective: an investigation of European regions', *Regional Studies* **52**(2): 159–171.

Capello, R. and Lenzi, C. (2019), 'Regional innovation evolution and economic performance', *Regional Studies* **53**(9): 1240–1251.

Cooke, P. (2004), 'Integrating global knowledge flows for generative growth in Scotland: life sciences as a knowledge economy exemplar', in OECD (ed.), *Global Knowledge Flows and Economic Development*, Paris: OECD, pp. 73–96.

Foray, D. (2009), 'Understanding smart specialisation', in Pontikakis, D., Kyriakou, D. and van Bavel, R. (eds), *The Question of R&D Specialisation*, Brussels: JRC, European Commission, Directorate General for Research, pp. 19–28.

Hollanders, H., Tarantola, S. and Loschky, A. (2009), 'Regional innovation scoreboard (RIS) 2009', Pro Inno Europe Paper no. 14, *Entreprise and Industry Magazine*, Brussels. http://www.proinno-europe.eu/page/regional-innovation-scoreboard.

Hollanders, H., Es-Sadki, N., MacAulay, B., Muller, E. and Zenker, A. (2014), 'European Service Innovation Scoreboard (ESIS) – key findings', ESIC European Service Innovation Centre Report. https://www.google.com/url?sa=t&rct=j&q=&esrc=s&source=web&cd=1&cad=rja&uact=8&ved=2ahUKEwiS-bLTkcvjAhXFyKQKHYpVDdcQFjAAegQIBBAC&url=http%3A%2F%2Fec.europa.eu%2FDocsRoom%2Fdocuments%2F12233%2Fattachments%2F1%2Ftranslations%2Fen%2Frenditions%2Fnative&usg=AOvVaw3KNORJXx1KJGfzZeCq4Fgz (accessed 23 July 2019).

Jensen, M.B., Johnson, B., Lorenz, E. and Lundvall, B.A. (2007), 'Forms of knowledge and modes of innovation', *Research Policy* 36(5): 680–693.

Landabaso, M. (2014), 'Guest editorial on research and innovaton strategies for smart specialization in Europe: theory and proactice of new innovation policy approaches', *European Journal of Innovation Management* 17(4): 378–389.

Licht, G. (2009), 'How to better diffuse technologies in Europe', Knowledge Economy Policy Brief 7.

Martin, R. (2010), 'Roepke Lecture I Economic Geography. Rethinking regional path dependence: beyond lock-in to evolution', *Economic Geography* 86(1): 1–27.

Martin, R. and Sunley, P. (2006), 'Path dependence and regional economic evolution', *Journal of Economic Geography* 6: 395–437.

Matusiak, M. and Kleibrink, A. (eds) (2018), *Supporting an Innovation Agenda for the Western Balkans: Tools and Methodologies*, Luxembourg: Publications Office of the European Union.

McCann, P. and Ortega-Argilés, R. (2015), 'Smart specialization, regional growth and applications to the European Union cohesion policy', *Regional Studies* 49(8): 1291–1302.

Navarro, M., Gibaja, J.J., Aguado, R. and Bilbao-Osorio, B. (2009), 'Pattern of innovation in the EU-25 regions: a typology and policy recommendations', *Environment and Planning C* 27(5): 815–840.

OECD (2009a), *How Regions Grow: Trends and Analysis*, Paris: Organisation for Economic Co-operation and Development.

OECD (2009b), *Regions Matter: Economic Recovery, Innovation and Sustainable Growth*, Paris: Organisation for Economic Co-operation and Development.

Pavlínek, P. (2002), 'Transformation of Central and East European passenger car industry: selective peripheral integration through foreign direct investment', *Environment and Planning A* 34: 1685–1709.

Simmie, J. (2012), 'Path dependence and new technological path-creation in the Danish wind power industry', *European Planning Studies* 20(5): 7553–7772.

Todling, F. and Trippl, M. (2005), 'One size fits all? Towards a differentiated regional innovation policy approach', *Research Policy* 34: 1203–1219.

Trippl, M., Grillitsch, M. and Isaksen, A. (2018), 'Exogenous sources of regional industrial change: attraction and absorption of non-local knowledge for new path development', *Progress in Human Geography* 42(5): 687–705.

Varga, A. and Schalk, H. (2004), 'Knowledge spillovers, agglomeration and macroeconomic growth: an empirical approach', *Regional Studies* **38**(8): 977–989.

Verspagen, B. (2010), 'The spatial hierarchy of technological change and economic development in Europe', *Annals of Regional Science* **45**(1): 109–132.

Wintjes, R. and Hollanders, H. (2010), 'The regional impact of technological change in 2020', Report to the European Commission, Directorate General for Regional Policy, on behalf of the network for European Techno-Economic Policy Support (ETEPS AISBL). http://ec.europa.eu/regional_policy/sources/docgener/studies/pdf/2010_technological_change.pdf.

World Bank (2009), *World Development Report 2009: Reshaping Economic Geography*, World Bank. https://openknowledge.worldbank.org/handle/10986/5991 License: CC BY 3.0 IGO.

6. Mapping innovation potential for place-based innovation policies

Hugo Hollanders and Monika Matusiak

6.1 INTRODUCTION

The notion of place-based innovation policies implies the existence of public actors (usually governments and administration) who want to design and implement such policies in order to improve the innovativeness and competitiveness of their countries or regions. This chapter focuses on innovation policy-making from the public investor's point of view, and provides more information at the policy design stage on which sectors or domains can bring the highest potential return on public investment in innovation (impact).

Significant efforts have been made to define priority domains for smart specialisation, a policy approach implemented throughout the European Union (EU) as a place-based innovation policy (Foray, 2015). Smart specialisation priority domains are understood as intersectoral groups of economic activities that can increase innovativeness and value added thanks to the input of knowledge into a region or country.

There are many approaches on how to identify the smart specialisation priority domains. Following the concept outlined in the previous paragraph, a first step towards identifying smart specialisation priority domains can be an economic analysis to identify economic specialisations using detailed industry-level data on employment, value added, wages and exports (see Chapter 2 in this book, on mapping economic specialisation). A second step involves the identification of the innovation potential of these preliminary priority domains by implementing an innovation potential mapping exercise. Mapping the innovation potential of regions should move from a generic and horizontal view of innovativeness, embodied in questions such as, 'What is the share of innovative companies in the national/regional economy?', to a more granular picture.

The innovation potential cannot be treated separately from the existing economic fabric. As a result, the main research questions for an innovation potential mapping exercise are: Which sectors present the highest innovative potential and engage in innovative activities? Does the type of innovative activity differ between sectors? Are the sectors with big critical mass (in terms of employment and value added) innovative? Do different sectors also have different innovation needs and paths? This chapter focuses on the first two of these questions. There is a rich literature on sectorial innovation differences (Pavitt, 1984; Marsili and Verspagen, 2001; Kirner et al., 2009, among others), but it is rarely connected with the complex view of innovation potential of territories. In the context of the smart specialisation concept, the main challenge here is the need to identify priority domains that are not necessarily sectorial, but combine a few sectors (sub-sectors), specialised knowledge inputs and have an inter-sectorial character. The standard datasets, publicly available at subnational – especially EU Nomenclature of Territorial Units for Statistics (NUTS) 2 level – are too generic for that purpose. In the EU, the mostly easily accessed disaggregated publicly available data, especially for data on innovation, are at Statistical Classification of Economic Activities in the European Community (NACE) two-digit level, which allows for distinguishing between manufacturing and agriculture, but does not permit understanding of which specific industries develop in the region, and what their interconnections and possible value chains are. This implies the need to access disaggregated datasets for the quantitative analysis and, at later stages, to move beyond quantitative analysis only in order to identify a set of potentially transformative innovative activities that can modernise the regional industries.

This chapter develops a methodology on how to use the information from business innovation surveys to identify the degree of innovativeness of industries and their level of innovation capacity. The approach taken uses the benefits of the smart specialisation strategy design process, where ownership by the public sector and a strong focus on available evidence is required. The participation of public actors, including statistical offices, allows access to disaggregated datasets – preferably at NUTS 2 level and NACE three or four-digit level. For the purpose of this research exercise, it was possible to access the detailed datasets for 25 Ukrainian regions showing different levels of innovation activities for four-digit NACE sub-sectors. The proposed methodology was then applied to this dataset. The conclusions for smart specialisation and connections with economic potential will be discussed.

This chapter then focuses on the implementation stage and distinguishes between innovative and potentially innovative companies as potential beneficiaries of public intervention. As the rationale for public intervention is market failure (Chaminade and Edquist, 2010), the main beneficiaries should be potentially innovative companies which need additional incentives to start investing in innovation, and not the already innovative companies which would continue to innovate even without public support. Some efforts to identify potentially innovative companies have been made in France (Marmuse and Godest, 2008), based on a set of financial indicators accessible from advanced databases. A new effort can be made using the updated 2018 Community Innovation Survey (CIS),[1] which includes a set of questions concerning business processes and knowledge flows in companies.

6.2   USING INNOVATION SURVEY DATA TO IDENTIFY INDUSTRIES WITH INNOVATIVE CAPACITIES

For mapping the innovation capacities of industries one can use data on research and development (R&D) activities, data on patent activities, or data on innovation activities. Patent statistics can only indirectly be linked to industries, as patents are classified according to technology fields (International Patent Classification, IPC) and these are not uniquely linked to industries based on industrial codes (NACE; the United Nations International Standard Industrial Classification of all Economic Activities, ISIC). R&D data identify only those innovation activities which are more directly linked to science-based technologies. Innovation in most industries and less-developed countries will not be based on R&D (Huang et al., 2010 show that half of European enterprises innovate without performing R&D), and a mapping analysis only based on R&D data would exclude too many industries. Innovation surveys, by directly surveying enterprises about their innovation activities, currently provide the best data to be used for mapping the innovation potential of industries. The broad view of innovation seems to be particularly important in transition economies, such as Ukraine, but also lagging regions and countries in the EU where a lot of non-technological innovations are introduced while the traditional industries, often with a high critical mass in terms of

---

[1]   The CIS is a survey of innovation activity in enterprises. The survey is designed to provide information on the innovativeness of sectors by type of enterprise, on the different types of innovation and on various aspects of the development of an innovation, such as the objectives, the sources of information, the public funding, the innovation expenditures, and so on. The CIS provides statistics broken down by countries, type of innovators, economic activities and size classes. Surveys are carried out with two-year frequency by EU member states and other European countries.

employment or value added, modernise and transform (or fail to) towards higher value added and more innovative activities. The case of transition economies highlights the need to apply the broader view of innovation (not only R&D and technology-oriented) that is recommended by the smart specialisation approach.

Innovation surveys are used in many countries in the world, but here we focus on the European CIS innovation survey, as this survey uses a harmonised questionnaire with a set of identical core questions used in most European countries. The CIS was first developed in the early 1990s and it has evolved into the largest and most well-known innovation survey in the world (see Arundel and Smith, 2013 for a historical overview). The CIS is conducted every two years and results are released both individually by national statistical offices and in a harmonised tabulated format by Eurostat, the statistical office of the European Union. The questionnaire itself is revised with every new round of the CIS, including the testing of new questions with enterprises (so-called cognitive testing). A major revision of the questionnaire took place for the 2018 CIS. Here we will discuss and use the questionnaires of both the 2016 CIS, as 2016 data are the most recent available data, and the 2018 CIS.

The CIS 2016 is used by most European countries, but there are differences in the national survey questionnaires as the CIS has two types of questions: obligatory and voluntary questions. Obligatory questions have to be included in the national questionnaires by all countries implementing the CIS; voluntary questions are only recommended to be included. In developing a methodology for mapping the innovation potential of countries and regions, the focus will be on using obligatory questions. The innovativeness of industries can be assessed by any of the indicators in Box 6.1, or a combination of these (with all questions being obligatory in the CIS 2016):

- Combining questions 2.1, 3.1, 8.1 and 9.1 will give the share of enterprises that introduced at least one type of innovation (product innovation, process innovation, organisational innovation or marketing innovation).
- Question 5.1 will give the share of enterprises with at least one innovation activity (in-house R&D; external R&D; acquisition of machinery, equipment, software and buildings; acquisition of existing knowledge from other enterprises or organisations; training for innovative activities; market introduction of innovations; design; or other).
- Combining questions 2.2, 3.2 and 7.2 will give the share of enterprises that have in-house capabilities to innovate (developed by the

enterprise itself; developed by the enterprise together with other enterprises or organisations; or the enterprise cooperated on any of its innovation activities with other enterprises or organisations).

BOX 6.1 POTENTIAL CIS 2016 QUESTIONS FOR MAPPING THE INNOVATION POTENTIAL OF COUNTRIES AND REGIONS

Question 2.1: During the three years 2014 to 2016, did your enterprise introduce ('product innovation'):

- Goods innovations: new or significantly improved goods.
- Service innovations: new or significantly improved services.

Question 2.2: Who developed these product innovations?

- Your enterprise itself.
- Your enterprise together with other enterprises or organisations.
- Your enterprise by adapting or modifying goods or services originally developed by other enterprises or organisations.
- Other enterprises or organisations.

Question 3.1: During the three years 2014 to 2016, did your enterprise introduce any ('process innovation'):

- New or significantly improved methods of manufacturing for producing goods or services.
- New or significantly improved logistics, delivery or distribution methods for your inputs, goods or services.
- New or significantly improved supporting activities for your processes, such as maintenance systems or operations for purchasing, accounting, or computing.

Question 3.2: Who developed these process innovations?

- Your enterprise itself.
- Your enterprise together with other enterprises or organisations.
- Your enterprise by adapting or modifying goods or services originally developed by other enterprises or organisations.
- Other enterprises or organisations.

Question 5.1: During the three years 2014 to 2016, did your enterprise engage in the following innovation activities:

- In-house research and development (R&D), i.e., R&D activities undertaken by your enterprise.

- External R&D, i.e., R&D contracted out to other enterprises or to public and private research organisations.
- Acquisition of machinery, equipment, software and buildings, to be used for new or significantly improved products or processes.
- Acquisition of existing knowledge from other enterprises or organisations, e.g., existing know-how, copyrighted works, patented and non-patented inventions for the development of new or significantly improved products or processes.
- In-house or contracted out training for your personnel for innovative activities.
- In-house or contracted out activities for the market introduction of new or significantly improved products.
- Design activities, in-house or contracted out, to alter the share, appearance of usability of goods of services.
- Other in-house or contracted our activities to implement new or significantly improved products or processes.

Question 7.2: During the three years 2014 to 2016, did your enterprise cooperate on any of your innovation activities with other enterprises or organisations?

Question 8.1: During the three years 2014 to 2016, did your enterprise introduce ('organisational innovation'):

- New business practices for organising procedures.
- New methods of organising work responsibilities and decision-making.
- New methods of organising external relations with other enterprises or public organisations.

Question 9.1: During the three years 2014 to 2016, did your enterprise introduce ('marketing innovation'):

- Significant changes to the aesthetic design or packaging of a good or service.
- New media or techniques for product promotion.
- New methods for product placement or sales channels.
- New methods of pricing goods or services.

6.3   CHALLENGES USING INNOVATION SURVEY DATA

The challenge for using CIS data is to be able to break down the samples used to produce data at the national level to representative data at the level of the region. The priority for most countries is to produce reliable national-level statistics, and the sample used for collecting responses to the questionnaire from enterprises is both large enough and balanced enough to correctly represent the different relative size of industries in the national economy. For most countries it is not possible to produce the same reliable and representative statistics at the level of the region as the sample size is too small, creating a trade-off between the desired statistics at the regional level and the statistics which can be made available at a sufficiently reliable level. Another complication is that for multi-establishment enterprises the innovation activities for different establishments will only be reported by the head office of the enterprise for the whole country. For producing representative regional data this creates a problem, since for regions with no head offices of multi-establishment enterprises their innovation activities will be underestimated, whereas for regions with many head offices their innovation activities will be overestimated. One possible solution is the one that has been used for many years in the European Commission's Regional Innovation Scoreboard (RIS)[2] by focusing on the activities of small and medium-sized enterprises (SMEs) only.

An additional issue with CIS data is that these data are not available for all industries. The CIS makes a distinction between 'core' and 'non-core' industries (see Box 6.2 for the list of core industries). Core industries need to be included in the national questionnaires by all countries implementing the CIS; non-core industries may be included on a voluntary basis. Many countries do not include non-core industries in their national questionnaire and thus do not collect any innovation survey data for these industries. This is an issue since not only are many service industries excluded, but also the agricultural sector (NACE A), which in many countries and regions is a very important sector employing a significant share of the population. Solely relying on CIS data to map the innovation potential

---

[2]   The Regional Innovation Scoreboard (RIS) assesses the innovation performance of European regions on a limited number of indicators. The report is published by the European countries every two years. The latest 2019 edition covers 238 regions across 23 EU countries, Norway, Serbia and Switzerland. In addition, Cyprus, Estonia, Latvia, Luxembourg and Malta are included at country level. The RIS report uses regional data for 17 indicators, of which six indicators use CIS data. Regional CIS data are not directly available from Eurostat and most national statistical offices, and a special data request was made to obtain regional NUTS 2 level data from 25 European countries for the following indicators: the share of SMEs with product or process innovations; the share of SMEs with marketing or organisational innovations; the share of SMEs innovating in-house (that is, which developed their innovations themselves, or together with other enterprises or organisations); the share of innovative SMEs collaborating with others; the share of non-R&D innovation expenditure by SMEs in total turnover; and the sales share of new-to-market and new-to-firm innovations by SMEs in total turnover. The report and the database with NUTS 2 level data is available at https://ec.europa.eu/growth/industry/innovation/facts-figures/regional_en.

could lead to the exclusion of important industries for certain countries and regions.

BOX 6.2   CORE INDUSTRIES IN THE CIS

Core industries include the following NACE Rev. 2 sections and divisions:

- B: Mining and quarrying.
- C: Manufacturing.
- D: Electricity, gas, steam and air conditioning supply.
- E: Water supply, sewerage, waste management and remediation activities.
- 46: Wholesale trade, except of motor vehicles and motorcycles.
- H: Transportation and storage.
- J: Information and communication.
- K: Financial and insurance activities.
- 71: Architectural and engineering activities; technical testing and analysis.
- 72: Scientific research and development.
- 73: Advertising and market research.

6.4   AN EXAMPLE USING UKRAINIAN INNOVATION SURVEY DATA

For a mapping exercise by the European Commission's Joint Research Centre (JRC) for Ukraine, detailed innovation survey data for all 25 Ukrainian regions[3] (Oblasts) were made available by the State Statistics Service of Ukraine. The data covered NACE industries B–E (mining and quarrying, B; manufacturing, C; electricity, gas, steam and air conditioning supply, D; and water supply, sewerage, waste management and remediation activities, E) at the four-digit industry level for two periods, 2012–2014 and 2014–2016, and included data for CIS questions 2.1, 3.1, 8.1 and 9.1:

- Share of enterprises that introduced product innovations.
- Share of enterprises that introduced process innovations.
- Share of enterprises that introduced organisational innovations.
- Share of enterprises that introduced marketing innovations.

---

[3]   Ukraine is administratively divided into 27 regions but there is no access to the data for two of them – the Autonomous Republic of Crimea and the city of Sevastopol – due to their annexation by Russia.

The JRC mapping of the innovation potential for 25 Ukrainian regions excluded agriculture (NACE A), construction (NACE F) and services (NACE G–S), as innovation survey data were not available. For mapping the innovation potential, the share of enterprises that introduced at least one type of innovation would be useful to use in the analysis, but these data were not available for the 25 Ukrainian regions. These shortcomings were partly overcome by the mapping of economic potential and a scientometric exercise (specialisation in patents and publications), and a qualitative process gathering feedback from experts and stakeholders. This part of the analysis is not presented in this chapter, as it focuses at the identification of innovation potential from a place-based perspective, but it was a part of the mapping exercise for Ukrainian regions. The innovation potential was calculated using two different but related criteria measuring the degree of specialisation.

First is specialisation relative to the region, which measures whether in relative terms an industry is more innovative than the regional economy (here: total industry NACE B–E). Specialisation is measured separately for product, process, organisational and marketing innovation, using location quotients (LQs):

$$LQ\text{-}1_i = (\%in\_x_i) / (\%in\_x)$$

Second is specialisation relative to the aggregate industry in the country, which measures whether in relative terms an industry is more innovative than the aggregate industry in the national economy (that is, total industry NACE B–E). Specialisation is measured separately for product, process, organisational and marketing innovation, using location quotients (LQs):

$$LQ\text{-}2_i = (\%in\_x_i) / (\%IN\_x_i)$$

where
$\%in\_x_i$ = share of type-x innovators in industry i;
$\%in\_x$ = share of type-x innovators in the regional economy;
$\%IN\_x_i$ = share of type-x innovators in the aggregate industry in the country;
x   = product or process or organisational or marketing innovation.

Industries have an innovation potential if the degree of specialisation is above predefined threshold values:

- An industry will have an innovation potential in 2014 if for at least two of the four types of innovations the LQ is above 1.25 both relative to the region (LQ-1$_i$) and relative to the aggregate industry in the country (LQ-2$_i$).

- An industry will have an innovation potential in 2016 if for at least two of the four types of innovations the LQ is above 1.25 both relative to the region (LQ-1$_i$) and relative to the aggregate industry in the country (LQ-2$_i$).

An industry is selected to have an innovation potential if it either passes all four criteria (the 'strict' rule; that is, relative to region and relative to aggregate industry in both 2014 and 2016) or at least three of the four criteria (the 'relaxed' rule). The proposed analysis focuses on one aspect of innovation potential of territories – innovation activities of enterprises – as it is a part of a wider approach (supplemented by the analyses of economic and scientific potential; see Chapters 2 and 8 in this book). It is also designed to have a practical application as an input to evidence-informed policy debate: that is, why it is preferable to limit the number of indicators analysed to make the information easier to absorb by stakeholders and policy-makers. That is also why a further qualitative process is proposed in the smart specialisation process[4] after the identification of the first results in order to refine and deepen the conclusions.

Looking at the results achieved, the number of selected industries differs significantly both across the regions for each individual criterion and across the different selection criteria (Table 6.1). For example, for the specialisation relative to the region in 2014, only three industries could be selected in Luhansk and as many as 42 in Dnipropetrovsk; and for the specialisation relative to the aggregate industry in 2014, also only three industries could be selected in Luhansk and as many as 38 in Kharkiv. Using the strict rule that an industry needs to pass all four criteria, at most 15 industries are selected in Lviv, representing almost 12 per cent of employment in that region, whereas no industry could be selected in Luhansk. For most regions using the strict rule of passing all criteria, this results in only a small number of selected industries. To be able to select more industries, the more relaxed rule of passing at least three of the four criteria is more appropriate. Using the relaxed rule increases the average number of selected industries by about 50 per cent and the average share of these industries in total regional employment by about 60 per cent. For some regions the number of selected industries is still small, and

---

[4] See Smart Specialisation Framework for WEU Enlargement and Neighbourhood Countries, https://s3platform.jrc.ec.europa.eu/.

Table 6.1 Number of identified industries in Ukrainian regions with innovation potential

	#1 Relative to region in 2014	#2 Relative to national industry in 2014	#3 Relative to region in 2016	#4 Relative to national industry in 2016	Innovation potential: all 4 criteria	Share in regional employment (%)	Innovation potential: at least 3 criteria	Share in regional employment (%)
Cherkasy	18	10	21	11	3	1.7	6	3.2
Chernihiv	14	14	20	14	6	2.7	10	5.9
Chernivtsi	10	10	15	10	7	8.5	8	10.6
City of Kyiv	34	24	45	44	14	2.2	23	3.7
Dnipropetrovsk	36	25	34	34	11	5.4	19	20.8
Donetsk	10	11	15	8	1	0.1	5	5.9
Ivano-Frankivsk	24	27	29	26	12	8.4	16	14.0
Kharkiv	35	37	37	37	14	11.0	22	17.5
Kherson	16	16	14	21	9	7.9	10	9.4
Khmelnytskiy	15	10	17	12	4	6.1	7	8.7
Kirovohrad	18	17	18	20	8	9.4	11	14.9
Kyiv	33	29	33	30	14	7.2	20	14.0
Luhansk	2	2	9	9	0	0.0	0	0.0
Lviv	32	35	28	26	14	10.3	19	11.8
Mykolayiv	17	19	16	17	9	16.7	9	16.7
Odesa	28	26	25	22	10	3.1	16	5.3
Poltava	15	11	23	20	7	6.0	11	9.6

Rivne	18	26	20	20	4	6.0	14	16.6
Sumy	14	14	15	15	9	10.8	10	11.2
Ternopil	11	11	17	19	10	11.3	11	15.4
Vinnytsya	23	26	19	17	6	4.7	13	13.6
Volyn	11	12	13	10	4	4.4	7	8.6
Zakarpattya	10	8	13	9	6	6.2	7	6.8
Zaporizhzhya	30	24	29	26	10	22.0	19	26.7
Zhytomyr	24	20	31	27	10	6.7	18	18.1

Note: The Autonomous Republic of Crimea and the city of Sevastopol were not covered in the mapping analysis.

Source: Based on detailed innovation survey data from the State Statistics Service of Ukraine.

the selection process could be further customised for these regions. The selected industries represent on average 7.3 per cent of regional employment using the strict rule, and 11.6 per cent using the relaxed rule, with highest employment shares for Zaporizhzhya. It is important to remember that the smart specialisation approach recommends the identification of a limited number of priorities that can render the highest possible impact from public investment into research and innovation. It also suggests focusing on niches where a territory (country or region) can achieve competitive advantage.

Across all 25 Ukrainian regions the more traditional industries have an innovation potential (Table 6.2) including, among others, the manufacture of furniture (14 regions), the manufacture of beverages (12 regions), and the manufacture of dairy products and of other food products (each 10 regions). This result suggests that in many Ukrainian regions the industry composition is geared towards producing more traditional products, but there is an ongoing modernisation effort.

The combination of CIS questions 2.1, 3.1, 8.1 and 9.1 helps to identify industries which are already involved in innovation activities by having introduced at least one type of innovation (product, process, organisational or marketing). For the mapping analysis, data from CIS question 5.1 could also be used, allowing a further differentiation between innovation activities based on R&D (either own R&D or contracted-out R&D) and other innovation activities not based on R&D, which are particularly dominant in many service industries and in less-developed countries. However, for Ukraine, the response rate to CIS question 5.1 is lower than those for CIS questions 2.1, 3.1, 8.1 and 9.1, and a further breakdown of the aggregate data into NACE three- or four-digit data at the regional level will lead to too many industries where the number of sampled enterprises is too small, resulting in a non-disclosure of these data for reasons of confidentiality by statistical offices. For the Ukrainian regions for too many industries data were therefore not available, and these data could not be used.

Another use of the CIS innovation survey is to use questions 2.2, 3.2 and 7.2 to identify enterprises with own innovation capabilities: that is, those enterprises which developed their product or process innovation either themselves or together with other enterprises or organisations (the first two answer categories in questions 2.2 and 3.2) or which collaborated with other enterprises or organisations on any of their innovation activities (question 7.2). More details on the use of these questions are given in the next section, discussing the use of the revised questionnaire of the CIS 2018.

Table 6.2   Ranking of industries with an innovation potential in Ukrainian regions

NACE	industry	Passed all 4 criteria	Passed at least 3 criteria
31	Manufacture of furniture	7	14
11	Manufacture of beverages	4	12
10.5	Manufacture of dairy products	6	10
10.8	Manufacture of other food products	6	10
10.7	Manufacture of bakery and farinaceous products	4	9
28.2	Manufacture of other general-purpose machinery	3	9
28.3	Manufacture of agricultural and forestry machinery	2	9
13.9	Manufacture of other textiles	8	8
20.1	Manufacture of basic chemicals, fertilisers and nitrogen compounds, plastics and synthetic rubber in primary forms	6	8
26.5	Manufacture of instruments and appliances for measuring, testing and navigation; watches and clocks	4	8
17.2	Manufacture of articles of paper and paperboard	5	7
20.4	Manufacture of soap and detergents, cleaning and polishing preparations, perfumes and toilet preparations	5	6
20.5	Manufacture of other chemical products	5	6
10.4	Manufacture of vegetable and animal oils and fats	4	6
28.9	Manufacture of other special-purpose machinery	4	6
10.3	Processing and preserving of fruit and vegetables	3	6
25.9	Manufacture of other fabricated metal products	3	6
10.2	Processing and preserving of fish, crustaceans and molluscs	5	5
16.1	Sawmilling and planing of wood	4	5
27.1	Manufacture of electric motors, generators, transformers and electricity distribution and control apparatus	4	5
29.3	Manufacture of parts and accessories for motor vehicles	4	5

Table 6.2   (continued)

NACE	industry	Passed all 4 criteria	Passed at least 3 criteria
25.2	Manufacture of tanks, reservoirs and containers of metal	3	5
10.1	Processing and preserving of meat and production of meat products	4	4
32.4	Manufacture of games and toys	4	4
32.5	Manufacture of medical and dental instruments and supplies	4	4
35.3	Steam and air conditioning supply	4	4
23.9	Manufacture of abrasive products and non-metallic mineral products n.e.c.	3	4
24.3	Manufacture of other products of first processing of steel	3	4
28.1	Manufacture of general-purpose machinery	3	4
23.6	Manufacture of articles of concrete, cement and plaster	2	4
36	Water collection, treatment and supply	2	4
26.3	Manufacture of communication equipment	1	4
20.3	Manufacture of paints, varnishes and similar coatings, printing ink and mastics	3	3
32	Other manufacturing	3	3
15.2	Manufacture of footwear	2	3
21.2	Manufacture of pharmaceutical preparations	2	3
23.1	Manufacture of glass and glass products	2	3
24.5	Casting of metals	2	3
27.3	Manufacture of wiring and wiring devices	2	3
30.2	Manufacture of railway locomotives and rolling stock	2	3
10.6	Manufacture of grain mill products, starches and starch products	1	3

Notes: The Autonomous Republic of Crimea and the city of Sevastopol were not covered in the mapping analysis. Only those industries are shown which have an innovation potential in at least three regions for at least three specialisation criteria.

Source: Based on detailed innovation survey data from the State Statistics Service of Ukraine.

6.5   REVISED CIS QUESTIONNAIRE

Available CIS data to be used in innovation mapping exercises are, at the time of writing of this chapter in December 2019, available for the CIS 2016 and earlier rounds of the CIS. The CIS has been a stable source for producing statistical data on innovation for European countries for nearly three decades. CIS data are widely used in both European and national policy reports on innovation, and in academic literature and research papers on innovation. There was, however, an increasing need to revise the CIS: among other reasons, to reflect the latest recommendations in the 2018 edition of the Oslo Manual, the international reference guide for collecting and using data on innovation (OECD/Eurostat, 2018).

The revised CIS 2018 questionnaire provides better information on the management, the strategies, the hampering factors, and the willingness of enterprises to change in a competitive environment. The revised questionnaire is now relevant to all enterprises, as most questions are being asked of both innovative and non-innovative enterprises. Using data from the CIS 2018 will help to better identify the innovation capabilities of enterprises and to differentiate between different types of enterprises with no innovation.

The most important changes in the old and new CIS questionnaire are shown in Figure 6.1. Up until the CIS 2016, the questionnaire differentiated between four types of innovators: product, process, organisational and marketing innovators. Enterprises were first asked whether they had introduced a product or process innovation (CIS 2016 questions 2.1 and 3.1) and, if so, who had developed these innovations (CIS 2016 questions 2.2 and 3.2), about their innovation activities (CIS 2016 question 5.1), and whether they had collaborated with others (CIS 2016 question 7.2). Enterprises with only organisational or marketing innovations (CIS 2016 questions 8.1 and 9.1) would not be asked any of these questions. The old questionnaire was biased towards enterprises with product and process innovations. Following the recommendations in the 2018 Oslo Manual, the CIS 2018 differentiates between only two types of innovators: product and business process innovators (CIS 2018 questions 3.1 and 3.6), with the latter incorporating the former process, organisational and marketing innovators. All enterprises with product or business process innovations will be asked who developed these innovations (CIS 2018 questions 3.4 and 3.7), about their innovation activities (CIS 2018 question 3.9), and whether they had collaborated with others (CIS 2018 question 3.15). The relevant CIS 2018 questions are shown in Box 6.3.

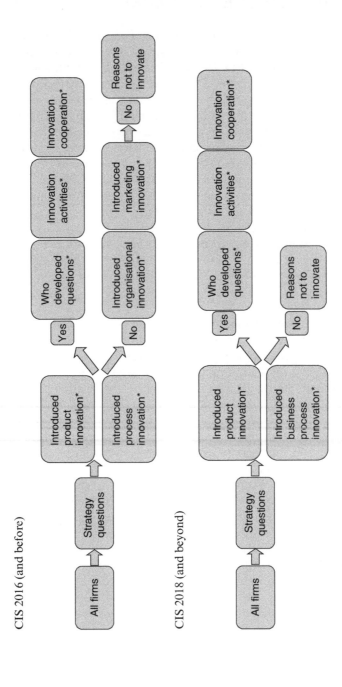

CIS 2016 (and before)

CIS 2018 (and beyond)

Note: * Obligatory CIS questions.

Figure 6.1 *A graphical presentation of the old and new structure of the CIS questionnaire*

BOX 6.3   POTENTIAL CIS 2018 QUESTIONS FOR MAPPING
THE INNOVATION POTENTIAL OF COUNTRIES
AND REGIONS

Question 2.1**: During the three years 2016 to 2018, how important were the following strategies to the economic performance of your enterprise (high, medium, low importance; or not important):

- Focus on improving your existing goods or services.
- Focus on introducing new goods or services.
- Focus on low price (price leadership).
- Focus on high quality (quality leadership).
- Focus on a broad range of goods or services.
- Focus on one or a small number of key goods or services.
- Focus on satisfying established customer groups.
- Focus on reaching out to new customer groups.
- Focus on standardised goods or services.
- Focus on customer-specific solutions.

Question 3.1*: During the three years 2016 to 2018, did your enterprise introduce any ('product innovation'):

- New or improved goods.
- New or improved services.

Question 3.2: Who developed these product innovations? (Same as CIS 2016 question 2.2.)

Question 3.6*: During the three years 2016 to 2018, did your enterprise introduce any of the following types of new or improved processes that differ significantly from your previous processes ('business process innovation'):

- Methods for producing goods or providing services (including methods for developing goods or services).
- Logistics, delivery or distribution methods.
- Methods for information processing or communication.
- Methods for accounting or other administrative operations.
- Business practices for organising procedures or external relations.
- Methods of organising work responsibility, decision-making or human resource management.
- Marketing methods for promotion, packaging, pricing, product placement or after sales services.

Question 3.7*: Who developed these process innovations? (Same as CIS 2016 question 3.2, but also including organisational and marketing innovation.)

Question 3.15*: During the three years 2016 to 2018, did your enterprise co-operate with other enterprises or organisations?

- On R&D.
- On other innovation activities (excluding R&D).
- On any other business activities.

Question 3.18***: During the three years 2016 to 2018, how important were the following factors in hampering your enterprises' decision to start innovation activities, or its execution of innovation activities (high, medium, low importance; or not important):

- Lack of internal finance for innovation.
- Lack of credit or private equity.
- Difficulties in obtaining public grants or subsidies.
- Costs too high.
- Lack of skilled employees within your enterprise.
- Lack of collaboration partners.
- Lack of access to external knowledge.
- Uncertain market demand for your ideas.
- Too much competition in your market.
- Different priorities within your enterprise.

Notes: * Obligatory question to be included in national questionnaire. ** Question highly recommended to be included in national questionnaire. *** Question recommended to be included in national questionnaire.

6.6   MAPPING INNOVATION POTENTIAL USING QUESTIONS FROM THE REVISED CIS

Future mapping exercises should use the data from the CIS 2018. This section explains the methodology that could be used to identify the degree of innovativeness of industries and their level of innovation capacities. The methodology also distinguishes between innovative and potentially innovative companies.

With only two types of innovations, the methodology explained above can be simplified, making it easier to implement as data availability will improve as data become available for more industries. Industries have a high degree of innovativeness if they show above-average shares of enterprises that have introduced an innovation by combining two degrees of specialisation.

First is specialisation relative to the region, which measures whether in relative terms an industry is more innovative than the regional economy.

Specialisation is measured separately for product and business process innovators, using location quotients (LQs):

$$LQ\text{-}1_i = (\%in\_x_i) / (\%in\_x)$$

Second is specialisation relative to the aggregate industry in the country, which measures whether in relative terms an industry is more innovative than the aggregate industry in the national economy. Specialisation is measured separately for product and business process innovators, using location quotients (LQs):

$$LQ\text{-}2_i = (\%in\_x_i) / (\%IN\_x_i)$$

where
$\%in\_x_i$ = share of type-x innovators in industry I;
$\%in\_x$ = share of type-x innovators in the regional economy;
$\%IN\_x_i$ = share of type-x innovators in the aggregate industry in the country;
x   = product or business process innovation.

Industries have a high degree of innovativeness if both degrees of specialisation are above predefined threshold values, for example 1.25 for both. The required data should be extracted from CIS 2018 questions 3.1 and 3.6.

If data are available for questions 3.5 and 3.7, the methodology can be refined by including only those enterprises which claim to have in-house capabilities to innovate. In their work on innovation modes, Arundel and Hollanders (2005) used the questions on who developed the innovation, and the question on innovation collaboration, to differentiate between four types of innovative enterprises. Innovative enterprises have in-house innovation capabilities if they developed the innovation either themselves or in cooperation with other enterprises. For 'strategic innovators', innovation is a core component of their competitive strategy and all of these enterprises have developed their product or process innovation fully or partly in-house. They perform R&D on a continuous basis to develop novel product or process innovations. The 'intermittent innovators' develop their product or process innovation fully or partly in-house, but innovation is not a core activity. 'Technology modifiers' modify existing products and processes initially developed by other enterprises or organisations. 'Technology adopters' innovate by adopting innovations developed by other enterprises or organisations.

The same rationale can be used to adapt the equations for the degrees of specialisation by including only those enterprises which answered 'yes' to either 'your enterprise itself' or 'your enterprise together with other enterprises or organisations' in CIS 2018 questions 3.2 and 3.7; or, if both questions were not answered by the respondent enterprise, which said that they cooperated with other enterprises or organisations on R&D or other innovation activities in CIS 2018 question 3.15.

Important for improving the innovativeness of industries is to identify potentially innovative enterprises, for which CIS 2018 questions 2.1 on business strategies and 3.18 on hampering factors can be used. Knowing how many enterprises have considered to innovate but decided not to do so should result in the design of appropriate policy support measures to make it easier for these enterprises to innovate in the near future. A distinction should be made between using CIS 2018 questions 2.1 and 3.18. Both are non-obligatory questions and are included by statistical offices in their national questionnaires on a voluntary basis. But whereas question 2.1 on business strategies is highly recommended by Eurostat to be included, question 3.18 on hampering factors is only recommended. One may therefore expect that for more countries data will become available for the question on business strategies.

For all enterprises not considered to be innovative – that is, all enterprises which did not introduce a product or business process innovation – potential innovators can be defined as those enterprises which attached a high degree of importance to any of the following business strategies: focus on improving existing goods or services; focus on introducing new goods or services; focus on reaching out to new customer groups; or focus on customer-specific solutions. CIS 2018 data can be used to calculate for each industry the share of potential innovators. Similarly to using the data for enterprises having introduced a product or business process innovation, two degrees of specialisation can be calculated, and an industry would have a high potential to innovate if both degrees of specialisation pass a predefined threshold. If data for CIS 2018 question 2.1 are not available, data for question 3.18 could be used to identify potentially innovative enterprises as those enterprises which attached a high degree of importance not to innovate for any of the following reasons: lack of skilled employees within the enterprise, lack of collaboration partners or lack of access to external knowledge. The other hampering factors are less relevant, for different reasons. Uncertain demand or too much competition results from perceived market situations, and policy should not interfere in competitive markets unless there are clear signs of market imperfections. High costs or difficulties in accessing different forms of finance are most likely biased by the status of the respondent enterprise, perceiving an innovation project as too risky and therefore too costly.

If costs are perceived as too high then the expected rate of return of the innovation is too low to warrant an investment, and policy should refrain from making funding available for investment projects with insufficiently high rates of return. Lack of skilled employees within the enterprise, lack of collaboration partners, or lack of access to external knowledge are factors that are real and where policy could make a difference to improve the supply of skilled employees, to raise awareness of the existence of collaboration partners by improving communications, and to make public knowledge more easily available.

6.7   DISCUSSION AND CONCLUSION

The identification of innovative potential of territories at sub-national level, with the purpose of using the results for policy-making, is a challenging exercise. On one hand, with the abundance of traditional and new sources of data, there is a risk of producing complex and often inaccessible analyses with unclear conclusions that will not be used by policy-makers. On the other hand, oversimplification can be equally harmful. The methodology for analysing the innovation potential at regional level presented in this chapter is one of the possible approaches, which should be used together with mapping the economic and scientific potential, economic complexity and other analyses. The results of all these should be also verified in a qualitative process in order to produce reliable conclusions for place-based innovation policies. Therefore, the approach described in this chapter should be seen as part of a bigger analytical toolbox.

The advantage of using Community Innovation Survey (CIS) data in European Union and other European countries is the general availability of necessary data (with the restraints of the size of the sample explained earlier in the chapter) and a widely accepted methodology that allows comparing and benchmarking territories. With the disaggregation at the regional and sub-industrial level it should allow precise identification of the sectors that should be the object of further analyses. The final objective of these analyses is the identification of domains and activities where the public investment into innovation can bring the highest potential impact, and contribute to the industrial transformation and spillover effects.

For this purpose, the analysis of location quotients has been modified to show the propensity of economic sub-sectors to innovate compared to the regional and national economy. This can be a starting point for further studies that will help in understanding the factors and reasons relating to the innovation activities and the types of public support needed. The comparison of specialisation indicators for innovative potential with economic data (classic specialisation analysis) and analysis of knowledge production in the region can contribute to a better understanding of the regional strengths and potential niches for investment.

The recent changes in the CIS 2018 are particularly beneficial from the perspective of public policy-makers, as they allow the identification of groups of potentially innovative companies. Having in mind the discourse on public policy interventions, which indicates the danger of pushing out private capital that would be otherwise invested in innovative activities, it is important to understand which companies will not innovate without some public support. The method shown in this chapter can be the first step in this direction, performed at aggregated level, which means showing a potential target group of beneficiaries and not individual companies.

There are further areas of research and methodological development including, for example, in relation to the delays in obtaining statistical data, which always shows a historical picture. The simplest way to overcome this obstacle is the addition of a qualitative analysis. However, statistical forecasting techniques can be used to give a more recent picture. Another interesting area of future research is the issue of the existing classifications, including those for economic activities (NACE). As with any model of the reality, they often do not adequately show the existing and, in particular, the emerging industries. Statistical mapping and analysis of new or transforming sectors is a promising area of future research.

Last but not least is the problem of bridging science and policy in an effort to develop evidence-informed policies. Here, the issue of communication and visualisation of results to policy-makers and other stakeholders taking part in the policy dialogue is an important factor that can determine whether the results of the analyses are used in practice. And while the practical aspects are not always the main goal of science, the increasing complexity of economic transformation, along with social and environmental challenges, calls for using scientific inputs. If scientific inputs are to be widely applied, they need to be accessible and understandable to a wider public, which leaves a lot of room for new developments.

REFERENCES

Arundel, A. and H. Hollanders (2005), 'EXIS: An Exploratory Approach to Innovation Scoreboards', Brussels: European Commission.

Arundel, A. and K. Smith (2013), 'History of the Community Innovation Survey', in F. Gault (ed.), *Handbook of Innovation Indicators and Measurement*, Cheltenham, UK and Northampton, MA, USA: Edward Elgar Publishing, pp. 60–87.

Chaminade, C. and C. Edquist (2010), 'Rationales for public policy intervention in the innovation process: Systems of innovation approach', in R. Smits, S. Kuhlman and P. Shapira (eds), *The Theory and Practice of Innovation Policy: An International Research Handbook*, Cheltenham, UK and Northampton, MA, USA: Edward Elgar Publishing, pp. 83–97.

Foray, D. (2015), *Smart Specialisation: Opportunities and Challenges for Regional Innovation Policy*, Abingdon, UK and New York: Routledge.

Huang, C., A. Arundel and H. Hollanders (2010), 'How firms innovate: R&D, Non-R&D, and technology adoption', UNU-MERIT Working Papers #2010-027, Maastricht University.

Kirner, E., S. Kinkel and A. Jaeger (2009), 'Innovation paths and the innovation performance of low-technology firms: an empirical analysis of German industry', *Research Policy*, **38**(3), 447–458.

Marmuse, C. and J.-C. Godest (2008), 'La détection des entreprises potentiellement innovantes: modélisation d'une approche de score pour l'accompagnement des entreprises à potentiel innovateur', Conférence Internationale de Management Stratétgique, Nice – Sophia Antipolis, 28–31 May.

Marsili, O. and B. Verspagen (2001), 'Technological regimes and innovation: looking for regularities in Dutch manufacturing', ECIS, Eindhoven University of Technology.

OECD/Eurostat (2018), *Oslo Manual 2018: Guidelines for Collecting, Reporting and Using Data on Innovation*, 4th edn, The Measurement of Scientific, Technological and Innovation Activities, Paris: OECD Publishing and Luxembourg: Eurostat.

Pavitt, K. (1984), 'Sectoral patterns of technical change: towards a taxonomy and a theory', *Research Policy*, **13** (6), 343–373.

7. Learning from similar regions: how to benchmark innovation systems beyond rankings

Susana Franco, Carlo Gianelle, Alexander Kleibrink and Asier Murciego

7.1 INTRODUCTION

National and regional benchmarking tools supporting industrial policy have become a boom business. Dozens of reports highlight every year which regions and countries are most competitive and where doing business is easiest.[1] Most debates in industrial and innovation policy in the past 30 years were triggered by the sudden and repeated identification of 'performance gaps' between economic powers: Europe lags behind the United States (US) and Japan in research and development, so Europe ought to learn from them how to improve (Cincera and Veugelers, 2013; O'Sullivan, 2007). The European Council made benchmarking a central element of the open method for coordination to achieve the Lisbon Strategy's goal of making the European Union (EU) the most competitive economic area by 2010, by 'establishing, where appropriate, quantitative and qualitative indicators and benchmarks against the best in the world and tailored to the needs of different Member States and sectors as a means of comparing best practices' (European Council, 2000).

Comparing countries or regions is not only useful for understanding their relative performance. Comparison is first and foremost an exercise through which policy-makers can learn how to improve welfare at home by introducing public policy innovations borrowed from others' experiences. This and other forms of learning are important tools for the creation and evolution of new policy designs in a complex and fast-

---

[1] See, for instance, the Regional Competitiveness Index produced by the European Commission (https://ec.europa.eu/regional_policy/en/information/maps/regional_competitiveness), or the Ease of Doing Business Index developed by the World Bank (www.doingbusiness.org).

changing world whose possible 'futures' are inherently uncertain. When the state of the environment and the system under scrutiny, as well as the processes aimed at generating novel states, cannot be fully determined in advance, the information needed in order to take sound policy decisions cannot, by definition, be derived solely from deterministic models. Given both cognitive boundaries and imperfect information about natural and social phenomena, a rational policy must necessarily rely on the systematic and iterative use of empirical evidence to support, update and rethink its underlying priors and basic assumptions, very much in line with the idea of a Bayesian learning process.

Policy-makers can learn from their own past experience, for instance through monitoring and evaluation activities (Sabel, 1993); or from experiences of others, by means of interaction, observation and analysis (Levy, 1994; Dobbin et al., 2007). Learning from others requires gathering and processing strategic information and insights from a range of stakeholders and insiders, and analysing practices adopted in other jurisdictions. At the regional level, in the EU and beyond, policy learning is increasingly supported through structured forms of participatory governance and joint search and discovery processes by pooling knowledge and information from relevant stakeholders and local actors, such as in the smart specialisation policy (Foray et al., 2012). Learning from others' experiences requires policy-makers to first identify candidates for meaningful comparison. Benchmarking methodologies essentially are heuristics to *ex ante* simplify such identification problems that otherwise may be extremely burdensome and practically unfeasible for resource-constrained policy-makers. The aim of benchmarking is precisely to preselect a limited number of peer candidates whose characteristics facilitate policy-makers to form expectations about the potential effects the policies implemented in those places would have at home.

If the Organisation for Economic Co-operation and Development (OECD) ranks Finland high on schoolchildren competences, we assume there must be something to learn from them to close the gap towards this top performer. Indeed, Finland became a destination for 'policy tourists' trying to grasp why Finnish children are doing so well in standardised tests (Grek, 2009). In innovation policy, the annually published scoreboards for EU member states and regions receive wide attention (Hollanders et al., 2009, 2019; Hollanders, 2019). While there is broad consensus that benchmarking is a necessary element of policy learning, there are diverging views regarding what criteria are best suited to determine which comparisons are conceptually sound, empirically relevant and ultimately conducive to effective learning. The tenet of this chapter is that transnational and transregional policy learning is facilitated when comparisons are made according to policy-relevant structural characteristics. Such characteristics have significant influence on the broad evolution of the socio-economic dimensions that the policy of interest is meant to change. They are by nature either constant in time, or little prone to short-term cyclical fluctuations, hence not immediately modifiable by the policy intervention itself. If regions benchmark themselves with other regions that are fundamentally different, and may therefore react differently to policy stimuli, policy learning is likely to be misguided. The core of benchmarking methods is therefore the selection of those structural characteristics most relevant for the policy area of interest.

In the last 20 years, policy learning has become a widely studied field in regional studies and economic development more broadly, drawing attention to the role of benchmarking as a learning enabler (Cooke, 2014; Borrás, 2011; Hausmann and Hidalgo, 2011; Lundvall and Tomlinson, 2002). Yet, most studies largely ignore varying contextual conditions and compare unlike with unlike. Several commonly used national and regional rankings used for benchmarking mix up information on both the structure of socio-economic systems (broad determinants of policy outcomes) and the performance of local actors (outcome of policy interventions). This makes it difficult, if not impossible, to identify viable peers to effectively learn from in the sense we have explained above (see, e.g., Hollanders, 2019).

This chapter addresses these shortcomings by proposing a novel methodology for benchmarking regions in order to effectively support transnational learning in innovation policy. We do this by measuring the degree of similarity between regions in terms of structural and theoretically relevant social, economic, institutional and geographical factors influencing innovation activities and innovation policy outcomes. We collect regional data for all EU member states covering several relevant structural dimensions, and we construct a full matrix of interregional 'distances' obtained by aggregating different dimensions. By exploring this matrix, even non-expert users interested in a given region can easily find suitable – that is, close enough – candidates for policy learning. Contrary to other studies, our methodology does not produce a unique ranking of regions (scoreboard) or a typology (clustering), but rather allows users to create different region-specific peer sets which we believe are of greater practical use and can better support policy learning in the design and implementation of regional development policies.

The chapter is structured as follows. Section 7.2 further characterises benchmarking and its potential contribution to policy learning. Section 7.3 presents the methodology for the identification of peer regions. Section 7.4 illustrates the results by examining the case of the Basque Country in

Spain and its peer regions. Section 7.5 concludes by presenting a set of policy implications for impactful benchmarking.

7.2 REGIONAL BENCHMARKING AND INNOVATION POLICY LEARNING

Benchmarking exercises were initially developed in the context of business studies to compare corporate strategies and performance. They have been progressively adapted to territorial contexts and policy learning only at a later stage. The main aim of applying benchmarking to policy learning was helping an entity – organisation or territory – to draw lessons from its own history and from others by restricting comparison to those entities with similar political conditions, close geographical proximity and comparable ideologies (Rose, 1993). Spatial applications include comparisons of state-level entities, outside and within the EU, and more recently, European regions (Koellreuter, 2002).[2] Most often, benchmarking has been understood as entailing the systematic comparison of one entity with another with the aim to identify and replicate 'best' practices (Lundvall and Tomlinson, 2001).

Transfer of policy practices between entities is meaningful only when it is supported by solid expectations of the effects the replicated measures will have on the recipient entity. Forming such expectations would require a great deal of analytical and information processing capacity, which is costly to build up and employ. To learn from other experiences generally requires carrying out three main activities: (1) gather relevant information about measures implemented by others; (2) for each measure, analyse the causal chain leading from inputs to results, and assess the impact of similar policy measures in different scenarios; and (3) select the solutions that best fit one's profile and objectives. All these activities require processing a possibly huge mass of complex information at a cost that can be considerable.

Policy learning under such demanding conditions can only be bounded, because of the inherently limited capacities of policy-makers to possess and process all relevant information (March and Simon, 1993). More specifically, in the presence of binding resource constraints, decision-making

---

[2]   As explained by Fagerberg (2003), the practice of comparison-based learning in the context of national policy-making has a long-standing tradition, although it has only recently been conceptualised. The most ambitious exercise in this sense was probably carried out in the late nineteenth century, when the Meiji government of Japan sent out emissaries to Western countries to bring back a blueprint for the design of a modern state.

agents usually try to simplify the process *ex ante* by resorting to heuristics or 'rules of thumb' based on common knowledge, experience or theory that allow for preselecting a limited number of cases to learn from. This is precisely the aim of benchmarking. Benchmarking requires three steps. First, focus on a homogeneous class of policy measures characterised by common objectives and with impact on the same variables. Second, identify the factors that determine (broadly) the evolution of the objective variables (usually long-term evolution) net of the effect of the considered measures. Third, focus policy learning only on those peer territories that share a similar endowment of factors identified in the previous step. Smith (2001, p. 268) emphasises that 'quantitative comparisons usually have to assume that there is qualitative uniformity among the objects being compared or counted: like has to be compared with like'.

In the case we examine in this chapter, the first step of benchmarking corresponds to focusing on innovation policy in EU regions. Next comes the selection of regions which are structurally homogeneous in a way that is relevant for innovation policy. Innovation-relevant structural characteristics are framework conditions that cannot be changed easily by policy interventions in the short to medium term. Rather, they affect regional development and define the broad innovation trajectory over a longer time horizon (Huggins, 2010; Papaioannou et al., 2006; Polt, 2002). Identifying such characteristics is particularly important because of the heterogeneity of economic structures and models (Smith, 2001), and the richness and diversity of regional innovation patterns and policy practices (Tödtling and Trippl, 2005; Nauwelaers and Reid, 2002). Territorial innovation systems are more complex than companies (Soete and Corpakis, 2003; Polt et al., 2001); they usually rely on political, economic and social factors which are beyond the control of a single authority (Iurcovich et al., 2006); and they are characterised by frequent trade-offs among the multiple goals the public sector seeks to pursue, often simultaneously (Schludi, 2003).

While several studies argue in favour of focusing on peer regions with similar innovation-relevant structural characteristics (Smith, 2001; Tödtling and Trippl, 2005; Nauwelaers and Reid, 2002), this approach has so far not been operationalised systematically. Regions have most often been compared to those that exhibit a better performance, resulting in rankings which give no hint of the different conditions at the origin of regions' relative performance (Huggins, 2010; Papaioannou et al., 2006; Polt, 2002). The use of performance-based comparison was also identified as one of the reasons why less-developed regions in the EU are reluctant to engage in benchmarking exercises (McCann and Ortega-Argilés, 2013). One of the few cases in which policy-relevant structural features are taken explicitly into account is the Index of the Massachusetts Innovation Economy (John Adams Innovation Institute, 2009), in which the economic and innovation performance of Massachusetts is compared only with the performance of the states in the U.S. that display significant concentration of employment in the same sectors in which Massachusetts exhibits a specialisation.

Regional typologies identifying sets of regions sharing similar features represent an increasingly popular benchmarking tool alternative to simple rankings. Examples in this vein can be found, for instance, in Dunnewijk et al. (2008), Hollanders et al. (2009), Verspagen (2010), OECD (2011) and Camagni and Capello (2013). Also in this case, the main problem rests in the choice of variables defining those typologies. Navarro and Gibaja (2009) examine a range of existing typologies that mix up variables of a very different nature, such as structural conditions, behavioural aspects and performance; this issue was also raised by Camagni and Capello (2013). Another way to take the policy-relevant context into account is to introduce control variables – for instance, size and industrial structure of the territory – in regression analyses that seek to explain the observed performance. Nevertheless, this approach does not allow the construction of a set of homogeneous regions to be used for comparison.

Based on a comprehensive literature review, we isolated seven classes of structural factors that play a prominent role in determining the regional innovation patterns and trends: (1) geo-demographic factors (for example, size of the market, age structure of the population); (2) human resources (for example, schooling); (3) technological specialisation (for example, patenting activity); (4) sectoral specialisation; (5) company structure (for example, firm-size distribution); (6) trade openness; and (7) institutions and values (for example, multi-level governance, social capital, entrepreneurial attitudes). The literature review is schematised according to those dimensions in Table 7.1.

The choice of dimensions allows one to control for the different stages of development of regions, namely through their technological and sectoral specialisation (Parteka, 2010; Parteka and Tamberi, 2013; Petralia et al., 2017), without the need to use the level of per capita gross domestic product (GDP). Income-based measures are typically endogenously related to innovation activities as they are both a determinant and a product of innovation (Lall, 2001). At the same time, two regions with very different structural conditions could reach the same level of development as a result of different sets of policies and strategies (Niosi, 2002). Hence, the inclusion of income-based measures of the stages of development may hamper rather than facilitate the identification of regions facing similar challenges arising from their common structural conditions.

Table 7.1 Literature review: classes of innovation-relevant structural factors

	1. Geo-demographic factors	2. Human resources	3. Technological specialisation	4. Sectoral specialisation	5. Company structure	6. Trade openness	7. Institutions and values	Others
Akerblom et al. (2008)				Industrial structure				
Andersson and Mahroum (2008)				Economic structure			Institutional framework	
Archibugi and Coco (2004)	Geography						Cultural factors	Economic factors
Archibugi et al. (2009)	Size and infrastructure	Human resources						Income
Arundel and Hollanders (2008)			Patterns of innovation					
Atkinson and Andes (2008)				Industrial structure				
Balzat (2006)							Social values & political goals, History	Economic development
Fagerberg and Srholec (2008)	Geography, demography and natural resources							
Fagerberg et al. (2007)	Geography, demography and natural resources						History	
Iurcovich et al. (2006)	Geography, size			Economic and industrial structure			Language	

John Adams Innovation Institute (2009)		Cluster structure			
Koellreuter (2002)	Geographical proximity	Economic and industrial activities			
Lall (2001)					Level of development
Nauwelaers et al. (2003)	Size	Economic specialisation	Firms size Openness	History, cultural & social capital	
OECD et al. (2004)	Size	Industry specialisation		Institutional factors	
OECD (2005)	Geography	Industrial structure		Policy context & culture	
Paasi (2005)	Size and natural resources	Economic structure		Culture & history	Development level
Schwab (2009)					GDP per capita
Smith (2001)	Size	Industrial structure			GDP per capita

Source: Navarro et al. (2014).

7.3 METHODOLOGY AND DATA

This section first describes the specific variables we included in the empirical analysis in order to fully reflect the multifaceted nature of each of the seven innovation-relevant structural dimensions. The variable selection is of course conditioned by data availability. Information at the regional level is usually quite scarce with regard to some crucial issues such as governance, social capital endowment or trade openness (Iurcovich et al., 2006; Dunnewijk et al., 2008). Fortunately, new databases have been developed recently in some of these fields which allowed us to progressively enrich the scope of the analysis, expanding the set of variables beyond what we had in earlier studies (Navarro et al., 2011, 2012, 2014).

We then illustrate the methodology for aggregating the variables in order to obtain a synthetic measure of regional distance. Finally, we construct a full matrix of pairwise regional distances in the EU. This approach allows us to obtain a full vector of distances for each region included in the matrix. While this analytical outcome is necessarily more complex to interpret and use than, for example, a cluster analysis, it is tailor-made to the needs of each region and therefore adds a useful degree of freedom to policy-makers in identifying the most suitable peers for policy learning among those reported in the distance vector.

7.3.1 Variable Selection

The seven dimensions we identified in the literature are often quite broad (for example, geo-demographic factors), comprise several different but related aspects (for example, institutions and values), or are difficult to grasp using a single indicator (for example, specialisation). Thus, we first divide them into constituting elements that we then match to quantitative indicators in order to identify the variables that can best measure or approximate those dimensions. Table 7.2 reports the 16 elements that we propose and the 42 variables that measure them. Our main units of analysis – that is, regions – are the EU territorial entities identified at level two of the Nomenclature of Territorial Units for Statistics (NUTS 2), except in Belgium, Germany and the United Kingdom, where level one territorial entities (NUTS 1) are used instead.

Geo-demographic factors
Within the geo-demographic dimension we included four elements: regional size (measured in terms of total population), urbanisation (percentage of population living in cities and related commuting zones), age structure of the population (percentage of the population aged 65

Table 7.2   Innovation-relevant structural elements and variables

Dimensions	Elements	Variables	Sources	Components
1. Geo-demographic factors	Regional size	Total population	Eurostat	Total population
	Ageing	Population ≥ 65 Population ≤ 15	Eurostat Eurostat	Ageing
	Urbanisation	Population in urban and commuting areas	DG REGIO	Population in urban and commuting areas
	Accessibility	Multimodal accessibility	ESPON (2009)	Multimodal accessibility
2. Human resources	HR educational level	Population with upper secondary and tertiary education	Eurostat	Population with upper secondary and tertiary education
3. Technological specialisation	Technological distribution (patents)	Electrical engineering Instruments Chemistry Mechanical engineering Other fields	OECD REGPAT OECD REGPAT OECD REGPAT OECD REGPAT OECD REGPAT	pat.f.01 pat.f.02 pat.f.03
	Technological concentration (patents)	Gini index of 35 sub-fields	OECD REGPAT	Gini index of 35 sub-fields
4. Sectoral specialisation	Economy's sectoral distribution	Agriculture, forestry and fishing (A) Industry (except construction) (B–E) Construction (F) Wholesale and retail trade, transport, etc. (B–I) Information and communication (J) Financial and insurance activities (K)	Eurostat LFS Eurostat LFS Eurostat LFS Eurostat LFS Eurostat LFS Eurostat LFS	emp.total.f.01 emp.total.f.02 emp.total.f.03

Table 7.2 (continued)

Dimensions	Elements	Variables	Sources	Components
		Real estate activities (L)	Eurostat LFS	
		Professional, scientific and technical activities (M–N)	Eurostat LFS	
		Public administration (O–Q)	Eurostat LFS	
		Arts, entertainment and recreation (R–U)	Eurostat LFS	
	Sectoral concentration	Employment share in the of five two-digit sectors (%)	Eurostat LFS	Top of 5 sub-sectors (2 digits) (% total employment)
	Industrial sectoral structure	Mining and quarrying (05–09)	Eurostat LFS*	
		Food, drinks and tobacco (10–12)	Eurostat LFS*	
		Textiles, apparel and leather (13–15)	Eurostat LFS*	
		Wood, paper and printing (16–18)	Eurostat LFS*	emp.ind.f.01
		Chemicals, pharmaceuticals, rubber, plastic and refined petroleum (19–22)	Eurostat LFS*	emp.ind.f.02
		Non-metallic mineral products (23)	Eurostat LFS*	emp.ind.f.03
		Basic metals and metal products (24–25)	Eurostat LFS*	emp.ind.f.04
		Electric, electronic, computer and optical equipment (26–27)	Eurostat LFS*	
		Machinery (28)	Eurostat LFS*	
		Transport equipment (29–30)	Eurostat LFS*	
		Other manufacturing (31–33)	Eurostat LFS*	
5. Company structure	Firm size	Average firm size	Eurostat SBS	Average firm size

	Trade openness	Total exports (% of GDP)	JRC and PBL	Total exports (% of GDP)
6. Trade openness				
7. Institutions and values	Multi-level government	Decentralisation	BAK Basel Economics	Decentralisation
	Social and institutional capital	Quality of institutions index	Charron et al. (2012)	social.inst.capital
		Feeling safe while walking alone in local area after dark	ESS	
		Most people can be trusted, or You can't be too careful	ESS	
	Entrepreneurial and innovative attitudes	Important to think new ideas and being creative	ESS	Ent.innov.att
		Important to try new and different things in life	ESS	

Notes:
* Data calculated from ad hoc request to Eurostat.
DG REGIO = Directorate-General for Regional and Urban Policy; ESPON = European Spatial Planning Observation Network; HR = Human Resources; OECD REGPAT = OECD Regional Patents Database; LFS = Labour Force Survey; SBS = Structural Business Statistics; JRC = Joint Research Centre; PBL = Planbureau voor de Leefomgeving / Netherlands Environmental Assessment Agency; ESS = European Social Survey.

Source: Navarro et al. (2014).

years or older; percentage of the population aged 15 years or younger) and accessibility (multimodal accessibility index computed by the European Spatial Planning Observation Network, ESPON).

Human resources
The human resources dimension corresponds to a single element capturing the education level of the population. We compute the percentage of the population aged 25–64 years that has reached an upper secondary or tertiary educational level.

Technological specialisation
The region's technological areas of specialisation are captured by two distinct elements: technological distribution and technological concentration. For the former, we estimate the share of Patent Cooperation Treaty (PCT) patents in five broad technology fields: (1) electrical engineering; (2) instruments; (3) chemistry; (4) mechanical engineering; and (5) other fields. Those fields are obtained from International Patent Classification (IPC) codes of the World Intellectual Property Organization (WIPO) by making use of WIPO's IPC technology concordance table. Data are computed on the basis of the OECD's January 2013 regional patent database. Given the small number of PCT patents in several regions, we opted for adding the patents applied for over the period 2005–2010. For the latter indicator, technological concentration, we compute the Gini coefficient across 35 different two-digit IPC technological fields for the period 2005–2010.

Sectoral specialisation
In order to characterise the regional sectoral specialisation, we identified three elements, all of which are based on employment statistics: the distribution of total employment, its concentration, and the distribution of employment across sectors within industry alone. To compute the distribution of total employment, we considered the employment share in ten major sectors from the Eurostat's regional economic accounts, based on Statistical Classification of Economic Activities in the European Community (NACE) rev. 2: agriculture, forestry and fishing (A); industry (except construction) (B, C, D, E); construction (F); trade, transportation, accommodation and food service activities (G, H, I); information and communication (J); financial and insurance activities (K); real estate activities (L); professional, scientific, technical, administration and support service activities (M, N); public administration, defence, education, human health and social work activities (O, P, Q); arts, entertainment, recreation and other services (R, S, T, U). Data are for the year 2011. The

concentration index is defined as the share of employment in the top five sub-sectors at NACE two-digit level in each region. In order to capture more subtle specialisation patterns within industry, we further calculate the share of industrial employment in 11 sectors based on the OECD's Structural Analysis (STAN) database classification. Data are extracted from the Eurostat Labour Force Survey for the year 2011.

Company structure
Company structure is assessed based on the average size of local units. Data are taken from Eurostat and then checked and, where necessary, adjusted on the basis of firms' average size at national level in order to avoid spurious regional patterns, as for instance in the case of German regions for which Eurostat data only report employment for units that have at least ten employees, thus overestimating company size.

Trade openness
The degree of trade openness of the economy is calculated as total exports over GDP in the year 2013. Regionalised data come from a database developed by the Joint Research Centre of the European Commission in collaboration with the Netherlands Environmental Assessment Agency according to the procedure described in Thissen et al. (2019).

Institutions and values
There are many relevant institutional aspects that characterise regions. We selected those for which we could find reliable data sources and focused on three elements: multi-level government; social and institutional capital; entrepreneurial and innovative attitudes. The first element refers to the level of decentralisation or devolution to sub-national levels of government, and it is measured using the composite index developed by BAK Basel Economics for the Assembly of European Regions (2009). In order to assess social and institutional capital, we used three indicators. First, an index on the quality of institutions computed at regional level by Charron et al. (2012). This index is based on survey data and appraises the level of corruption, protection of the rule of law, governmental efficiency and accountability. Second, the general situation regarding social stability in a region is operationalised through the subjective perception reported in the European Social Survey for 2008 (responses to the statement 'Feeling of safety of walking alone in local area after dark'). Social capital is also captured through a second variable from the same survey (responses to the statement 'Most people can be trusted or you can't be too careful'). Finally, entrepreneurial and innovative attitude is proxied using two variables from the European Social Survey (responses to the statements 'It is

important to think of new ideas and be creative' and 'It is important to try new and different things in life').

7.3.2   Constructing the Regional Pairwise Distance Matrix

In order to construct the regional pairwise distance matrix based on the set of variables and components described above, we applied several transformations to the original variables, tested different aggregation techniques and performed sensitivity analysis. The main steps we undertook are described below.

Corrections for outliers, asymmetry and kurtosis, normalisation and concentration of components

First, each variable was corrected for outliers, asymmetry and kurtosis using the procedure outlined in Appendix 7A.1. Second, in order to add them up, variables were normalised using the mini-max method, rescaling them so that all values fall between 0 and 100. We next proceeded to concentrate the information conveyed by the full set of 42 variables grouped according to the 16 elements in as few components as possible. The correspondence between variables and components is reported in the last column of Table 7.2. We applied the following procedure: when an element is measured by a single variable, the variable is kept; when it is measured by two variables (for example, age structure of the population), we aggregated them by means of a simple arithmetic average; finally, when an element is measured by more than two variables (for example, technological specialisation), we carried out a principal component analysis (PCA) and we retained the minimum number of components explaining most of the variability in the underlying data.[3] As a result, we obtained 22 components.

Weighting

The following step consisted in assigning weights to each of the components. As explained for instance in JRC European Commission and OECD (2008), there are different ways to do so. We explored two main alternatives.

The first was assigning equal weights. We considered three different possibilities: (1) equal weights to each of the 22 components; (2) equal weights to each of the components within one dimension, and then equal

---

[3]   This generally means keeping components with an eigenvalue greater than one, which individually explain at least 10 per cent of the variability of the data and together at least 60 per cent of such variability.

weights to each of the seven dimensions; and (3) equal weights to each of the components within a macro-dimension, and then equal weights to each macro-dimension. The macro-dimensions are defined based on the frequency with which the seven dimensions are cited in the literature. As we can see in Table 7.1, geo-demographical factors, sectoral structure, institutions and values are mentioned more often than the other four dimensions included in the analysis. Hence, we considered four macro-dimensions, the first three being equal to the most-cited ones and the fourth being the aggregation of the other four: human resources, technological specialisation, company structure and trade openness.

The second alternative was assigning weights based on the factor loadings of principal components. The three aforementioned possibilities were also explored in this context. Hence, a single PCA incorporating all 22 components was performed, as well as PCAs for each of the seven dimensions and the four macro-dimensions. In each case, we retained the components with highest factor loading. In the first case, the weights for each component were computed by aggregating the squared factor loadings in each of the retained components which were multiplied by the percentage of the variance each component explains. In the second and third cases, the procedure had to be iterated once more, performing a PCA with the seven dimensions (four in the case of the macro-dimensions). The resulting weights from the different weighting methods are reported in Appendix 7A.2.

Aggregation

Once the components' weights are set, there are different alternatives to aggregate them in order to calculate a summary distance indicator. We explored two alternative aggregation methods. The first is additive quadratic aggregation. The total distance between two regions is calculated through the following formula:

$$d(i,i') = \sum_{j=1}^{k} m_j(x_{ij} - x_{i'j})^2$$

where i is the first region, i' the second region, x is the value of a specific variable j, k is the total number of variables to be aggregated, and m_j is the weight assigned to the variable. This method allows for compensation in a non-linear way.

The second is geometric aggregation. In this case the distance is calculated as:

$$d(i,i') = \prod_{j=1}^{k} (1 - |x_{ij} - x_{i'j}|)^{m_j}$$

This is also an alternative for non-linear compensability.

Obtaining the distance matrix

The formulas illustrated above allow us to compute a full row vector of pairwise regional distances for each region *I*; all distance vectors together form the distance matrix. Among all the possible distance matrices calculated according to the weighting methods presented above, we gave preference to the matrix obtained with weights based on a single PCA analysis on the 22 components altogether. This allows for variability of the weights according to the variability observed in the data without constraining the weights to conform to the seven dimensions or four macro-dimensions. Between the two alternative aggregation methods, we gave preference to the additive quadratic aggregation.

Sensitivity analysis

The sensitivity of the results was tested for by means of Spearman correlation coefficients. This was done by computing the correlation coefficients between the distance vectors for each region obtained with different combinations of weights and aggregation methods. The 205 resulting coefficients were then averaged in order to obtain an indication of the correlation between the sets of peer regions obtained according to different combinations of weighting and aggregating methods. The results are presented in Appendix 7A.3. The Spearman correlation coefficients are quite high, ranging on average between 0.84 and 0.92. This means that the region-specific peer sets obtained with our preferred method would be quite similar to what we would obtain using other combinations of weighting and aggregating methods.

The row vector containing the distances between a given region and all the others can be extracted from the distance matrix and rearranged based on the distance values. In this way a set of peer candidates, meaning close-enough regions, can be easily identified. This procedure, although somewhat more complex than a standard cluster analysis, is superior to the latter technique in our view at least for two reasons: (1) it provides all regional pairwise distances, helping the user to make a judgement on the appropriateness of each peer candidate; and (2) it allows the user to define ad hoc sets of peers of various dimensions.

7.4   REGIONS SIMILAR TO THE BASQUE COUNTRY

Using the difference matrix that has been computed giving weights through PCA to the 22 components and aggregating them using the additive quadratic method, in this section we present regions similar

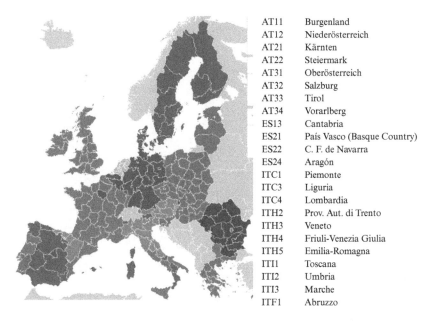

AT11	Burgenland
AT12	Niederösterreich
AT21	Kärnten
AT22	Steiermark
AT31	Oberösterreich
AT32	Salzburg
AT33	Tirol
AT34	Vorarlberg
ES13	Cantabria
ES21	País Vasco (Basque Country)
ES22	C. F. de Navarra
ES24	Aragón
ITC1	Piemonte
ITC3	Liguria
ITC4	Lombardia
ITH2	Prov. Aut. di Trento
ITH3	Veneto
ITH4	Friuli-Venezia Giulia
ITH5	Emilia-Romagna
ITI1	Toscana
ITI2	Umbria
ITI3	Marche
ITF1	Abruzzo

Source: Navarro et al. (2014).

Figure 7.1 Regions similar to the Basque Country using the cluster approach

to the Basque Country for illustrative purposes, both according to the cluster approach and the individual approach. The former (presented in Figure 7.1) provides a division of regions in groups that have a strong national bias. In the case of the Basque Country, it is grouped with some of the regions in northern Spain, but also with regions in the north of Italy and Austria. For the individual approach depicted in Figure 7.2, we have chosen the same number of regions (23, including the Basque Country) that had resulted from the cluster approach. This allows for a better comparison between both groups of regions. We notice that the individual approach provides a spread of regions from a larger variety of countries, maintaining the Spanish regions that were in the cluster group and even including another Spanish region (Catalonia). Most of the Italian and Austrian regions disappear and are substituted by regions mainly from Germany and the United Kingdom, and a few from other countries. We consider that the characteristics of the similar regions from the individual approach indeed fit better with those of the Basque Country. Therefore, they constitute a reasonable group of regions to be considered in further stages of a benchmarking exercise.

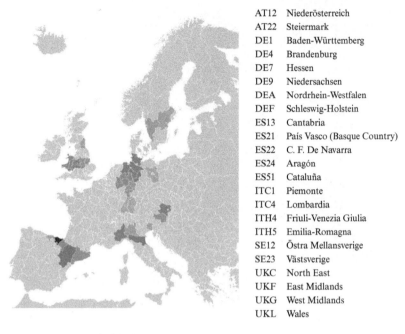

AT12	Niederösterreich
AT22	Steiermark
DE1	Baden-Württemberg
DE4	Brandenburg
DE7	Hessen
DE9	Niedersachsen
DEA	Nordrhein-Westfalen
DEF	Schleswig-Holstein
ES13	Cantabria
ES21	País Vasco (Basque Country)
ES22	C. F. De Navarra
ES24	Aragón
ES51	Cataluña
ITC1	Piemonte
ITC4	Lombardia
ITH4	Friuli-Venezia Giulia
ITH5	Emilia-Romagna
SE12	Östra Mellansverige
SE23	Västsverige
UKC	North East
UKF	East Midlands
UKG	West Midlands
UKL	Wales

Source: Navarro et al. (2014).

Figure 7.2 Regions similar to the Basque Country using the individual approach

In a second step, we compare the characterisation of structural conditions in the Basque Country and its similar regions to EU and Spanish averages. Compared to the EU regions' average, and in terms of geo-demography, human resources education and technological specialisation (see Table 7.3), the Basque Country and its similar regions are characterised by a large ageing population (in terms of both larger proportions of elders and smaller proportions of youngsters), a high degree of urbanisation and connectivity, and by their technological specialisation in mechanical engineering and instruments. Regarding Spanish regions, the Basque Country's specialisation reproduces the aforementioned patterns. It stands out in terms of more developed human capital. Finally, in comparison with the similar regions, the Basque Country is more urbanised, and specialised in mechanical engineering.

As Table 7.4 displays, the Basque Country and its similar regions are strongly specialised in industry and professional, scientific and technical activities; and, within manufacturing, in basic metals and metal products, machinery and transport equipment. This specialisation is more

Table 7.3   Characterization of the Basque Country and its similar regions in terms of geo-demography, human resources education and technological specialisation

Dimensions	Elements	Variables	Basque Country	RR (individ. app.)	RR (cluster app.)	EU	Spain
1. Geo-demography	Regional size	Total population (millions)	2.1	4.4	2.0	2.4	2.7
	Ageing	Population >= 65 years old (%)	20.1	19.5	20.3	17.6	18.0
		Population <15 years old (%)	14.3	15.6	14.9	16.4	15.4
	Urbanisation	Pop. in urban and comm. areas (%)	80.0	72.5	54.6	60.9	70.6
	Accessibility	Multimodal accessibility index	93.4	107.7	98.4	86.2	68.9
2. Human resources educational level	Human resources educational level	Pop. with upper secondary and tertiary ed. (%)	68.1	73.9	69.3	73.6	54.8
3. Technological specialisation	Technological distribution (patents)	Electrical engineering (% of total)	11.4	17.1	16.4	19.0	12.4
		Instruments (% of total)	15.0	15.1	13.3	13.4	12.7
		Chemistry (% of total)	21.4	25.4	21.3	27.5	29.1
		Mechanical engineering (% of total)	37.1	31.2	33.6	29.2	29.6
		Other fields (% of total)	15.2	11.2	15.3	11.0	16.3
	Technological concentration (patents)	GINI index of 35 subfields	0.4	0.5	0.5	0.6	0.5

Note: **RR** = reference regions.

Source: Navarro et al. (2014).

Table 7.4   Characterisation of the Basque Country and its similar regions in terms of sectoral structure

Dimensions	Elements	Variables	Basque Country	RR (individ. app.)	RR (cluster app.)	EU	Spain
4. Sectoral structure	Economy's sectoral distribution	Agriculture, forestry and fishing (A) (%)	1.3	2.6	3.9	6.6	5.2
		Industry (except const.) (B–E) (%)	21.0	19.5	21.2	17.4	15.3
		Construction (F) (%)	6.1	7.1	8.2	7.3	7.3
		Wholesale and retail trade, transport,... (B–I) (%)	23.4	23.7	25.6	23.8	28.5
		Information and communication (J) (%)	3.3	2.7	2.1	2.4	2.4
		Financial and insurance activities (K) (%)	2.8	2.8	3.0	2.6	2.2
		Real estate activities (L) (%)	0.4	0.8	0.6	0.7	0.5
		Professional, scientific and technical activities (M–N) (%)	11.1	9.7	8.5	7.9	8.9
		Public administration (O–Q) (%)	23.5	25.2	20.8	24.4	22.4
		Arts, entertainment and recreation (R–U) (%)	7.3	5.6	6.2	5.0	7.5
	Sectoral concentration	Top of 5 subsectors (2 digits) (% total employment)	8.4	8.5	8.3	8.4	9.1

Industrial sectoral structure					
Mining and quarrying (05–09) (%)	3.8	9.1	7.3	12.0	11.2
Food, drinks and tobacco (10–12) (%)	6.0	10.8	10.5	15.4	20.7
Textiles, apparel and leather (13–15) (%)	0.9	3.2	6.9	6.0	5.2
Wood, paper and printing (16–18) (%)	6.2	7.1	8.4	8.1	7.2
Chem., pharm., rubber, plastic and refined petroleum (19–22) (%)	8.9	9.8	8.6	9.6	8.6
Non-metallic mineral products (23) (%)	3.7	3.4	5.0	4.1	4.7
Basic metals and metal products (24–25) (%)	26.8	16.1	16.7	13.2	14.6
Electric, electronic, computer and optical equipment (26–7) (%)	8.1	7.9	8.6	6.8	4.0
Machinery (28) (%)	12.0	10.4	9.4	6.3	4.5
Transport equipment (29–30) (%)	18.4	13.5	8.0	8.4	9.1
Other manufacturing (31–3) (%)	5.2	8.9	10.6	10.1	10.3

Note: RR = reference regions.

Source: Navarro et al. (2014).

Table 7.5   *Characterisation of the Basque Country and its similar regions in terms of firm size, openness and institutions and values*

Dimensions	Elements	Variables	Basque Country	RR (individ. app.)	RR (cluster app.)	EU	Spain
5. Firm size	Firm size	Average firm size (number of employees)	6.5	8.8	6.1	6.5	4.5
6. Openness	Trade openness	Total exports (% GDP)	22.0	24.5	28.0	27.5	14.6
7. Institutions/ values	Multilevel government	Decentralization index	58.0	56.4	53.1	47.4	58.0
	Social and instituional capital	Quality of institutions index	0.7	0.6	0.2	0.1	0.2
		Feeling of safety of walking alone in local area after dark (1 very safe – 4 very unsafe)	2.0	2.0	2.0	2.0	1.9
		Most people can be trusted or you can't be too careful (0 You can't be too careful – 10 Most people can be trusted)	5.6	5.1	4.9	4.8	5.0
	Entrepreneurial and innovative attitudes	Important to think of new ideas and be creative (1 Very much like me – 6 Not like me at all)	2.4	2.4	2.4	2.5	2.5
		Important to try new and different things in life (1 Very much like me – 6 Not like me at all)	2.8	2.9	2.8	2.9	2.9

Note: RR = reference regions.

Source: Navarro et al. (2014).

pronounced in the Basque Country than in the other similar regions. There are also noticeable differences among Basque Country and its peer group, on the one hand, and the EU regions average, on the other, concerning the level of decentralisation, quality of institutions and, to a lesser extent, social capital (see Table 7.5). We observe the same pattern in the comparison between the Basque Country and Spain, except for the degree of decentralisation. Finally, we observe that the Basque Country's values are closer to those of similar regions coming from the cluster approach than the individual approach. This is related to a fact previously highlighted: national factors having a strong influence in cluster analysis results. Usually, dimensions such as geo-demography, education, institutions and values are more homogeneous within a country than across countries; and the opposite occurs in sectoral and industry specialisation in large countries.

7.5 CONCLUSIONS

We have presented a methodology to identify similar regions as a first step for policy learning, which avoids making odious comparisons. Although the method outlined in this chapter can be used to identify similar regions for any EU region, the comparability principle is even more important for less-developed regions. Less-developed regions might feel discouraged by the very demanding process of designing comprehensive evidence-based innovation strategies because the examples and practices they are faced with usually come from successful regions with which they do not have much in common.

Our findings support the idea of federalism driving policy innovations. Regions in large decentralised countries may benefit most from comparing themselves to peers inside their country. The Basque Country, on the other hand, shares many structural features with regions across the EU and less so within its own country. Effective policy learning depends, thus, on these scope conditions that should be considered when looking for 'good practices'.

Our method shows why existing typologies and rankings are generally not useful to identify truly similar regions. Firstly, they tend to mix variables and dimensions of different nature. Secondly, they provide an uneven number of regions in each of the groups, which might result in some small groups that do not offer a significant number of regions for the benchmarking exercise. Finally, the statistical grouping of regions might exclude similar regions that have been assigned to a different group or category. The approach followed in this chapter offers an alternative to these shortcomings: the proximity of regions is only assessed on the basis of structural conditions and there is no prior restrictive grouping of regions. Yet our approach is only the first step in a full-fledged benchmarking exercise. The list of comparable regions should be narrowed down on the basis of qualitative and more detailed quantitative data or analysis. For instance, there are likely to be meaningful data that are not available for all European regions but might be accessed for the more restricted group of comparable regions.

Once the final group of similar regions has been identified, their performance can be assessed. It is then possible to focus on the best-performing regions in order to understand the reasons of success or failure and draw lessons in order to strengthen the regional strategic positioning ('be unique') and their operational efficiency. For the benchmarking exercise to be useful, these lessons should not remain at the academic or advisory level, but they should be implemented at the operational level. Finally, collecting data on similar regions and a region's positioning vis-à-vis other regions is a necessary but not sufficient condition for policy learning. The insights gained here must feed into the whole policy process and be reflected in the monitoring and evaluation mechanism.

One of the main policy implications of this chapter is that benchmarking is highly relevant for designing and implementing the next generation of innovation strategies. An intelligent regional benchmarking of policy and innovation systems should follow several steps. First, it should identify comparable regions. Once they have been identified, those with better performance should be prioritised in a second step. These regions are more likely to provide replicable lessons on how to improve a region's own performance.[4] Empirical comparisons establish then 'good' or 'bad' performance (Lall, 2001; Balzat, 2006; Edquist, 2008). In a third step, benchmarking determines what causes these performances to be better or worse. Otherwise, benchmarking runs the risk of remaining at the stage of 'leagues' or simplistic regional rankings. In that case, it would certainly raise the awareness of existing problems, but it would fail to identify their

---

[4]   Certainly, it might also make sense to consider the others later on. As Polt (2002) and Salazar and Holbrook (2004) point out, unsuccessful cases and those that do not achieve the best results can also provide information and be a source of learning. But, as Iurcovich et al. (2006) argue, apart from being more difficult to get complete information about those that are mediocre or worst-in-class, there would be more scepticism in one's own region with regard to knowledge taken from those worse-performing regions. There would also be a lack of certainty to get things right if they are done somehow differently from the worst cases.

underlying causes.[5] As noted by Edquist (2001), a proper diagnosis consists of both the identification of performance problems and the analysis of their causes. Weak performers should reflect on how they differ (in terms of framework conditions, activities or input indicators) from regions with better performance (OECD et al., 2004). Finally, benchmarking exercises must be embedded in the entire policy process (Balzat, 2006; Paasi, 2005; Polt, 2002). Proper implementation, aside from requiring a complete understanding of the changes needed in the system, should involve policy-makers and stakeholders, their coordination and a continuous evaluation (Nauwelaers and Reid, 2002; Nauwelaers et al., 2003). In this way, benchmarking goes beyond mere rankings of regions that often are a mixed bag of factors.

REFERENCES

Akerblom, M., Bloch, C., Foyn, F., Leppälahti, A., Mortenssen, P., Mansson, H., et al. (2008). Policy relevant Nordic innovation indicators. NIND Project.

Andersson, T. and Mahroum, S. (2008). Policy relevant Nordic innovation indicators: objectives and rationales in Nordic and European innovation policies. NIND Project.

Archibugi, D. and Coco, A. (2004). A new indicator of technological capabilities for developed and developing countries (ArCo). *World Development* **32** (4): 629–654.

Archibugi, D., Denni, M. and Filippetti, A. (2009). The technological capabilities of nations: the state of the art of synthetic indicators. *Technological Forecasting and Social Change* **76**: 917–931.

Arundel, A. and Hollanders, H. (2008). Innovation scoreboards: indicators and policy use. In Nauwelaers, C. and Wintjes, R. (eds), *Innovation Policy in Europe*, Cheltenham, UK and Northampton, MA, USA: Edward Elgar Publishing, pp. 29–52.

Assembly of European Regions (2009). *From Subsidiarity to Success: The Impact of Decentralisation on Economic Growth. Part 1: Creating a Decentralisation Index. Researched and produced by BAK Basel Economics.* Brussels and Strasbourg: Assembly of European Regions (AER).

Atkinson, R. and Andes, S. (2008). *The 2008 State New Economy Index: Benchmarking Economic Transformation in the States*, Washington, DC: Information Technology and Innovation Foundation.

Balzat, M. (2006). *An Economic Analysis of Innovation. Extending the Concept of National Innovation Systems*, Cheltenham, UK and Northampton, MA, USA: Edward Elgar Publishing.

---

[5] The Expert Group on Benchmarking S&T Productivity (European Commission, 2002) emphasised that '[b]enchmarking must aim at deeper insights into the processes behind performance' and it 'must not stop at the quantitative comparison of different indicators'. Benchmarking in this understanding is only the first step of deeper analysis.

Borrás, S. (2011). Policy learning and organizational capacities in innovation policies. *Science and Public Policy* **38** (9): 725–734.

Camagni, R. and Capello, R. (2013). Regional innovation patterns and the EU regional policy reform: towards smart innovation policies. *Growth and Change* **44** (2): 355–389.

Cincera, M. and Veugelers, R. (2013). Exploring Europe's R&D deficit relative to the US: differences in the rates of return to R&D of young leading R&D firms. iCite Working Papers 2013-001, Universite Libre de Bruxelles (ULB).

Cooke, Philip (2014). Systems of innovation and the learning region. In Fischer, M.M. and Nijkamp, P. (eds), *Handbook of Regional Science*, Berlin and Heidelberg: Springer, pp. 457–474.

Dobbin, F., Simmons, B. and Garret, G. (2007). The global diffusion of public policies: social construction, coercion, competition, or learning? *Annual Review of Sociology* 33: 449–472.

Dunnewijk, T., Hollanders, H. and Wintjes, R. (2008). Benchmarking regions in the enlarged Europe: diversity in knowledge potential and policy options. In Nauwelaers, C. and Wintjes, R. (eds), *Innovation Policy in Europe: Measurement and Strategy*, Cheltenham, UK and Northampton, MA, USA: Edward Elgar Publishing, pp. 53–105.

Edquist, C. (2001). Innovation policy – a systemic approach. In Archibugui, D. and Lundvall, B.-Å. (eds), *The Globalizing Learning Economy*, Oxford: Oxford University Press, pp. 219–238.

Edquist, C. (2008). Design of innovation policy through diagnostic analysis: identification of systemic problems (or failures). CIRCLE, Lund University paper no. 2008/06.

ESPON (2009). Territorial dynamics in Europe. Trends in Accessibility. Territorial Observation No. 2, November.

European Commission (2002). *Report from the Expert Group on Benchmarking S&T Productivity*, Brussels: European Commission.

European Council (2000). Lisbon European Council 23 and 24 March 2000 presidency conclusions. https://www.europarl.europa.eu/summits/lis1_en.htm.

Fagerberg, J. (2003). The Potential of Benchmarking as a Tool for Policy Learning. IPTS Report 71: 13–19.

Fagerberg, J. and Srholec, M. (2008). National innovation systems, capabilities and economic development. *Research Policy* 37: 1417–1435.

Fagerberg, J., Srholec, M. and Knell, M. (2007). The competitiveness of nations: why some countries prosper while others fall behind. *World Development* **35** (10): 1595–1620.

Foray, D., Goddard, J., Goenaga, X., Landabaso, M., McCann, P., Morgan, K., et al. (2012). *Guide to Research and Innovation Strategies for Smart Specialisation (RIS 3)*, Brussels: European Commission, Regional Policy.

Grek, S. (2009). Governing by numbers: the PISA 'effect' in Europe. *Journal of Education Policy* **24** (1): 23–37.

Hausmann, R. and Hidalgo, C.A. (2011). The network structure of economic output. *Journal of Economic Growth* **16** (4): 309–342.

Hollanders, H. (2019). *European Innovation Scoreboard 2019 – Methodology Report*, Brussels: European Communities.

Hollanders, H., Es-Sadki, N. and Merkelbach, I. (2019). *Regional Innovation Scoreboard 2019 – Methodology Report*, Brussels: European Communities.

Hollanders, H., Tarantola, S. and Loschky, A. (2009). *Regional Innovation Scoreboard (RIS) 2009*, Brussels: European Communities.

Huggins, R. (2010). Regional competitive intelligence: benchmarking and policy-making. *Regional Studies* **445**: 639–658.

Iurcovich, L., Komninos, N., Reid, A., Heydebreck, P. and Pierrakis, Y. (2006). Blueprint for regional innovation benchmarking. Mutual Learning Platform, Regional Benchmarking Report, Luxembourg: IRE Secretariat.

John Adams Innovation Institute (2009). *2008 Index of the Massachusetts Innovation Economy*, Westborough, MA: Massachusetts Technology Collaborative.

JRC European Commission and OECD (2008). *Handbook on Constructing Composite Indicators*. http://www.oecd.org/dataoecd/37/42/42495745.pdf.

Koellreuter, C. (2002). Regional Benchmarking as a tool to improve regional foresight. Paper for the STRATA-ETAN Expert Group Action on 'Mobilising Regional Foresight Potential for an Enlarged EU', European Commission Research DG.

Lall, S. (2001). Competitiveness indices and developing countries: an economic evaluation of the Global Competitiveness Report. *World Development* **29** (9): 1501–1525.

Levy, J.S. (1994). Learning and foreign policy: sweeping a conceptual minefield. *International Organization* **48** (2): 279–312.

Lundvall, B.-Å. and Tomlinson, M. (2001). Learning-by-comparing: reflections on the use and abuse of international benchmarking. In Sweeney, G. (ed.), *Innovation, Economic Progress and the Quality of Life*, Cheltenham, UK and Northampton, MA, USA: Edward Elgar Publishing, pp. 120–136.

Lundvall, B.-Å. and Tomlinson, M. (2002). International benchmarking as a policy learning tool. In Maria Rodrigues (ed.), *The New Knowledge Economy in Europe: A Strategy for International Competitiveness and Social Cohesion*, Cheltenham, UK and Northampton, MA, USA: Edward Elgar Publishing, pp. 203–231.

March, J. and Simon, H.A. (1993). *Organizations*, Cambridge, MA: David Blackwell.

McCann, P. and Ortega-Argilés, R. (2013). Smart specialisation, regional growth and applications to EU cohesion policy. *Regional Studies* **49** (8): 1291–1302.

Nauwelaers, C. and Reid, A. (2002). Learning innovation policy in a market-based context: process, issues and challenges for EU candidate-countries. *Journal of International Relations and Development* **5** (4): 357–379.

Nauwelaers, C., Veugelers, R. and Van Looy, B. (2003). Benchmarking national R&D policies in Europe: lessons from Belgium. Final Report for the Federal Public Service for Scientific Affairs.

Navarro, M. and Gibaja, J.J. (2009). Las tipologías en los sistemas regionales de innovación. El caso de España. *Ekonomiaz* **70**: 240–281.

Navarro, M., Franco, S., Murciego, A. and Gibaja, J.J. (2012). Metodología de benchmarking territorial: la necesidad de identificación de las regiones de referencia. *Información Comercial Española* **869**: 115–132.

Navarro, M., Gibaja, J.J., Franco, S. and Murciego, A. (2011). El análisis de benchmarking y la identificación de regiones de referencia: aplicación al País Vasco. In Navarro, M. (ed.), *Indicadores de innovación y benchmarking. Reflexión y propuesta para el País Vasco*, Zamudio: Innobasque, pp. 298–371.

Navarro, M., Gibaja, J.J., Franco, S., Murciego, A., Gianelle, C., Hegyi, F.B. and Kleibrink, A. (2014). Regional benchmarking in the smart specialisation process: identification of reference regions based on structural similarity. JRC Technical Report JRC89819, European Commission, Joint Research Centre.

Niosi, J. (2002). National Systems of innovations are 'x-efficient' (and x-effective): why some are slow learners. *Research Policy* **31**: 291–302.

OECD (2005). *Micro-Policies for Growth and Productivity: Synthesis and Benchmarking User Guide*, Paris: OECD.

OECD (2011). *Regions and Innovation Policy*, OECD Reviews of Regional Innovation, Paris: OECD Publishing.

OECD, Ministry for Trade and Industry and Inside Consulting (2004). *Benchmarking Innovation Policy and Innovation Framework Conditions*, January.

O'Sullivan, M. (2007). The EU's R&D deficit and innovation policy. Report of the Expert Group on Knowledge for Growth, European Commission DG Research.

Paasi, M. (2005). Collective benchmarking of policies: an instrument for policy learning in adaptive research and innovation policy. *Science and Public Policy* **32** (1): 17–27.

Papaioannou, T., Rush, H. and Bessant, J. (2006). Benchmarking as a policy-making tool: from the private to the public sector. *Science and Public Policy* **33** (2): 91–102.

Parteka, A. (2010). Employment and export specialisation along the development path: some robust evidence. *Review of World Economics* **145**: 615–640.

Parteka, A. and Tamberi, M. (2013). Product diversification, relative specialisation and economic development: import–export analysis. *Journal of Macroeconomics* **38**: 121–135.

Petralia, S., Balland, P.-A. and Morrison, A. (2017). Climbing the ladder of technological development. *Research Policy* **46**: 956–969.

Polt, W. (2002). Benchmarking. In Fahrenkrog, G., Polt, W., Rojo, J., Tübke, A. and Zinöcker, K. (eds), *RTD-Evaluation Toolbox Assessing the Socio-Economic Impact of RTD-Policies*, European Commission, IPTS Technical Report Series EUR 20382 EN.

Polt, W., Rammer, C., Gassler, H., Schibany, A. and Scharting, D. (2001). Benchmarking industry–science relations: the role of frameworks conditions. *Science and Public Policy* **28** (4): 247–258.

Rose, R. (1993). *Lesson-Drawing in Public Policy*, Chatham, NJ: Chatham House.

Sabel, C.F. (1993). Learning by monitoring: the institutions of economic development. Working Paper No. 102, New York: Center for Law and Economic Studies, Columbia University School of Law.

Salazar, M. and Holbrook, A. (2004). A debate on innovation surveys. *Science and Public Policy* **31** (4): 254–266.

Schludi, M. (2003). Chances and limitations of 'benchmarking' in the reform of welfare state structures: the case of pension policy. AIAS Working Paper no. 10.

Schwab, K. (ed.) (2009). *The Global Competitiveness Report 2009–2010*, Geneva: World Economic Forum.

Smith, K. (2001). Comparing economic performance in the presence of diversity. *Science and Public Policy* **28** (4): 267–276.

Soete, L. and Corpakis, D. (2003). R&D for competitiveness and employment: the role of benchmarking. *IPTS Report* **71**: 2–12.

Thissen, M., Ivanova, O., Mandras, G. and Husby T. (2019). European NUTS 2 regions: construction of interregional trade-linked Supply and Use tables with consistent transport flows. JRC Working Papers on Territorial Modelling and Analysis No. 01/2019, JRC115439, Seville: European Commission.

Tödtling, F. and Trippl, M. (2005). One size fits all? Towards a differentiated regional innovation policy approach. *Research Policy* **34**: 1203–1219.

Verspagen, B. (2010). The spatial hierarchy of technological change and economic development in Europe. *Annals of Regional Science* **45**: 109–132.

Yeo, I.-K. and Johnson, R. (2000). A new family of power transformations to improve normality or symmetry. *Biometrika* **87**: 954–959.

APPENDIX 7A.1   PROCEDURE FOR THE CORRECTION OF POSSIBLE OUTLIERS, ASYMMETRY AND KURTOSIS

Steps for the correction of possible *outliers*, asymmetry and kurtosis:

1. Tests of asymmetry and kurtosis are calculated.
   a. If the probability of rejecting the hypothesis of the variable being symmetric and mesokurtic are above 0.05, the variable is not corrected.
   b. Otherwise, the presence of *outliers* is tested for in step 2.
2. The number of possible *outliers* is calculated according to the following criteria: number of observations that are outside the $[Q_1 - 1,5(Q_3 - Q_1), Q_3 + 1,5(Q_3 - Q_1)]$ interval, where Q_1 y Q_3 are, respectively, the first and third quartiles.
   a. If the number of *outliers* is less or equal than 10 (5% of observations), winsorization takes place. Winsorisation implies assigning the greatest value within the interval to all observations that are greater than the highest extreme of the interval. Equivalently, the minimum value within the interval is assigned to the observations that fall below the lowest extreme of the interval. Then, asymmetry and kurtosis tests are recalculated.
      i. If the probability of rejecting the hypothesis is above 0.05 the winsorized variable is kept.
      ii. Otherwise, the procedure continues with the original variable in step 3.
   b. If the number of *outliers* is above 10, the procedure continues with step 3.
3. Yeo–Johnson transformation (Yeo and Johnson, 2000) is applied, choosing the λ value that best corrects the asymmetry.

APPENDIX 7A.2

Table 7A.1   Alternative weights for components (%)

	Equal			PCA		
	22 components	7 Dimension	4 Macro-dimensions	22 components	7 Dimension	4 Macro-dimensions
dem.pop.avg	4.55	3.57	6.25	5.23	3.05	4.50
dem.aging	4.55	3.57	6.25	3.89	5.41	7.98
dem.pop.urban.sh	4.55	3.57	6.25	4.75	4.06	5.98
mmaccess.2006	4.55	3.57	6.25	5.49	3.68	5.42
educ.isced3_6.sh	4.55	14.29	3.57	4.00	17.30	4.56
pat.f.01	4.55	3.57	3.57	3.49	3.67	5.61
pat.f.02	4.55	3.57	3.57	5.72	2.43	3.71
pat.f.03	4.55	3.57	3.57	3.75	2.35	3.59
pat.pct.field.gini.35	4.55	3.57	3.57	5.05	3.50	5.34
emp.total.f.01	4.55	1.79	3.13	5.43	1.81	3.16
emp.total.f.02	4.55	1.79	3.13	5.02	1.77	3.11
emp.total.f.03	4.55	1.79	3.13	4.23	1.75	3.06
emp.ind.f.01	4.55	1.79	3.13	5.07	1.85	3.24
emp.ind.f.02	4.55	1.79	3.13	4.28	1.90	3.32
emp.ind.f.03	4.55	1.79	3.13	4.30	1.80	3.16
emp.ind.f.04	4.55	1.79	3.13	4.57	0.51	0.90
emp.total.top5	4.55	1.79	3.13	5.29	1.77	3.09
firm.size.avg	4.55	14.29	3.57	3.93	15.22	4.56
open.exports.gdp	4.55	14.29	3.57	5.01	13.65	4.56
inst.decentralisation	4.55	4.76	8.33	3.99	3.83	6.47
social.inst.capital	4.55	4.76	8.33	5.45	3.77	6.37
entrepreneurship	4.55	4.76	8.33	2.06	4.92	8.31

Source: Navarro et al. (2014).

193

APPENDIX 7A.3

Table 7A.2 Spearman correlation between different alternative weightings and aggregation methods

	22 equal	22 equal G	dim 4	dim 4 G	dim 7	dim 7 G	pca 22	pca 22 G	pca dim 4	pca dim 4 G	pca dim 7	pca dim 7 G	Average
22 equal		0.989	0.965	0.956	0.853	0.844	0.994	0.983	0.976	0.965	0.821	0.811	0.923
22 equal G	0.989		0.955	0.965	0.839	0.847	0.983	0.993	0.965	0.975	0.808	0.814	0.921
dim 4	0.965	0.955		0.988	0.804	0.795	0.958	0.948	0.987	0.975	0.768	0.758	0.900
dim 4 G	0.956	0.965	0.988		0.795	0.801	0.949	0.957	0.977	0.987	0.759	0.764	0.900
dim 7	0.853	0.839	0.804	0.795		0.985	0.827	0.814	0.844	0.832	0.992	0.978	0.869
dim 7 G	0.844	0.847	0.795	0.801	0.985		0.818	0.821	0.835	0.840	0.978	0.992	0.869
pca 22	0.994	0.983	0.958	0.949	0.827	0.818		0.989	0.964	0.953	0.791	0.781	0.910
pca 22 G	0.983	0.993	0.948	0.957	0.814	0.821	0.989		0.953	0.961	0.779	0.784	0.907
pca dim 4	0.976	0.965	0.987	0.977	0.844	0.835	0.964	0.953		0.988	0.817	0.807	0.919
pca dim 4 G	0.965	0.975	0.975	0.987	0.832	0.840	0.953	0.961	0.988		0.805	0.812	0.917
pca dim 7	0.821	0.808	0.768	0.759	0.992	0.978	0.791	0.779	0.817	0.805		0.985	0.846
pca dim 7 G	0.811	0.814	0.758	0.764	0.978	0.992	0.781	0.784	0.807	0.812	0.985		0.844

Note: 'G' denotes the use of the geometric aggregation method.

Source: Navarro et al. (2014).

8. Identifying specialisation domains beyond taxonomies: mapping scientific and technological domains of specialisation via semantic analyses

Enric Fuster, Francesco A. Massucci and Monika Matusiak

8.1 INTRODUCTION

Smart specialisation, as a place-based innovation policy concept, is entering its second period of implementation in the European Union (EU). Introduced for the programming period 2014–2020, it will be further continued in the years 2021–2027 (European Commission, 2018), as the so-called 'enabling condition' for access to the European Structural and Investment Funds, in particular the European Regional Development Fund for investments in the area of research and innovation. The application of the concept in the period 2014–2021 required a lot of institutional and stakeholder learning in EU member states and regions, as smart specialisation is supposed to be an interdisciplinary and inter-sectoral approach (Balland et al., 2017) that is informed by knowledge and evidence, but also by participative processes. The coming new period has a chance to become a period of refinement, when regions and countries will look for more advanced analytical techniques and take more informed collective decisions.

The main analytical challenge at a policy level is to identify and combine the information coming from different data sources, and to allow stakeholders to engage meaningfully with the processes and results of the analysis. The smart specialisation approach focuses specifically on the identification of a limited number of priorities that can guide public and private investment into research and innovation projects. This chapter focuses specifically on methods for the identification of the scientific and technological potential of territories, but it is important to underline that the results of such analysis have to be considered jointly with analysis of the economic fabric, innovative potential of territories, societal and environmental challenges, and so on. In this context, scientific and technological knowledge is considered not as an output as such, but as evidence of localised capabilities: an input for a wider process of building knowledge-based competitive advantage and socio-economic transformation.

In particular, this chapter focuses on new methods that can be used at the interface of science and policy for the identification of the localised domains of specialisation in science and technology. While the notion of localised scientific specialisation can be derived from the stickiness of knowledge, especially in the tacit dimension (Granovetter, 1985), most policy-targeted analyses (if any) performed as a part of the smart specialisation exercise in the years 2014–2020 were based on standard classifications and pre-existing taxonomies such as industry and International Patent Classification (IPC)[1] classes and science domains. In this chapter we explore semantic methodologies which, by analysing the textual content of science and innovation-related documents (such as policy and project descriptions, scientific publications, patents and clinical trials) go beyond classifications, allowing the identification of emergent topics and domains, as well as mapping and benchmarking the local capabilities in specific domains of interest (such as specific societal challenges, targeted industrial niches or emerging technologies).

8.2   THE IDENTIFICATION OF TERRITORIAL SPECIALISATIONS IN THE AREA OF SCIENCE AND TECHNOLOGY

The notion of localised competitive advantage goes back to the works of Alfred Marshall (1920) where the development of specialisation is due to the specialised workforce, social and technical infrastructure and knowledge spillovers, all of which can appear only at a certain level of concentration of specific industries. The theoretical work on clusters (Porter, 1998) built heavily on these early works, but focused not only on the spatial concentration of industries but also on co-localisation of related industries. New economic geography further developed the

---

[1]   International Patent Classification (IPC). See: https://www.wipo.int/classifi cations/ipc/en/.

concept of the economics of agglomeration (Fujita and Thisse, 2002), which can be applied not only to pure economic concentrations but also to scientific and innovative activities (Meusburger, 2000). Understanding territories as complex systems brought advancements such as related variety (Boshma and Iammarino, 2009) and spatially embedded networks (Berthelemy, 2011). All of these concepts are used, with different levels of success, for the analysis of territories performed for policy-making purposes. In particular, the analysis of territorial potential performed as a part of the smart specialisation strategic process is usually an exercise performed by regional or national authorities or experts. Policy-makers and practitioners face two main types of demands or requirements on mapping scientific and technological domains of specialisation, which differ by their starting point and could be labelled as 'emergent' and 'targeted' analysis.

In 'emergent analysis', the main challenge is to understand what exists and happens in the territory: which topics, what industries and scientific fields and technologies, what relative specialisation, which actors, which internal and external linkages, and so on, are present and how they have been evolving in time. Although the overall specialisation domains resulting from an emergent analysis will rarely surprise the experts and policy-makers, they can contribute to a definition of research and innovation policies better adapted to the local science, technology and innovation (STI) and socio-economic context, by:

- a finer weighting of the vitality of well-known specialisation domains;
- pinpointing smaller but growing domains;
- better understanding science, technology and industrial specialisation misalignments (particularly between academic and research institutions and the private sector); and
- assessing and characterising distinctive capacities in comparison to other geographic areas.

In 'targeted analysis', for some externally defined science, technology and innovation domains, the challenge is to understand what are the territory's assets and activities, and how they compare to benchmarks. Domains of interest may be, for instance, 'Industry 4.0', nanotechnology in the life sciences, or climate change adaptation. In this case, the specialisation domain of interest may not be a distinctive feature of the territory at hand, but there is a strategic interest in assessing the possibility of investing in that direction. Targeted analyses are relevant because:

- science and innovation networks are internationally related,[2] and relevant policies framed by European[3] or global policy trends (such as the United Nations Science, Technology and Innovation Roadmaps for Sustainable Development Goals[4]), and territorial governments may be required to respond and contribute to these trends;
- the implementation of societal-challenge or mission-oriented approaches to research and innovation requires the definition of innovation objectives (in health, social welfare, energy, the environment, infrastructure, and so on) unrelated to the current territory's science and innovation capabilities;
- there is the necessity of inserting local ecosystems into global value chains and reacting to emerging technological and market opportunities.

The main policy decisions addressed by a targeted analysis are:

- Is there a current or potential capacity to contribute and/or compete in this domain? How does it compare with benchmark territories? How is it evolving?
- Who are the actors (in science, technology, industry, society) already active in the domain, and could they become the backbone of a future specialisation?
- How is the territory's STI ecosystem complementary with external actors?
- Which are the main gaps (sub-domains, enablers, institutional missions) to be addressed?

8.3   THE CHALLENGES OF USING TAXONOMIES WHEN MAPPING SCIENTIFIC AND TECHNOLOGICAL DOMAINS OF SPECIALISATION

Quantitative analyses of territorial science and technology specialisation patterns, of the two types presented above, usually rely on aggregate

---

[2]   United Nations, *Harnessing Science, Technology and Innovation to achieve the Sustainable Development Goals*, https://sustainabledevelopment.un.org/tfm#roadmaps.

[3]   In the European Union, it happens due to the growing importance of research and innovation and interregional collaboration in Cohesion Policy, as well as the budget increases in the Research and Innovation Framework Programmes.

[4]   https://sustainabledevelopment.un.org/tfm#roadmaps.

indicators, classified according to standard taxonomies. Statistical offices provide indicators of sectoral added value, employment or company innovation by NACE codes.[5] Patents and trademarks are categorised following international classification systems such as the IPC. Bibliometric database vendors organise journals (and, therefore, scientific publications) in bibliometric categories. Territorial policy-makers and the competent line ministries and agencies must compile, integrate and analyse these data to design, implement and monitor place-based science and innovation policies, such as smart specialisation.

Unfortunately, taxonomies present several fundamental shortcomings that undermine the tailor-made and place-based approach characterising these policy models, in particular:

1. Individual records may be incorrectly assigned to the categories of the taxonomy (Jacobs and O'Neill, 2003; Shu et al., 2019).
2. Taxonomies may lack the necessary granularity (Foray and Goenaga, 2013; Gianelle et al., 2017) and nuance (Zitt, 2005) to adequately define a domain of interest in the territory. For instance, they may not distinguish between crop types (within agricultural taxons) or renewable energy sources, and present difficulties with interdisciplinarity and enabling domains.
3. Taxonomies evolve slowly and may be unfit to characterise emerging domains (Rotolo et al., 2015). This difficulty is compounded by the forward-looking nature of innovation policies, which usually target newly defined domains such as smart manufacturing or personalised medicine. Also, if the definition of specialisation priorities evolves during policy implementation, with the entrepreneurial discovery process (EDP)[6] understood as a continuous process (Marinelli and Perianez-Forte, 2017), taxonomies must evolve at the same pace, obfuscating the definition of priority perimeters and jeopardising policy monitoring.
4. Taxonomies are data source-specific, complicating integrative specialisation analysis across the diverse data sources which represent the multiple dimensions of science and technological innovation in a territory. How are scientific disciplines to be reconciled with technological domains and industrial sectors? Taxonomical concordance tables can

---

[5] Statistical Classification of Economic Activities in the European Community (NACE). See https://ec.europa.eu/eurostat/statistics-explained/index.php/Glossary: Statistical_classification_of_economic_activities_in_the_European_Community_(N ACE).

[6] See: https://s3platform.jrc.ec.europa.eu/entrepreneurial-discovery-edp.

be developed, but they are also subject to the three issues indicated above (Kortum and Putnam, 1997).

Furthermore, if a new place-based innovation policy defines specialisation priority domains, a new taxonomy is created, with labels such as 'civilian security' or 'new technologies and process management for the aerospace industry'.[7] To support implementation and monitoring, publicly funded research and development (R&D) projects, innovation support services, clusters or innovative companies are organised and classified according to this new taxonomy.

However, these ad hoc taxonomies are not compatible with earlier information sources (such as R&D projects funded by a previous policy), are hard to concord with external data sources and do not allow benchmarking, since nobody outside of the specific territory is classifying science and innovation activities according to this new taxonomy. Smart specialisation being, by definition, an outward-looking effort, not being able to benchmark the starting point or the evolution of a priority domain is a fundamental shortcoming.

8.4 A SEMANTIC APPROACH TO MAPPING SCIENTIFIC AND TECHNOLOGICAL DOMAINS OF SPECIALISATION

Science and technology data sources are growing in number, dimension, coverage, quality and data richness. Governments and public agencies are opening access to data of their science and innovation policies,[8] and linking single projects to their scientific, technological and socio-economic results. Some notable cases are the Flanders Research Information Space, the Catalan Research and Innovation Strategies for Smart Specialisation (RIS3) mapping platform (RIS3-MCAT), OpenCoesione and Gateway to Research.[9] Also, open-minded European and international communities and stakeholders are launching new data infrastructure and repositories,

---

[7] These examples have been taken from 'Eye@RIS3: Innovation Priorities in Europe', a tool developed by the Smart Specialisation Platform (Joint Research Centre – European Commission).

[8] See the European Commission's Community Research and Development Information Service (CORDIS) or the French ScanR.

[9] See: https://researchportal.be/en/about-fris, http://catalunya2020.gencat.cat/en/plataforma-ris3-mcat/, https://opencoesione.gov.it/en/progetto/, https://gtr.ukri.org/resources/about.html.

supporting open science, open innovation and open data.[10] In publication abstracts, patent descriptions, R&D project objectives, and so on, these sources provide a wealth of textual[11] information describing in detail the current challenges, the proposed or demonstrated advances, and the expected impacts of innovations.

In parallel, data science is becoming more accessible, thanks to cost and running time reductions and the arrival of new cohorts of social scientists and engineers trained in these techniques. In particular, natural language processing (NLP) is increasingly used in scientometrics and technometrics, and in foresight (Gordon and Pease, 2006), to analyse the semantic content of science and technology-related textual records.

Making the most of these converging trends, we describe in this chapter three semantic approaches to map scientific and technological domains and the science and innovation ecosystems that contribute to them, which share the following three traits:

1. Analyse each single science and technology-related textual record individually, avoiding taxonomy-based aggregates.
2. Build ad hoc text-based perimeters of the domains of interest, cutting across taxonomies to allow for the transversal analysis of several data sources at once.
3. Systematically analyse the records of the territory of interest, together with records outside of the territory, to allow for benchmarking and relative specialisation analysis as well as the identification of actual or potential external knowledge or value chain partners; as international collaboration has been proven essential (Fitjar and Rodríguez-Pose, 2011) for companies' sustained innovation efforts, particularly in peripheral geographies (Copus and Skuras, 2006; Eder and Trippl, 2019).

We describe in the following sections three methods that can be used to classify STI-related textual records into categories that can be used to help address the two policy demands previously described. All these methods make use of some NLP techniques and assume that textual records may be machine-processable. The first method proposed is topic modelling, an

---

[10]   See, for instance, the growing links between CORDIS, Zotero and OpenAire at the European level.

[11]   Many open access repositories not only allow text and data mining, but also actively encourage them, following The Hague Declaration on Knowledge Discovery in the Digital Age. See PLOS and the League of European Research Universities (LERU): 'The right to read is the right to mine', LERU Statement: https://www.leru.org/files/LERU-statement-The-Right-to-Read-is-the-Right-to-Mine.pdf.

approach that aims at discovering hidden topics linked to a collection of texts. The second method is based on the construction and application of a controlled vocabulary, while the third one exploits an initial collection of texts (a seed corpus) to identify sets of records that share some semantic properties with it. It is worth stressing that the first and the last methods usually link the analysed records with the thematic areas of interest with a continuous weight, rather than a clear-cut unique association: this implies that some weight threshold must be defined and that univocal document to classes linkage is not guaranteed.

8.4.1   Technique 1: Identifying and Mapping Emergent Science and Technology Domains through Topic Modelling

Recently, several techniques have been proposed to coarse-grain the outputs of scientific production. Some examples in this sense include methods for extracting maps of words (Van Eck and Waltman, 2009), or statistical methods to retrieve topics in large datasets (Griffiths and Steyvers, 2004). Beyond their technical differences, all those efforts have the common goal of automatically clustering large text corpora and of tagging them with (sensible) labels emerging from the texts themselves. Ideally, those emerging labels should help a human analyst to quickly discern the themes tackled by each different cluster of texts.

Within those efforts, topic modelling (TM) is a field of machine learning that aims at 'discovering' the unknown topics to which a collection of texts belongs (Blei et al., 2003). For this reason, TM is an extremely useful tool to gain an emergent analysis of the research focus of local STI ecosystems and thus to address the first policy demand outlined at the beginning of this chapter; see the Application Case 1 below for an overview of a practical example of how TM can be used to tackle this policy demand. Different methods (Hofmann, 2017; Choo et al., 2013) have been proposed to detect the topics, but all share the idea that the observed collection of texts was produced by some generative model (Blei, 2004): for all of them, the topics provided are stacks of tightly related words that co-appear consistently in the observed texts.

The advantages of topic modelling with respect to taxonomic classifications and keyword extraction are that:

- The topics emerge from – and are characterised by – the language actually used by specialists (scientists, engineers, technicians, policy officers, project managers, and so on).
- The process allows for the identification of transversal concepts which contribute to several topics.

- The technique accepts polysemy, where words have a different meaning in unrelated topics, as in 'solar cell' versus 'tumoral cell'.
- Topics are related to each other with diverse strengths, allowing for partial overlapping, vertical and horizontal relationships as well as the existence of transversal or fundamental topics.

It is worth stressing, however, that the linkage from documents to topics provided by TM is not categorical: that is, documents do not belong exclusively to one topic, but instead, documents can belong strongly to several topics, and weakly to others. In turn, all the words in the text corpus may belong to several topics, with different strengths (from a negligible to strong relationship).

The usefulness of TM becomes clear when one exploits all metadata associated to the texts analysed. For instance, by exploiting the geographical or organisational information linked to documents, it is possible to see how different sub-regions, institutions and individuals contribute to each single topic: this helps one to understand which organisations within a certain geographical boundary are focusing their research and innovation efforts on some specific topic of interest. In terms of the analysis of localised scientific and technological potential, the result for the territory is therefore seen as the sum of the contributions and achievements of the organisations located in a specific region but operating within wider scientific and technological networks and collaborations (especially collaboration research and innovation projects, co-patenting and co-publishing). Furthermore, if the publication year of each document is known, one can use TM to monitor how the incidence of certain research topics varies in time, providing a view of which are the emerging and diminishing topics, both locally (at the regional level) and globally (at the national or European level), and enabling one to perform extremely targeted benchmark analyses.

TM is turning out to be a key method in STI research intelligence: in the context of smart specialisation, given a certain perimeter of interest (that being a regional STI ecosystem, or a subset of organisations) and a textual corpus of research inputs and outputs records (publications, patents, research projects), TM can provide a very synthetic yet effective summary of the emerging research and innovation portfolio. Despite its usefulness in yielding synthetic snapshots of research portfolios, TM does have some shortcomings.

TM returns lists of topics by leveraging on the statistical co-occurrence of words in texts. Although this correspondence is often driven by the conceptual proximity of the terms, other factors may actually affect the co-appearing patterns. A typical example is provided by the geographical provenance of the texts at hand: indeed, authors may be talking about the application of some technique of interest in their specific geographical context. TM would therefore compound together the technical terms related to the technique of interest with a series of location names that do not convey any useful information (and that render the interpretation of the topics rather cumbersome). This problem, which is fairly well known to researchers (Chang et al., 2009), requires (at least partial) human supervision of the automated technique. Although some solutions to embed the supervision in the algorithm itself have been proposed (Gallagher et al., 2017), there is not a golden standard yet, and specific efforts must be devoted to iteratively refining results and carefully labelling the topics with accessible and self-contained names.

Another recurring issue is that, depending on the analysis to be carried out, some words should be completely ignored by the algorithm. For instance, when analysing STI texts, words like 'study', 'analysis', 'project' should all ideally be skipped and inserted into so-called blacklists; that is, lists of terms that are ignored by the algorithm. However, as mentioned, the specific choice of the blacklisted terms is strongly dependent on the specific objectives of the categorisation effort and on the textual source at hand. The above shortcomings highlight the fact that economic and human resources must be dedicated to the specialisation analyses: skills and knowledge are needed from both the policy and the technical side, to ensure the quality of the categorisation efforts and to implement targeted algorithms, respectively.

8.4.2   Technique 2: Mapping Science and Technology Domains with a Controlled Vocabulary

Sometimes, domain experts are able to build relatively comprehensive vocabularies of terms pertaining to a given topic. This is what is usually called a 'controlled vocabulary', in the sense that it does not result from algorithms, but from expert knowledge. Therefore, a controlled vocabulary usually consists of lists of words and phrases that are exploited to unequivocally tag records. Typically, controlled vocabularies are employed to ease the retrieval of information by leveraging on key terms that are simple enough to use and understand by a user who is after some specific information. Quoting the definition provided by the web pages of the European Union:[12] 'Controlled vocabularies are meant to organise

---

[12]   https://publications.europa.eu/en/web/eu-vocabularies/controlled-vocabularies.

knowledge that is classifiable in nature. They can be approached from a broad perspective or a more purpose-specific context.'

Because controlled vocabularies are built on carefully selected terms, positively linked with specific domains of interest, they allow for a clear cut identification of textual records assuredly related with some theme of interest. This is at odds with methods based on taxonomy mappings (which can lead to the inclusion of false positives when the sector of interest crosses taxonomic boundaries) or on topic modelling (which may yield topics only partly aligned with the thematic perimeter at stake). The bypass of taxonomies is especially relevant, for example, for decision-makers if they want to know how many research projects on 'pest resistance' for 'a specific type of crop' were funded in their region by the Horizon 2020 programme (H2020), instead of having to deal with the wealth of information contained in the H2020 programme taxon 'Sustainable agriculture and forestry'. Therefore, in the context of the smart specialisation strategies (S3), the 'purpose-specific context' case scenario mentioned in the EU web pages typically applies. This is because regional stakeholders are interested in quantifying local STI efforts in specific niches of strategic relevance. Therefore, the use of controlled vocabularies is better adapted than topic modelling for tackling the second policy demand described at the beginning of this chapter (targeted analysis).

Hence for a specific domain of policy interest, controlled vocabularies define semantic boundaries and are used to tag records with labels that summarise their content. The tagging effort is carried out either manually (that is, via human indexers who actually read content and assign sensible labels) or via some automated method which indexes records by detecting the presence of key terms. Controlled vocabularies are useful in that they allow one to circumvent taxonomies and to get direct access to information at a fine-grained level; a practical example is provided in Application Case 2 below, where a controlled vocabulary was used to detect cancer research and innovation activities in Spain.

Examples of controlled vocabularies are the Medical Subject Headings (MeSH) taxonomy (Rogers, 1963), employed by the widely used Pubmed database developed by the National Library of Medicine and the National Institute of Health in the United States, or the thesaurus of the Institute of Electrical and Electronics Engineers (IEEE),[13] used to tag publications in accordance with engineering, technical and scientific terms.

However, for most of the sources and thematic perimeters which are relevant in the context of the S3, records are not indexed, or there is an

---

[13]   'IEEE Thesaurus', https://www.ieee.org/publications/services/thesaurus.html.

utter lack of relevant controlled vocabularies. This fact implies that, to carry out targeted and useful analyses, vocabularies need to be built and documents need to be indexed *ex novo*. To deal with this problem, a methodology must be developed to quickly and efficiently build controlled vocabularies from an initial set of pertinent terms. For instance, machine learning techniques may be used to learn synonyms of the initial set of words (Mikolov et al., 2013), and extensive, automated searches on knowledge-based repositories, such as DBpedia (Lehmann et al., 2015) and Wikidata (Vrandečić and Krötzsch, 2014) can be exploited to retrieve a series of terms related to the set initially identified; an approach of this kind may allow easy scaling-up up by about a factor of ten from the initial selection of terms.

It is worth stressing that, if records are not labelled, STI documents must be positively associated to the terms in the crafted vocabulary. To successfully carry out this task, a series of pattern matching rules must be defined to capture possible variants of the same concept within texts, such as permutations of words within the concept and/or the presence of null words to be skipped. For instance, the term 'agricultural export subsidies' should be matched by the patterns 'subsidies to agricultural exports' as well as 'agricultural and goods export subsidies'. For this reason, matching rules (based, for instance, on regular expressions) must be carefully crafted to take into account variations, permutations and distance of words featured within a term of the controlled vocabulary. Again, specific resources must be devoted to the creation of the vocabulary and to its implementation in indexing pertinent records; these resources must allow bringing together domain expertise, technical expertise and technological infrastructures to accomplish the tasks of identifying relevant documents and actors.

8.4.3 Technique 3: Mapping Science and Technology Domains from a Seed Text Corpus

To meet the second policy demand and provide a targeted analysis of STI activities within a very specific domain, there is room for an intermediate approach between the bottom-up (topic modelling) and the top-down (controlled vocabulary) processes described in the preceding two sections. In fact, it is always possible to define the boundaries of the domain by identifying a reference collection of documents (which for the sake of synthesis we will call a 'seed corpus' in the following), which deal with the specific theme of interest, and to use those documents to retrieve further records related to the theme, rather than specifying a whole vocabulary for it. For instance, one can identify the abstract of the projects funded by the

H2020 programme 'Future Internet: Software, Hardware, Infrastructures, Technologies and Services' as a seed corpus dealing with information and communication technology (ICT) infrastructures and services catering for the web. Once a suitable seed corpus has been identified, the idea is that, by NLP techniques, textual records from the seed corpus can be clustered together with a wider text corpus of interest, such as all the patents, research projects or publications from a specific region, identifying those that are semantically similar to the seed corpus (for example, 'future internet') and discarding all the rest.

To be able to perform the clustering effort, texts must be transformed into vectors that can be treated by a machine. Some possible NLP methods to perform this operation are, for instance, a vectorisation based on the well-established term frequency–inverse document frequency (TF-IDF) metric (Salton and McGill, 1983), or on more modern techniques based on neural networks, such as the paragraph vector (Le and Mikolov, 2014). TF-IDF assigns, for each word in a document (and thus, for the non-null dimensions of the associated vector), a value proportional to the frequency of the word within the document and inversely proportional to the overall word frequency. The second method trains a neural network at predicting the expected word and document, given their semantic context.

On top of these vectors, clustering methods can be used to identify which records in the reference corpus can be grouped with the seed corpus. For carrying out this task, one can use traditional (and widely popular) clustering techniques such as K-means clustering and hierarchical clustering (Lloyd, 1982; Rokach and Maimon, 2005). With this approach, one may for instance link to the domain of interest all documents belonging to clusters where the majority of members belongs to the seed corpus. Another approach is based on calculating the similarity between the records in the seed corpus and those in the set of interest by means of similarity scores such as the cosine similarity (Singhal, 2001).

Similarly to the controlled vocabulary approach, the seed corpus provides the semantic content of the domain of interest, but at odds with the controlled vocabulary approach, terms appearing in the seed corpus are not controlled. This fact presents advantages and disadvantages: on the one hand, if the documents to be analysed are not indexed by a controlled vocabulary, the effort for identifying a suitable seed corpus and performing this clustering analysis is typically much lower than that of specifying a vocabulary for the area of interest and using it to tag and retrieve documents. On the other hand, with the seed corpus one has only loose control over the terms that are used to cluster and tag documents as belonging to the domain of interest. For this reason, it is fundamental to identify a series of terms that should be excluded (in technical jargon, blacklisted) and ignored in the analyses.[14] Again, the allocation of economic and human resources for carrying out these tasks is a central issue: both qualitative knowledge of the field of interest, and technical skills to develop suitable algorithms to produce useful results, must be secured by the political will.

8.4.4   Application Case 1 (Topic Modelling): Emergent Scientific and Technological Mapping for Preliminary Priority-Setting

In the context of the S3 Platform project 'Smart Specialisation and Organisational Development in Enlargement and H2020 Associated Countries', the Joint Research Centre (JRC) of European Commission launched a project on 'Characterisation of Preliminary Priority Areas for Smart Specialisation in Moldova' (unpublished), with the objective of mapping science, technology and innovation activities in Moldova to support priority-setting and to organise the Entrepreneurial Discovery Process in the country, including the regional dimension of the process. This exercise built upon and complemented the previous work 'Mapping of Economic, Innovative and Scientific Potential in the Republic of Moldova' (unpublished), by H. Hollanders, also funded by the JRC.

For the purpose of the analysis, several data sources representing different dimensions of science, technology and innovation ecosystems were gathered (EU[15] and nationally[16] funded research and innovation (R&I) projects, internationally indexed publications[17] and patents;[18] a total of 8000 records for a ten-year period), and their titles, abstracts or descriptions analysed through topic modelling (Technique 1, presented above), to provide an emergent set of S3 preliminary priority analysis (Figure 8.1).

Given the semantic heterogeneity of this body of text,[19] it was found that the optimal number of emergent topics, best describing the whole text

---

[14]   For instance, all ambiguous terms should be excluded as they may yield false positive matches. In the case of STI documents, terms of this kind may be, for example, 'analysis', 'study', 'research'.
[15]   Source: Community Research and Development Information Service (CORDIS).
[16]   Source: EXPERT On-line – Moldovan S&T Proposal Submission and Evaluation System.
[17]   Source: Scopus (Elsevier).
[18]   Source: Moldovan State Agency on Intellectual Property (AGEPI).
[19]   The number of topics is chosen by minimising the Schwarz Bayesian information criterion, a standard approach in statistics for optimal model selection (see Schwarz, 1978).

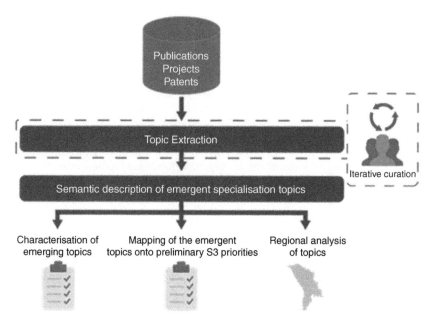

Figure 8.1   Methodology schema of the extraction of specialisation topics

corpora, was 15. Inspecting the top keywords appearing in each topic, we proceeded to give an explanatory label to the topics (see Table 8.1).

Once the topics were identified and labelled, it was then possible to proceed to perform traditional quantitative analysis to inform priority-setting and policy-making. First, we looked at the distribution of the data sources in each topic, finding that some topics appeared more frequently in publications, or in patents, evidencing different positions in the science–technological innovation spectrum. Notably, some of the topics presented a very balanced distribution of records, which means that there is a large semantic overlap and alignment between scientific activity (publications) and technological innovation (patents) (Table 8.2).

The results of this exercise are not considered definitive and, as mentioned above, serve as an input to the further analyses and stakeholder dialogue. Thus, this characterisation of the topics would us allow to better organise the entrepreneurial discovery process (EDP)[20] and to shape

---

[20]   To overcome biases in the representativeness of the types of actors who are invited to and participate in EDP activities, where universities and research institutions are usually overrepresented in relation to companies and social actors (see Edwards and Marinelli, 2018, p. 28).

Table 8.1   Proposed label and top 20 words for five of the 15 emergent topics

Proposed label	Top 20 words in the topic
Surfaces and nanofabrication	film zno layer surface gas sensor oxide substrate device thin semiconductor nanoparticles deposition response electron x-ray diffraction microscopy optical deposit
Alcohol and food processing	wine temperature mass mixture dry product food oil acid extract preparation waste grape alcohol fermentation separation mix vegetable substance food-industry
Equipment for process industries	pipe chamber heat liquid air valve pump gas outlet capacity tube inlet supply engine channel discharge cylinder reservoir hole electric
Agriculture and biotechnology	agriculture seed cultivation soil strain plant biotechnology acid fruit nutrient extract biomass feed concentration aqueous root grow bee tree preparation
Prosthetics and medical devices	bone implant suture tissue treat incision muscle cavity dental wound administer patient surgical tube surgery skin defect claimed anesthesia teeth

Table 8.2   Characterisation of the topics by the relative presence of the different types of records (data sources)

Publication-intense topics (science-oriented)	Balanced topics (science + technological innovation)	Patent-intense topics (technological innovation-oriented)
Surfaces and nanofabrication	New manufacturing processes	Mechanical systems
Materials science	Agriculture and biotechnology	Alcohol and food processing
Advanced materials	Medicine and pharmacology	Electrical and electronic equipment
Formal sciences (including computing)		Equipment for process industries
Quantum and photonics I		Prosthetics and medical devices
Quantum and photonics II		
Varied topics, related to public policies		

different support policies or policy mixes adapted to the different nature of the topics.

Second, the temporal evolution of the topics was charted; a relevant factor in the selection of priorities, and also useful to better adapt the

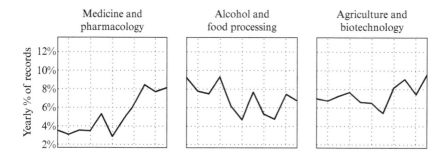

Figure 8.2   Yearly distribution of the presence of the topics in the whole body of texts (selection)

policy to growing, stable or declining domains. For instance, medicine and pharmacology, and surfaces and nanofabrication, were growing strongly; while mechanical systems, and equipment for process industries, were declining. These divergent situations may require different policy approaches (Figure 8.2).

Third, the regional distribution of the records was analysed and the specialisation index was computed. In Moldova, where academic and innovative activity is very centralised in Chisinau, the capital city, it was nevertheless possible to identify technical and industrial concentration in the peripheral regions, particularly related to mechanical, electric and electronic, oil and gas, and food industries. Fourth, regional, national and international collaboration networks were mapped, overall and for each of the preliminary priority domains, identifying national leaders, key public–private collaborations and top international partners (scientific institutions, companies, nations).

8.4.5   Application Case 1bis (Taxonomical + Topic Modelling): Hybrid Scientific and Technological Mapping for Preliminary Priority-Setting

Independently from the purely emergent analysis above, a hybrid methodology for the Moldovan case was also developed, starting from a taxonomic identification of preliminary priorities for smart specialisation, followed by a semantic analysis (topic modelling) of the records from the science and innovation (S&I) data sources included in each preliminary priority.

In the 'Mapping of Economic, Innovative and Scientific Potential in the Republic of Moldova' project, Hollanders identified an initial set of S3 preliminary economic priority areas in Moldova ('Agriculture and food processing', 'Textiles, apparel, footwear and leather goods (TAFL)', 'ICT', 'Renewable energy', and a set of 'Other' sectors[21]) based on statistical analysis of the economic, innovation and scientific potential. To widen the analysis, the 'Other' sectors of interest identified by Hollanders were singled-out (such as 'Health, biomedicine and pharmaceuticals' and 'Production technology and heavy machinery', and proceeded to manually align each of the preliminary priorities with the original taxonomies of the data sources to be analysed. For this manual alignment, it is necessary to understand the content of the proposed preliminary priorities, parse the taxonomies of the original data sources, and select the taxons that are deemed to belong to the priority. R&I projects funded by the Moldovan Academy of Sciences were aligned by their classification in Strategic Directions (a set of thematic priorities defined by the national government), internationally indexed publications were aligned by their subject areas and subject fields (the bibliometric categories defined by Scopus) and patents were aligned by the International Patent Classification (IPC[22]) (Figure 8.3).

With this alignment, it was then possible to analyse each single Moldovan S&I record assigned to one or several of the preliminary priorities, and to develop specialisation analysis (Table 8.3).

For the records corresponding to each of the preliminary priorities topic modelling was run, to better describe and understand the semantics of the content of the priorities, as presented in the example preliminary priorities in Box 8.1.

With these results, it was very interesting to merge the purely emergent semantic methodology (topic modelling) with the hybrid methodology presented in the previous paragraphs (taxonomic classification + topic modelling). It is important to observe that each S&I record is assigned a certain weight to any given topic resulting from topic modelling, so it is possible to identify the records that belong to one (or several) taxonomic priority and to an emergent topic, and to build a correspondence matrix between the classification systems resulting from the first and the second methodology.

With this correspondence in hand, the analysis was finalised by combining the insights of the two methodological approaches, overcoming most of the limitations of taxonomies and exploiting the full semantic expressiveness of the science and innovation records gathered from the Republic of Moldova (Figure 8.4). The summary schema presents the final results of the preliminary S3 prioritisation proposal. It consists of four main sectors (including their innovative subdomains) and a set of knowledge base

---

[21] These 'Other' sectors presented good indicators for priority-setting but had not been selected in the final recommendations.

[22] https://www.wipo.int/classifications/ipc/en/.

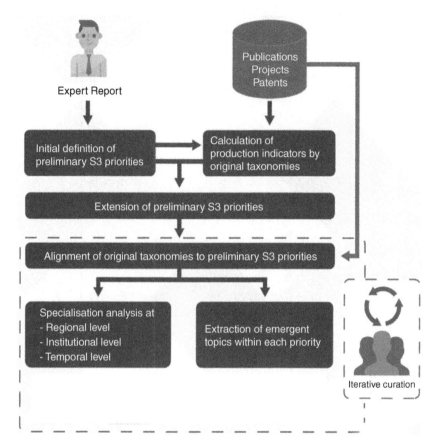

*Figure 8.3   Methodology schema for the hybrid taxonomical–semantic
mapping*

domains supporting innovation in the sectors as well as potential transfer
activities towards emerging sectors.

8.4.6   Application Case 2 (Controlled Vocabulary): Cancer Research and Innovation in Spain – Targeted Analysis to Improve Current Policies and Valorise the Ecosystem

In 2018, three Spanish philanthropic institutions – Asociación Española
Contra el Cáncer (AECC), 'la Caixa' Foundation and Asociación Española
de Investigación Sobre el Cáncer (ASEICA) – with the support of SIRIS
Academic, produced the first report on cancer research and innovation in
Spain (Fuster et al., 2018), which mapped the strengths and weaknesses

Table 8.3 Document distribution by preliminary priority

Priority	Publications		EC Projects		ASM projects		National patents	
	No. docs	% docs	No. docs	% docs	No. docs	% docs	No. docs	% docs
Agriculture and food processing	226	6	5	7	180	15	784	28
TAFL	0	0	0	0	0	0	14	0
ICT	373	10	16	24	0	0	140	5
Energy	114	3	2	3	47	4	99	4
Health, biomedicine and pharmaceuticals	600	15	5	7	249	21	764	27
Chemical industries, materials and nanotechnology	1771	45	5	7	378	31	762	27
Production technology and heavy machinery	298	8	3	4			482	17
Electrical and electronic technologies	611	16	1	1			232	8
Environmental industries, services and sciences	130	3	9	13	130	11	180	6
Vulcanized and fired materials	0	0	0	0	0	0	46	2
Paper industry	0	0	0	0	0	0	2	0
Furniture	0	0	0	0	0	0	15	1
No priority	1030	26	22	32	220	18	175	6

Note: EC = European Commission research and innovation projects; ASM = Academy of Science of Moldova.

BOX 8.1   TOPICS BY SECTOR

Agriculture and Food Processing
Six of the topics are patent-intensive, focusing on farming, food processing, alcohol production and food industry machinery. Two of the topics are publication-intensive, focusing on biotechnology and genetics. European projects are mostly connected to the latter field.

ICT
Three topics within the domain are patent-intensive, related to the development of mobile devices and applications, super/semiconductive materials and circuitry. European projects are mainly devoted to building e-infrastructure for research and innovation activities. Publication-intensive topics are instead more focused on frequency modulators and switches, photonics (at both theoretical and experimental level), algorithmic complexity and parallel computing. The implementation of e-infrastructures topic, already highlighted in the case of European projects, also features noticeable contribution from publications.

Energy
The four patent-intensive topics focus on electro-technical equipment, biofuels, electricity generation and electronics. The four publication-intensive topics focus on quantum and nano-technology, spectrometry, biomass-based energy production and electric motors.

---

of the Spanish cancer ecosystem and provided policy insight by comparing with leading countries in the area of cancer research and innovation. Through the integration and analysis of multiple data sources, it aimed to cover most of the domain, including public[23] and philanthropic-funded[24] research and innovation projects, scientific publications,[25] clinical trials[26] and patents.[27]

The report also had the objective of analysing the alignment between soci-

---

[23]   Sources: Agencia Estatal de Investigación, Instituto de Salud Carlos III and European Commission's Community Research and Development Information Service (CORDIS).

[24]   Source: ad hoc survey.

[25]   Sources: PubMed (National Institute of Health), Scopus (Elsevier) and SCImago Journal & Country Rank.

[26]   Source: https://clinicaltrials.gov/ct2/home; 'ClinicalTrials.gov is a Web-based resource that provides patients, their family members, health care professionals, researchers, and the public with easy access to information on publicly and privately supported clinical studies on a wide range of diseases and conditions.'

[27]   Source: European patents applications and specifications database (European Patent Office).

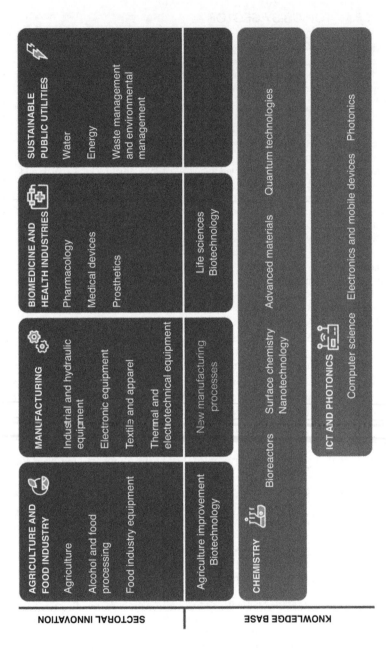

Figure 8.4   Summary schema of the preliminary S3 priorisation proposal

etal needs, expressed as cancer incidence and mortality by type of cancer, and the portfolio of research and innovation funding, activities and results,[28] to identify the areas of specialisation of the Spanish cancer ecosystem, describe the alignment or mismatching of activities across the science-to-clinical-application process and to identify underfunded cancer types. To provide coherent and comprehensive results and policy insights, it was necessary to analyse these data sources transversally, all at the same time.

As discussed in section 8.4.2, 'Mapping Science and Technology Domains with a Controlled Vocabulary', the National Library of Medicine maintains a controlled vocabulary for the medical and life science fields, Medical Subject Headings (MeSH), which is then applied to classify all publications in Medline[29] (which can be retrieved through PubMed[30]) and all clinical trials in ClinicalTrials.gov. Thus, for two important data sources in the analysis the individual records (publications and clinical trials) that addressed cancer in general and a specific cancer type in particular could be retrieved almost directly.[31]

Because the remaining two data sources (funded projects and patents) were not indexed by MeSH and no original taxonomy allowed for the identification of cancer-related records, not cancer types, it was decided to apply an NLP approach and automatically tag each record with a MeSH term characterising each cancer type.[32] To accomplish this, a technique based on keyword matching was applied, enhanced with the use of regular expressions to fully identify variations, permutations and distance of words characterising each cancer type. This keyword matching technique was applied to the textual fields describing projects (titles and descriptions) and patents (titles and abstracts) (Figure 8.5).

---

[28] The report also included portfolio analysis according to two other dimensions: (a) scientific disciplines; and (b) research areas of the Common Scientific Outline of the International Cancer Research Partnership (see https://www.icr partnership.org/cso).

[29] See: https://www.nlm.nih.gov/bsd/medline.html; 'MEDLINE is the US National Library of Medicine® (NLM) premier bibliographic database that contains more than 25 million references to journal articles in life sciences with a concentration on biomedicine. A distinctive feature of MEDLINE is that the records are indexed with NLM Medical Subject Headings (MeSH®).'

[30] See: https://www.ncbi.nlm.nih.gov/pubmed/.

[31] It was still necessary to define a synthetic list of cancer types (based on the World Health Organization 10th revision of the International Classification of Diseases, ICD-10 standard: 26 types, according to their localisation) and to map this list to hundreds of relevant MeSH terms.

[32] And some general, basic or transversal terminology that, although not connected to a specific cancer type, allowed records to be identified as cancer-related (for instance, related to basic research).

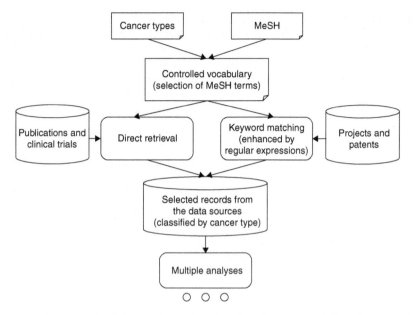

*Figure 8.5   Methodology schema for the identification and classification of
pertinent records*

This classification effort enabled the classification of records by cancer types and, therefore, identification of all records associated with cancer research and innovation from the data sources. So, with the same process, it was possible to both define the global perimeter of cancer research and innovation, and to classify the records in this selected corpus by cancer type.

The infographic in Figure 8.6 presents statistics and scientometric/ technometric indicators computed ad hoc on the perimeter of cancer-related research and innovation records, which allows Spain to be compared with the selected benchmark countries in terms of scientific output and impact, clinical research, technological innovation and competitiveness in European research and innovation funding.

With all the S&I records (publications, clinical trials, patents, European and national research and innovation projects) classified by cancer type, it was then possible to analyse the alignment between the different sources, and to compare the figures with health indicators (incidence and mortality by cancer type[33]) (Figure 8.7).

---

[33] Sources: Instituto Nacional de Estadística and Mapa de incidencia del cáncer, Observatorio del Cáncer, AECC. Retrieved 1 August 2018.

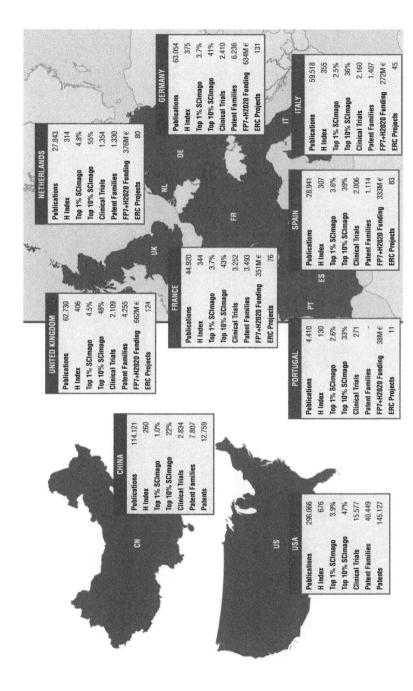

Figure 8.6   Benchmark of indicators of cancer science and innovation, funding, activities and outputs

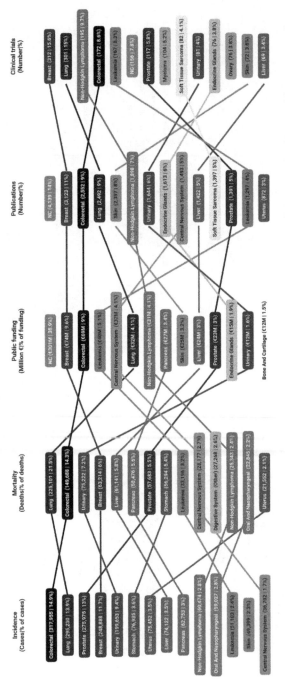

Figure 8.7   Parallel analysis of presence of cancer types in incidence, mortality, public R&I funding, publications and clinical trials

Although several caveats related to the nature of S&I funding, institutions and activities, as well as health and health policy factors, demand caution in the interpretation of these data, a few insights resulted, notably:

- Cancers affecting the liver, stomach, digestive system, urinary system, oral and nasopharyngeal areas, lung and larynx, and pancreas, amongst others, seemed to receive relatively lower funding in relation to their social burden.
- The number of clinical trials has little correlation with the mortality by cancer type: urinary tract, stomach, digestive system, liver and pancreas cancers are the object of relatively little clinical research.

The report resulted in the proposal of a Spanish Cancer Research and Innovation Strategy, which would aim to address the shortcomings of the ecosystem and better align the R&I portfolio with the needs of the patients and society at large.

8.4.7   Application Case 3 (Seed Corpus): Identifying and Mapping Competences in Industry 4.0

In the context of the actions promoted by the National Plan Industry 4.0[34] launched by the Italian Ministry of Economic Development, the Department of Industry of Regione Toscana started in 2016 a series of EDP (Entrepreneurial Discovery Process as recommended by the Smart Specialisation methodology) activities. This lead the Directorate to the creation of the Regional Platform for Industry 4.0 (http://www.cantieri40.it/i40), a structure aimed at connecting the needs of private companies to the skills in Industry 4.0 offered by the local Higher Education and Research Institutions (HERIs). Among the main objectives of the platform were to map the local skills and to match the private demand and HERI offer in Industry 4.0, and to help design ad hoc policies and tools to favour the transition.

The skills mapping problem was particularly challenging, since Industry 4.0 is a new topic, built upon several pre-existing disciplines and technological domains; as a domain, it is hard to define and it certainly it does not appear in existing taxonomies. To try to carry out this mapping, the region circulated a survey across HERIs to identify people and related skills. The response rate to the survey was relatively low, however, mainly because of

---

[34]   Piano nazionale Industria 4.0, see: https://www.mise.gov.it/index.php/it/19 8-notizie-stampa/2036244-piano-nazionale-industria-4-0.

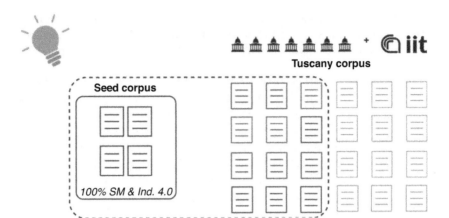

Figure 8.8   A sketch of the methodology used to identify Tuscan publications on Industry 4.0

the difficulties in getting hold of actors in the sphere of higher education and research. Indeed, HERIs are complex structures which, with the proliferation of schools, departments and laboratories, make it hard to get access to the relevant actors; for a field as transversal as Industry 4.0, the relevant skills may actually be in unexpected places. Additionally, communications are hindered by a misalignment between the offer and demand vocabularies: researchers use a technical jargon which, even for overlapping domains, may be poorly aligned with the terminologies used by policy-makers.

To help the region carrying out this mapping exercise, SIRIS Academic developed a methodology that exploited a seed corpus dealing with Industry 4.0 (Figure 8.8) to classify all publications produced by the regional HERI ecosystem and to identify, in turn, all authors and related affiliations. Specifically, the seed corpus was selected by gathering the abstracts of all the publications that were either produced by some research project funded by the Factories of the Future initiative of the European Commission,[35] or indexed via one of the keywords 'industry 4.0', 'smart manufacturing' (SM) or 'advanced manufacturing'.

The seed corpus was clustered with the roughly 50 000 publications produced by the Tuscan HERI ecosystem in the time period 2010–2015 to identify, within the latter dataset, all records focused on Industry 4.0 (I4.0) R&D. This effort enabled to identify 11 000 Tuscan publications on

---

[35]   https://ec.europa.eu/digital-single-market/en/factories-future.

Industry 4.0 and, in turn, 2000 authors based in a regional HERI with the relevant skills (including PhD students and untenured staff). The regional government of Tuscany performed quantitative and qualitative checks, to ensure that researchers were still in those institutions, and that inferred I4.0 skills were correct. About 1000 professors within the identified pool of researchers did confirm the findings (Figure 8.9).

Notably, a topic modelling extraction was also performed on the identified publications to understand the focal research themes in Tuscany, within Industry 4.0. The topics were finally mapped onto a list of standard competencies defined by the Italian Ministry of Economic Development (Table 8.4).

8.5 LIMITATIONS AND CONSIDERATIONS

The semantic–scientometric approaches presented above, as with all quantitative methods, are sensitive to biases from the nature and the coverage of the data sources used. Textual data richness is fundamental for analytical reliability and, consequently, for the strength and the level of detail of the qualitative conclusions extracted from it. We list here some of the main data-related limitations and considerations that can fundamentally affect the analysis and policy conclusions of any place-based sectoral, disciplinary or challenge-oriented analytical exercise, in particular.

First is bias against lower-technology sectors, traditional sectors and non-technological innovation: many of the traditional data sources are biased towards the natural sciences and technological innovations, and industrial sectors present different publication and patenting propensities (Camerani et al., 2018; Debackere et al., 2002). The potential relative absence of non-technological research and innovation activities – which can have an important role in smart specialisation strategies – and the low propensity to publish, to protect intellectual property and to participate in R&D projects of lower-technology and traditional sectors, have to be taken into account.

The lower presence of non-technological research and innovation activities (such as design-based industries or tourism) in the data sources should not be taken at face value (absence of evidence is not evidence of absence); it is essential to complement the analysis with analysis of additional sources, and especially, with qualitative, participatory and expert-based methods, as well as to combine it with other analyses focusing on concentration, specialisation and growth dynamics of employment, value added, trade patterns, innovation and so on. Multifaceted analysis of a territory, including quantitative, semantic and qualitative inputs, can better identify

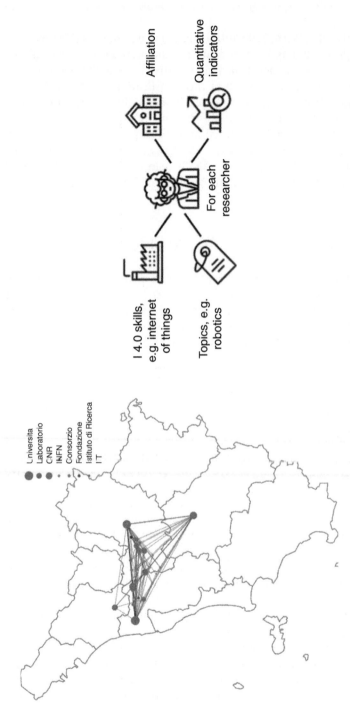

Note: Left: the Tuscan network of institutional collaborations in research on Industry 4.0. Right: the fine-grained results obtained at the level of single researchers.

Figure 8.9   An overview of the results obtained

Table 8.4   *The topics extracted via topic modelling, from the Tuscan publications on Industry 4.0*

Topic label	Main words in topic
Big data, and information and communication technology (ICT)	data, image, algorithm, analysis
ICT for manufacturing	technology, process, product, advanced
Design and testing of intelligent systems	performance, test, vehicle, safety
Distributed computing	service, data, cloud, platform
Theoretical computer science	function, problem, system, set
Green energy production and storage	frequency, surface, power, device
Algorithms	algorithm, solution, optimisation, method
Big data management	user, information, web, system
Business models	market, analysis, research, Italian
Advanced processes for manufacturing	experimental, test, pressure, effect
Multifunctional materials	magnetic, graphene, field, interaction
Internet of Things	wireless, sensor, node, traffic
Additive manufacturing	material, film, chemical, layer
Natural language processing	analysis, language, logic, fuzzy
Robotics	control, robotic, force, hand
Sustainable manufacturing	water, environmental, plant, production
Bio-nanomaterials	tissue, scaffold, protein, nanoparticles
Advanced human–machine interaction	instrument, detector, telescope, energy
ICT in medicine	clinical, medical, treatment, disease
Modelling and simulation	detector, collision, decay, mass

the realities of complex adaptive innovation systems, lead to a better understanding of place-based specificities, and inform and support richer and more fine-grained participatory priority-setting and policy-making.

Second is uneven representation of institutional typologies, over-representation of academic actors and under-representation of companies, non-governmental organisations (NGOs), governments, and so on, developing innovation or applying technology: as a consequence of the limitations mentioned above, it can be expected that companies, NGOs, governments, and so on are under-represented in the data sources and thus in the results of the analysis. Additional care must be taken when analysing results and interpreting conclusions related to priority-setting and the market or society-oriented innovation and application capacity of specialisation domains, policy instruments and activities.

Third is bias in the coverage of scientific publications in peripheral geographies, local languages and some disciplines: science and innovation fields that tend to publish in local journals and/or in local languages (typically within the domains of law, social sciences and the humanities) are not covered as extensively in both proprietary databases and international open access repositories as those fields that publish in international journals.

For the reasons given above, it is essential to gather and use local data sources and repositories[36] and to integrate the analysis with qualitative, participatory and expert-based methods. In any case, these data-related limitations and considerations also affect non-semantic sciento- and technometric analysis, compounded by additional issues presented above in section 8.3, 'The Challenges of Using Taxonomies when Mapping Scientific and Technological Domains of Specialisation'. We put great hope in the rapid growth and development of open access and open data initiatives and sources in science, technology, innovation, policy and administration, which are increasingly providing a wealth of structured and unstructured data, which include ever-richer textual fields, essential to perform the techniques presented.

Language affects semantic approaches in an additional fundamental way: although science, technology and innovation is more and more English-speaking (Gordin, 2015), in most contexts there will be a need to analyse records in two (local plus English) or more languages. Due to the very large size of the usual datasets in place-based analysis, this poses a feasibility threat that, unless automatic translation reaches a higher level of quality (especially for technical terms, acronyms, and so on), will curtail semantic analysis.

Especially in the case of topic modelling (Technique 1) and other emerging and non-supervised methodologies, where the results of the analysis emerge from the specific body of textual information, insights and conclusions are more difficult to compare across geographies. This indicates that there is a trade-off in bypassing taxonomies and traditional methods: difficulty in benchmarking results, diverging methodologies, and atomisation of the analytical frameworks that are especially detrimental in the case of smart specialisation, an EU-wide innovation policy model. Since semantic techniques will continue to be used by policy-makers and actors at all levels, common, open standards, infrastructures and resources would greatly diminish the risks.

---

[36] Note that when using local data sources and repositories the possibility of analysing local activities and results in an international context, as well as benchmarking, may be jeopardised.

These techniques are supported by large data sources (in the form of databases, platforms and repositories) which are costly to create, run[37] and maintain. Also, they are demanding in terms of human resources, since they require advanced data science skills and extensive manual curation which are rare and in great demand in the private sector. Regarding territorial cohesion, as new open data and open science platforms, which provide a wealth of information available for semantic analysis, are developed in more advanced regions and countries, we will witness a divergence in resources and capacities available to policy-makers and actors in lagging regions and countries.[38]

Finally, the application of these techniques can be experienced by policy-makers and actors as a 'black box': an insurmountable amount of data is ingested and transformed by opaque algorithms, crafted by specialists, and yields results which require reworking and interpretation for which they lack context. It is essential to present them with the nature and limitations of the techniques, include them in the key methodological choices, and involve them in the iterative steps that lead to the final result. Following the principles of open science, when possible, the data used should be open and the algorithms open source, to allow for replicability and to facilitate the updating of the analysis in later periods.

8.6   FINAL REMARKS

The methods presented above are new, and there are plenty of lines of future development, to better integrate them with other widespread techniques and to contribute to new policy-making trends, research and innovation activities and economic niches. In particular, we deem particularly interesting the following.

First is integration with global value chains analysis. The outward-looking nature of smart specialisation requires investment priorities to be (potentially) well positioned in global value chains (GVCs) (Brennan and Rakhmatullin, 2015). Integrating the semantic analysis of place-based data with maps and flows of GVCs would provide additional insight for priority-setting, policy design and policy implementation.

Second is relatedness. The techniques presented are multidimensional

---

[37]   Recently, concerns about the sustainability and carbon footprint of machine learning techniques have also been raised, due to the energy usage required to run the computations (see Strubell et al., 2019).

[38]   See the Joint Research Centre project, 'RIS3 Support to Lagging Regions', https://s3platform.jrc.ec.europa.eu/ris3-in-lagging-regions.

and continuous, and directly provide indications of proximity between topics and domains, as well as of transversality. Connecting and mapping these results with analysis of technological relatedness and related variety (Boschma and Gianelle, 2014) would allow for defining finer-grained priorities and policies supporting regional branching.

Third is challenge and mission-oriented policy-making. The European Commission,[39] member states and leading regions are exploring challenge and mission-oriented policy-making, which will demand finer-grained analysis and the inclusion in place-based analysis of key objectives and indicators well outside the research, technology and innovation domain. For instance, Navarre[40] has established a series of specific challenges (*retos*) in the S3 priorities defined by indicators such as 'number of public fast and semi-fast electric car recharge points' and 'total land surface dedicated to sustainable agricultural production'. Some of the key elements to be tackled in this new context are:

- The necessity to include in the analysis domain-specific objectives and indicators (beyond statistics and scientometrics) and to work in coordination with units and experts producing innovative territorial indicators.[41]
- The necessity to analyse evidence and data within a systemic approach, capable of disentangling contexts, means and solutions (innovations, technologies), actors, impacts, outcomes, and so on, and the relations amongst these concepts.
- The key role of the line ministries and departments (Health, Public Administration, Agriculture and Rural Development, Sustainable Development, Energy, and so on), not only those for Science and Innovation and/or Economic and Regional Development. The need to establish wider science and innovation policy governance and inter-departmental workgroups as a tool to guarantee coherence, coordination, policy design, implementation, monitoring amongst these actors.
- The leadership, methodologies and resources to extend open government and open science data practices to these new domains.

---

[39] European Commission, Directorate-General for Research and Innovation, 'A New Horizon for Europe', 2018; see: https://op.europa.eu/en/publication-detail/-/publication/00d78651-a037-11e8-99ee-01aa75ed71a1/language-en/format-PDF/source-77975709.

[40] See: http://www.sodena.com/descargas/S3/INFORME%20SEGUIMIENTO%20RETOS%20S3%20JUNIO%202018.pdf.

[41] See: https://ec.europa.eu/knowledge4policy/event/workshop-territorial-indicators_en.

Fourth is directionality of research and innovation, value creation and value destruction. In a context of increasing social polarisation and sustainability threats, policy-makers and other stakeholders are increasingly concerned (Weber and Rohracher, 2012) with the directionality of research and innovation (Schot and Steinmueller, 2018), and how the innovations transform social systems (who wins, who loses, how social values such as equality or cohesion are affected, and so on); how to map and understand where value is created and destroyed in innovation processes is key. Semantic techniques could be explored in that direction (akin to sentiment analysis) but a participatory approach to science and innovation policy design, implementation and monitoring, and an open analysis of public response to innovations and other changes to the status quo, can help to anticipate and address these concerns.

It seems clear that new data sources and analytical techniques can provide new, accurate and richer information, and are worth exploring further in the context of place-based innovation policy. Nevertheless, there are also some practicalities at the level of national and sub-national policy-making that can make wider application problematic. One of the key challenges is the capacity of policy-makers and stakeholders to absorb and practically apply non-standard advanced analytical methods. Also, the cost of such analysis is significantly higher than standardised traditional approaches, which can be a barrier to some local and regional authorities.

On the other hand, the recently observed applications of the concept of smart specialisation at local and sub-regional level, at macro-regional level (for international and cross-border cooperation[42]) and also beyond the EU present a new set of challenges and opportunities. Especially on other continents, where the European understanding of regions (Nomenclature of Territorial Units for Statistics, NUTS 2) and available datasets make it difficult to localise the analysis below the national level and achieve place-based dimension of policies, there is a call for different approaches and techniques that could be applicable in very different (and changing) territorial contexts. As scientometrics and semantic methods go to the level of single institutions and actors, they allow for adapting the scope of analysis to various territorial realities. Also, we expect that adaptability of these techniques, especially in precisely defining fine-grained multidisciplinary and inter-sectorial smart specialisation priority domains, societal challenges or missions will be especially relevant for the second period of

---

[42]   For example, the Thematic Platforms for Smart Specialisation launched by the Joint Research Centre; see https://s3platform.jrc.ec.europa.eu/s3-thematic-platforms.

implementation of smart specialisation strategies: Smart Specialisation 2.0.

In the age of complex global challenges, there is an increasing need for evidence-informed policy approaches and understanding the localised territorial potentials that can be mobilised to answer them. Mapping of the scientific and technological potential is one of many parts of such an analysis, and can indicate the thematic concentration of knowledge and the participation in the international networks. Jointly with the identification of the specialised areas of economic advantage, key challenges and actors, it can be a good basis for the business–research–society dialogue and a stronger cooperation on specific topics that can contribute to the knowledge-based economic transformation of territories. In order to address some of the difficulties in the practical application mentioned above, it is important to develop accessible science–policy interfaces that will be open to policy-makers and the wider public and offer the well-communicated results of the analysis and the possible implications. Also, with the increased territorial cooperation, joint resources can be pooled to improve the financial accessibility of such analyses. Last but not least, the results of different studies and reports need to feed into building the knowledge-based consensus and collaborative learning. With time, the capacity of policy-makers and stakeholders can be expected to increase. Practical experience shows that the publication of the results and transparency of the process can diminish the negative effects of lobbying or policy pressures. In terms of building social acceptance for the adopted policies, the joint discussion of results of different analyses helps not only to better interpret the conclusions, but also to build consensus and understanding.

REFERENCES

Balland, P.-A., Boschma, R., Crespo, J., Rigby, D. (2017), Smart specialization policy in the EU: relatedness, knowledge complexity and regional diversification. Utrecht University Papers in Evolutionary Economic Geography 17.17.

Berthelemy, M. (2011), Spatial networks. *Physics Reports*, **499**(1–3), 1–101.

Blei, D.M. (2004), Probabilistic models of text and images. Doctoral dissertation, University of California, Berkeley.

Blei, D.M., Ng, A.Y., Jordan, M.I. (2003), Latent Dirichlet allocation. *Journal of Machine Learning Research*, **3**(Jan), 993–1022.

Boschma, R., Gianelle C. (2014), Regional branching and smart specialisation policy. S3 Policy Brief Series No. 06/2014, Joint Research Centre, European Commission, Luxembourg: Publications Office of the European Union.

Boschma, R., Iammarino S. (2009), Related variety, trade linkages and regional growth in Italy. *Economic Geography*, **85**(3), 289–311.

Brennan, L., Rakhmatullin, R. (2015), Global value chains and smart specialisation strategy. Thematic work on the understanding of global value chains and their analysis within the context of smart specialisation. EUR 27649 EN.

Camerani, R., Rotolo, D., Grassano, N. (2018), Do firms publish? A cross-sectoral analysis of corporate. *STI 2018 Conference Proceedings*.

Chang, J., Gerrish, S., Wang, C., Boyd-Graber, J.L., Blei, D.M. (2009), Reading tea leaves: how humans interpret topic models. Advances in Neural Information Processing Systems 22: 23rd Annual Conference on Neural Information Processing Systems 2009. Proceedings of a meeting held 7–10 December, Vancouver, British Columbia, Canada. https://papers.nips.cc/paper/3700-reading-tea-leaves-how-hu mans-interpret-topic-models.

Choo, J., Lee, C., Reddy, C.K., Park, H. (2013), Utopian: user-driven topic modeling based on interactive nonnegative matrix factorization. *IEEE Transactions on Visualization and Computer Graphics*, **19**(12), 1992–2001.

Copus, A., Skuras, D. (2006), Business networks and innovation in selected lagging areas of the European Union: a spatial perspective. *European Planning Studies*, **14**(1), 79–93.

Debackere, K., Verbeek, A., Luwel, M., Zimmermann, E. (2002), Measuring progress and evolution in science and technology – II: The multiple uses of technometric indicators. *International Journal of Management Reviews*, **4**(3), 213–231.

Eder, J., Trippl, M. (2019), Innovation in the periphery: compensation and exploitation strategies. *Growth and Change*, **50**(4), 1–21.

Edwards, J., Marinelli, E. (eds) (2018), *Higher Education for Smart Specialisation: A Handbook*, Version 1.0, Seville: European Commission.

European Commission (2018), Communication from the Commission to the European Parliament, the European Council, the Council, the European Economic and Social Committee and the Committee of the Regions. https://eur-lex.europa. eu/resource.html?uri=cellar:c2bc7dbd-4fc3-11e8-be1d-01aa75ed71a1.0023.02/ DOC_2&format=PDF.

Fitjar, R.D., Rodríguez-Pose, A. (2011), When local interaction does not suffice: sources of firm innovation in Urban Norway. *Environment and Planning A*, **43**(6), 1248–1267.

Foray, D., Goenaga, X. (2013), The goals of smart specialisation. European Commission, Joint Research Centre, S3 Policy Brief Series No. 1/2013.

Fujita, M., Thisse, J.-F. (2002), *Economics of Agglomeration: Cities, Industrial Location and Regional Growth*, Cambridge: Cambridge University Press.

Fuster, E., Velasco, A., Massucci, F., Quinquillà, A., Capdevila, M., Figueroa, A., Puyol, M. (2018), Comprometidos con la investigación en cáncer. Primer informe sobre la investigación e innovación en cáncer en España 2018, Version V1. Zenodo.

Gallagher, R.J., Reing, K., Kale, D., Ver Steeg, G. (2017), Anchored correlation explanation: topic modeling with minimal domain knowledge. *Transactions of the Association for Computational Linguistics*, **5**, 529–542.

Gianelle, C., Guzzo, F., Mieszkowski, K. (2017), Smart specialisation at work: analysis of the calls launched under ERDF operational programmes. JRC Technical Reports JRC106974.

Gordin, M. (2015), *Scientific Babel*, Chicago, IL: University of Chicago Press.

Gordon, T., Pease, A. (2006), RT Delphi: an efficient, 'round-less' almost real time Delphi method. *Technological Forecasting and Social Change*, **73**(4), 321–333.

Granovetter, M. (1985), Economic action and social structure: the problem of embeddedness. *American Journal of Sociology*, **91**, s.481–510.

Griffiths, T.L., Steyvers, M. (2004), Finding scientific topics. *Proceedings of the National Academy of Sciences*, **101**(Suppl. 1), 5228–5235.

Hofmann, T. (2017), Probabilistic latent semantic indexing. *ACM SIGIR Forum*, **51**(2), 211–218.

Jacobs, G., O'Neill, C. (2003), On the reliability (or otherwise) of SIC codes. *European Business Review*, **15**(3), 164–169.

Kortum, S., Putnam, J. (1997), Assigning patents to industries: tests of the Yale Technology Concordance. *Economic Systems Research*, **9**(2), 161–176.

Le, Q., Mikolov, T. (2014), Distributed representations of sentences and documents. *International Conference on Machine Learning*, pp.1188–1196. https://arxiv.org/pdf/1405.4053.pdf.

Lehmann, J., Isele, R., Jakob, M., Jentzsch, A., Kontokostas, D., Mendes, P.N., et al. (2015), DBpedia – a large-scale, multilingual knowledge base extracted from Wikipedia. *Semantic Web*, **6**(2), 167–195.

Lloyd, S. (1982), Least squares quantization in PCM. *IEEE transactions on Information Theory*, **28**(2), 129–137.

Marinelli, E., Perianez-Forte, I. (2017), *Smart Specialisation at Work: The Entrepreneurial Discovery as a Continuous Process*, Luxembourg: Publications Office of the European Union. doi:10.2760/514714.

Marshall, A. (1920), *Principles of Economics*, 8th edition, London: Macmillan.

Mikolov, T., Sutskever, I., Chen, K., Corrado, G.S., Dean, J. (2013), Distributed representations of words and phrases and their compositionality. Advances in Neural Information Processing Systems 26. https://www.researchgate.net/publication/257882504_Distributed_Representations_of_Words_and_Phrases_and_their_Compositionality.

Meusburger, P. (2000), The spatial concentration of knowledge: some theoretical considerations. *Erdkunde*, **54**(4), 352–364.

Porter, M.E. (1998), Clusters and the new economics of competition. *Harvard Business Review*, November–December, 77–90.

Rogers, F.B. (1963), Medical subject headings. *Bulletin of the Medical Library Association*, **51**, 114–116.

Rokach, L., Maimon, O. (2005), *Clustering Methods, Data Mining and Knowledge Discovery Handbook*, Boston, MA: Springer.

Rotolo, D., Hicks, D., Martin, B. (2015), What is an emerging technology? 11 February, SWPS 2015-06. Available at SSRN: https://ssrn.com/abstract=2743186.

Salton, G., McGill, M.J. (1983), *Introduction to Modern Information Retrieval*, New York: McGraw-Hill.

Schot, J., Steinmueller, W.E. (2018), Three frames for innovation policy: R&D, systems of innovation and transformative change. *Research Policy*, **47**(9), 1554–1567.

Schwarz, G. (1978), Estimating the dimension of a model. *Annals of Statistics*, **6**(2), 461–464.

Shu, F., Zhang, L., Larivière, V., Julien, C.A., Zhang, J. (2019), Comparing journal and paper level classifications of science. *Journal of Informetrics*, **13** (2019), 202–225.

Singhal, A. (2001), Modern information retrieval: a brief overview. *Bulletin of the IEEE Computer Society Technical Committee on Data Engineering*, **24**(4), 35–43.

Strubell, E., Ganesh, A., McCallum, A. (2019), Energy and policy considerations for deep learning in NLP. 57th Annual Meeting of the Association for Computational Linguistics. arXiv:1906.02243 [cs.CL].

Van Eck, N., Waltman, L. (2009), Software survey: VOSviewer, a computer program for bibliometric mapping. *Scientometrics*, **84**(2), 523–538.

Vrandečić, D., Krötzsch, M. (2014), Wikidata: a free collaborative knowledge base. *Communications of the ACM*, **57**(10). https://dl.acm.org/doi/10.1145/2629489.

Weber, K.M., Rohracher, H. (2012), Legitimizing research, technology and innovation policies for transformative change. *Research Policy*, **41**(6), 1037–1047.

Zitt, M. (2005), Facing diversity of science: a challenge for bibliometric indicators. *Measurement*, **3**(1), 38–49.

Index